LAST RAMPAGE

LAST RAMPAGE

THE ESCAPE OF GARY TISON

JAMES W. CLARKE

The University of Arizona Press

Tucson

The University of Arizona Press
www.uapress.arizona.edu

© 1988 by James W. Clarke
Reprinted by special arrangement with Houghton Mifflin Company
First University of Arizona Press paperbound edition 1999

Printed in the United States of America
22   21   20   19   18   17   7   6   5   4   3   2

ISBN-13: 978-0-8165-1967-5 (paper)

Library of Congress Cataloging-in-Publication Data
Clarke, James W., 1937–
Last rampage : the escape of Gary Tison / James W. Clarke.
p.   cm.
Originally published: Boston : Houghton Mifflin, 1988.
Includes bibliographical references (p. [295]–307) and index.
ISBN 0-8165-1967-6 (pbk.)
1. Tison, Gary Gene, 1935–1978. 2. Criminals—United States
Biography. 3. Serial murders—Southwest, New Case studies.
4. Escapes—Arizona Case studies. 5. Fugitives from justice—United States
Biography. 6. Arizona State Prison. I. Title.
HV6248.T56C54   1999
365'.641—dc21
[B]   99-29166
CIP

British Library Cataloguing-in-Publication Data
A catalogue record for this book is available from the British Library.

♾ This paper meets the requirements of ANSI/NISO Z39.48-1992
(Permanence of Paper).

To the memory of my father and mother,
Alonzo Peterson Clarke and Beatrice Weston Clarke

I, the Lord thy God, am a jealous God, visiting the iniquity
of the fathers upon the children unto the third and fourth
generation of them that hate me.

Exodus 20:5

I have so many mixed emotions about Gary, ranging from
the love I had for him to hatred for what he has done to
our sons, and so many other people, that I probably will
never know myself just how I feel about Gary.

Dorothy Tison

CONTENTS

Part IV · Consequences

ILLUSTRATIONS

Following page 144

Dorothy Tison
Raymond Curtis Tison
Ricky Wayne Tison
Donald Joe Tison

Bobby Tuzon
Gary Tison
Warden Harold Cardwell

John Lyons
Donnelda Lyons
Christopher Lyons
Theresa Tyson
Margene and James Judge

Randy Greenawalt
Randy Greenawalt, Ricky Tison, Ray Tison

A NOTE FROM THE AUTHOR

It is indeed gratifying and fitting to publish this new, updated edition of *Last Rampage* with the University of Arizona Press. The events recounted in these pages stretch beyond the "true crime" genre. They describe, as well, the lingering vestiges of an outlaw tradition that was as real in 1978 as it was a century before when Johnny Ringo and the Clanton brothers were strolling the streets of Tombstone. The story of the Tison Gang extends our understanding of that tradition in Arizona history and the frontier culture of the Great Southwest.

PREFACE

In August 1978, I had a frightening brush with death while camping in southwestern Colorado. Unknown to me, for four days I repeatedly crossed paths with five fugitives — desperate men, two of them escaped murderers — who had killed a family of four in Arizona a few days before after stealing their car. One night in particular, I experienced a foreboding sense of danger in the unusual blackness that surrounded my campsite near the Dolores River. It was too still. I was unable to sleep, gradually becoming convinced that some malevolent force lurked beyond that impenetrable darkness. Although I didn't know it, a young couple, trout-fishing as I was, had been abducted and murdered that day, their van commandeered by the same five men. A few days later, the couple's belongings were found along the river close to the spot where I had spent the night.

The awareness of how narrowly I had missed having my own name added to the list of victims Gary Tison and Randy Greenawalt killed that summer aroused my interest in the case, which I followed closely in the newspapers. In 1983, I began more systematically to research the story of the prison escape and the last rampage of Gary Tison. This book is the result.

The easiest way to describe the years of research that went into this project is to compare it to assembling a large jigsaw puzzle whose pieces are scattered geographically over an area that included seven western states and extend back in time to the Great Depression. I had the edges and broad contours of the story in mind before I started, but surprises, even astonishment, followed as I began to piece in the more complicated interior. The story was much more complex than I imagined, hinging on bizarre relationships, extraordinary behavior, and astonishing coincidences. I could see how mood and emotion had shaded, then had defined, the reality of many of those involved as much as the events themselves. The psychological landscapes were often deceptive, like the vistas of the Sonoran desert, where much of this story takes place. Intentions and emotions changed with the angle of light, making interpretation difficult. One could not always be sure whether pieces that *seemed* to fit together actually did.

The story has its sociological roots in many of the same themes that John Steinbeck pursued in *The Grapes of Wrath*. The Joads moved west from Oklahoma and eventually reached Kern County, California, where they worked as pickers in the fields. The Tisons followed the same road west, worked the same fields, under the same hot sun, for the same low wages that Steinbeck wrote about. Both families struggled to thread their way through the contradictions of dusty, windblown poverty in a land of frontier promises and dreams. And the similarities go on. The oldest son, the central figure in this story, however, is not the selfless Christ figure that Steinbeck's Tom Joad was.

This story is about people who moved west a half century too late. It addresses the turbulence and uncertainty of life, after the frontier, on the edges of society — the dreary, unromantic marginality of people who traveled west in dilapidated automobiles, not covered wagons; who were called Okies rather than pioneers; who battled not colorful and savage Indians but employers, bankers, and landlords. Unlike their earlier counterparts, they did not "win" the West; instead, too many lost out to it. As Oklahoma poet Wilma Elizabeth McDaniel put it, describing the desperation of the Dust Bowl years:

> a man could get religion in a
> God forsaken
> place like this.

And many did. But the same pressures that pushed some into the pews and pulpits of cinderblock churches pushed others into granite-walled prisons and early graves. This is a story about both kinds of people, and the curious — and ultimately tragic — family relationships that developed within the moral vacuum left between authoritarian fundamentalism and lawlessness.

The story is drawn from a variety of sources: official police and court records; interviews with persons directly, or indirectly, acquainted with specific individuals, events, or eras; and newspaper accounts. What follows is based on this carefully documented material, or very tight logical inferences from it. In some instances, I have taken the liberty of reconstructing conversations and events that were described by only one of the parties; in a few others, I have inferred dialogue, without quotation marks, based on the mood and circumstances of specific situations, and my familiarity with the speech patterns and the personalities of the subjects involved. Sometimes I have transposed sentences in statements and remarks people have made. In a few cases, I have cut and combined materials from interviews that occurred at different times, or in different sequences, always, however, with care not to alter the meaning or significance of what was said. Occasionally, I did the same with secondary material, such as newspaper accounts — again, I believe, without distorting meaning or significance. All the persons I formally interviewed on tape were given transcripts of those interviews for their own records, with the understanding that editorial changes might be made in the transition from voice to print.

When the subject is crime, and particularly heinous crime, as it is in this book, different points of view and different perceptions of how things happened are to be expected. There are many reasons to lie, or shade the truth, some of them well intentioned. I made every attempt to take such differences into account before reaching my *own* conclusions. I did this, whenever possible, by considering and weighing information from a variety of sources, instead of relying solely on any single source.

Beyond this conventional research, I have spent a good bit of time retracing old trails, looking and listening in the places where events occurred — experiencing a specific time of day, or night, or a particular season — in order to reconstruct, as best I could, the circumstances of life and death in this story. Throughout, I have tried to be truthful.

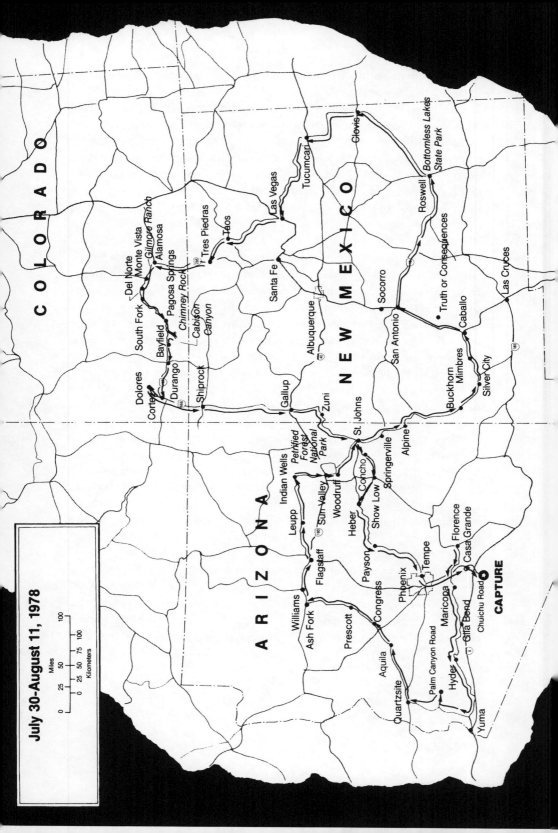

LAST RAMPAGE

Prologue

The Escape:
July 30–31, 1978

In times past, Florence, Arizona, was a thriving little town. Situated in a broad desert valley, just a few miles south of where the Gila River flows out between the Dripping Springs and Tortilla mountains, the town used to be a rest stop on the only paved road between Tucson and Phoenix. The Interstate changed all that. Yet Florence still recalls the faded styles and moods of the era of two-lane travel and independent ownership. If it weren't for the Circle K convenience store and the late-model pickups parked on the streets, Florence would look like a photograph of one of those lonely Western towns depicted in *Life* in the 1940s. About five thousand people live in Florence. There are only four stoplights in town, and three of them blink.

The center of town is dominated by the spire of the old Pinal County Courthouse. Built in the last century, the three-story brick structure sits at the edge of a modern complex of asphalt and tan stucco in which the county's affairs are now conducted. Apart from these buildings, the town still retains a lot of the dusty, sun-bleached authenticity of the old Southwest. On unpaved backstreets, Mexican adobe buildings—some with cracked plaster exposing the mud-and-straw bricks and saguaro ribs of the last century—stand next to mobile homes in sunlight that filters down through the branches of gnarled mesquite and tamarisk trees.

An old hitching rail, worn smooth from use, used to stand a couple of steps down from the plank porch of what was once the town's only hotel. Today the plank porch and hitching rail are gone, and the Florence Hotel stands vacant except for transient businesses that occasionally struggle and die in the space that once was its lobby. Overnight visitors now stay at the Blue Mist Motel, a prefabricated complex directly across U.S. Highway 89 from the town's most prominent and cheerless landmark, the Arizona State Prison.

Within the prison's high beige walls, in the grassy center of the maximum-security compound, near the truck-size gates that open into the industrial yard, is a one-story building of weathered pink brick about the size of a single-car garage. It looks like a run-down storage building. An evaporative cooler sits rusting against one wall. An old-fashioned stovepipe rises high — too high, some thirty feet — from the center of its flat roof. It has no windows, only four steel doors thick with years of gray paint. Three are standard size, the other is wide enough to wheel a gurney through. An old metal sign, white with rust streaking down from the bolts that hold it in place, marks one of them: CONDEMNED CELL, it says in faded black letters. Inside that door, through another doorway and a few steps beyond, stands one of the prison's few modern structures: the gas chamber. With its aerodynamic, gleaming stainless steel and glass, it looks like a space capsule. Inmates joke that it is the ultimate trip.

On Sunday, July 30, 1978, at 8:30 A.M., the temperature was already climbing toward 90. The sun burned in through the windshield and curled the cracked vinyl on the dashboard of a green Ford Galaxie moving slowly down the access road to the prison. The car's air conditioner was going full blast and roaring so loud that the three men inside could barely hear the weather forecast on the radio — clear skies and a high of 107 degrees expected in Phoenix — when they pulled into the parking lot east of the main gate. The driver punched off the radio and a stocky young man with collar-length brown hair, dressed in Levi's and a dark T-shirt, got out of the rear door and walked across the road to a building marked TRUSTY ANNEX. When he disappeared inside, the car turned and drove off back the way it had come.

The Annex was less intimidating than the main prison across the road, whose walls bristled with razor wire, guard towers, and searchlights. Built as a women's facility, the Annex had only two years before been converted to a medium-security unit for men. The lower walls and cyclone fence that enclosed it were softened on the inside by mulberry trees and neatly trimmed grass and flower beds. An ordinary-looking entryway opened directly to the road. If you had to do time at the Arizona State Prison, this was the best location, no doubt about it. The fortunate few inmates who resided here were given preferred work assignments and the luxury of dormitory-style housing, two men to a room, in contrast to the noisy corridors and stark, cramped cages across the road.

The young man walked to the guard's screened window, said good morning, and signed in to visit inmate 28354, his father, Gary Gene Tison. Raymond Tison was eighteen and had made these weekend visits to see his dad as long as he could remember. He customarily came with his mother and two older brothers on Sundays. It was a weekly ritual for the Tison family. The guards who had been around for a while were on a first-name basis with the family and had watched Ray and his brothers grow up over the last fifteen years that their dad had been in prison. It was an easygoing ("Morning, Ray, how're you doing?") relationship, the kind you might develop with the cashier at a grocery store or the local bank teller. It seemed as though Gary Tison had always been in prison; guards, walls, searches, and schedules had become just a normal part of life for Ray and his brothers. No big deal, they said. They were used to it.

At the buzz of the door release, Ray walked from the pale green entrance foyer into a smaller room, where he was given the casual routine search he was accustomed to. The brown paper bag he carried contained a six-pack of Coke and a couple of ham sandwiches. Satisfied, the guard nodded an O.K. and released a second door. Ray entered a vestibule that opened into an outdoor visitation area, where the grass and mulberry trees grew and sprinklers sprayed the flowers that blossomed along the buildings. Ray was already seated at one of the picnic tables when the gate to the confinement area opened and his father walked in.

Gary Tison was a physically imposing man. Not that he was especially tall — five foot ten or so, he was only an inch taller than his son. It was his beefy wide shoulders and his thickness from chest to back you noticed. For the past six months, he had worked as the chief cook in the galley and his weight had ballooned to over 250 pounds, a lot of it spilling out over a sagging western belt buckle. The buttons strained and pulled his shirt tight across his big belly. At the back, his prison-issue jeans hung loosely from his surprisingly small hips and rear. It seemed as if all his weight was concentrated in his thick, muscular arms and bulky torso. Though he carried the excess weight well because of his broad frame, it nevertheless had given him a jowly appearance. At forty-two, he retained only remnants of the angular handsomeness of his youth. He favored long, neatly trimmed sideburns, worn cowboy style to the bottom of his ears, and his thinning blond hair, receding above his temples, was combed straight back and cut close around his ears. He had always combed his hair straight back without a part. As a young man, he liked it when people said he looked like country rocker Jerry Lee Lewis. Jerry Lee, he said, played good music and was a hell-raiser like he was. But Gary's most striking physical feature — the thing most people noticed and never forgot — was his deep-set, expressionless, mismatched eyes, the right one an icy blue, and the left an eerie, translucent amber, like the eye of a cat. It was as if his eyes had no connection with any emotion he expressed. Whatever his mood — whether he was angry, jovial, or anything in between — his eyes remained the same. Empty. It was impossible to tell what Gary was actually thinking or feeling by looking at his eyes. And no one knows if they ever shed tears, for no one ever saw Gary cry. His stare was riveting, unsettling, with a malign intensity. What people remembered most about Gary were those cold, hard eyes.

Gary Tison had been in and out of jails and prisons since he was sixteen, first for stealing one thing or another, then for armed robbery. Now he was working on the eleventh year of two consecutive life sentences for killing a prison guard in 1967. The sentence made him madder than anything: the idea that when he died he'd still have time to do grated on him. It was as if he somehow believed he would have another life after the first one, and they were going to make him spend that one behind bars, too. He thought it was very unfair. So did Dorothy, his wife.

The father and son exchanged greetings, a few pats on the back, and seated themselves on the same side of a picnic table in clear view of the entryway. Ray snapped open one of the Cokes, offered it to his dad, and took a long pull when Gary waved him off. Gary shook out a Pall Mall and lit it with the silver Zippo he carried in his shirt pocket, never once looking at Ray or taking his eyes off the guard office across the yard.

A moment later he nudged Ray with his elbow. Another inmate, Randy Greenawalt, had walked to the guard office and knocked on the door. Greenawalt worked as a clerk-typist in the office, and if it's possible for a 240-pound man to look like a clerk-typist, the twenty-nine-year-old Greenawalt did. At five foot nine, Randy had a flaccid, spongy look. The features of his soft, round, little boy's face were now too small to accommodate the flesh they supported. His chin receded into heat-mottled rolls that sagged on the collar of a damp white extra-large T-shirt, which fit him like a salami skin. Thick dark-rimmed glasses rested on puffy cheeks, and his dark brown hair was parted and slicked down flat across a wide forehead marked with worry lines. His upper lip extended over his lower, which was drawn in as if in childlike uncertainty, or maybe self-pity. He had a thin little voice that sounded downright weird coming from that goiter-thick throat of his.

Like Tison, Greenawalt was considered a model prisoner — at least by the warden and his immediate staff. He also was serving life for murdering a truck driver. Actually, he had killed two, probably three, maybe four truck drivers in separate, nasty events, but he had only been tried and convicted for one. Randy had hated truck drivers ever since one roughed him up at a warehouse where he worked for a while outside Denver. He also knew drivers often carried a lot of cash. His "M.O." (mode of operating), he liked to explain with a shy little smile, made him a serial killer. Something special. The shrinks thought serial killers were more interesting than ordinary murderers, especially when they had IQs in the genius range like Randy's.

Randy had come to the guard office, as he did every Sunday, to type the next day's work assignments, "gang sheets," as they were called. Once he was admitted he walked over to his typewriter and sat down, his perspiring mass fairly enveloping the small secretarial chair.

Marquis Hodo was the sergeant in charge that morning. Hodo, a thin, wiry man with a deep voice scorched to a gravelly tone by a lot of cigarettes and a daily pot of strong black coffee, had just come up to the visitor area to relieve the guard at the registration window when two familiar young men entered the foyer — Ricky and Donald Tison. It was almost 9:00 A.M., and Hodo was unaware that Ray had come in about twenty minutes earlier. But there was nothing unusual about the Tison boys coming to see their father on the weekend. Their mother usually came with them on Sunday, but she would probably be along later. As a rule, as the boys grew older they left before she did, probably so she and Gary would have some time to themselves, if you can call being under constant surveillance in a visiting area with other visitors time to themselves. But that was another story.

All nice enough boys, the Tisons. Friendly and always polite. At nineteen, Ricky (so named because his mother loved the *Ozzie and Harriet* show) still had some growing up to do, but he had an appealing boyish charm. With that toothy grin, he always seemed to be in a good mood. You couldn't help smiling back. Except for that easy smile, he looked more like his dad than the other two. Ricky was a little taller and clearly a lot thinner than his father, but an onlooker might guess that Gary had had Ricky's tapered, athletic build when he was younger. Ricky's hair was light like his dad's, but he wore it longer, like his brothers — but not longer than their father allowed. Gary hated bikers and hippies, and he didn't want his sons looking like either one, especially around the prison. No longer than the bottom of their ears, he told them, and absolutely not over their collars. And that was a concession to their mother, who was trying to keep peace in the family. One time when they came to visit, Gary sent Donny home because his hair was too long. The following week when Donny showed up for visiting hours, his hair had been cut to the approved length.

Donny had always seemed more independent than his brothers. More of an outsider. He was twenty, looked more serious than his brothers, and acted more mature. He was stocky and had hair a shade in between his brothers'. As soon as he was old enough to drive, he had started visiting his dad alone, often departing when the others arrived. Then he joined the marines. He had told his father that he wanted to quit school, and Gary had said he'd approve only if Donny joined the marines. That made sense to Donny. His dad had been a military man during the war — or so he had been told. Once, on leave, Donny came to the prison in uniform. Gary seemed real proud of him. After he was discharged, Donny mentioned to one of the guards that he was thinking about a career with the state police and was taking courses in criminal justice at the community college. Gary claimed to have had a hand in that decision, too. In contrast to Donny, the younger two boys seemed to stick pretty close to home, and their mother.

As Ricky approached the registration window, Donny set the cardboard box he carried on a table located near the window. Visitors were permitted to bring ice chests and picnic baskets into the visiting area on weekends. The box, labeled "Salem Cigarettes" and covered with a tablecloth, would be searched when they entered the control room. Ricky filled out the visitor registration form and slid it back through to Hodo. When Hodo looked up from his paperwork seconds later, he saw Ricky's familiar grin — and then, tilting up beneath it, the muzzle of a sawed-off shotgun aimed directly at his face.

Prison visitors Fernando and Susanne Armenta were sitting on a bench across the room when the two brothers entered. While Ricky was standing at the registration window, Mr. Armenta got up and tried to set his own ice chest down next to the Salem box on the table. Donny suddenly elbowed him aside and, waving a .38 automatic in his direction, warned him to keep away from the box. Until that moment neither of the Armentas had noticed the shotgun in Ricky's hands. Susanne, who was holding their baby, immediately fled to the far corner of the room, crying and pleading for their safety. Ricky never took his eyes from the astonished Hodo while all this occurred. Donny softened his tone as he spoke again and began trying to reassure the terrified couple. "You behave, and don't do nothing wrong, and nobody will get hurt," he kept repeating. "We don't want to hurt anyone."[1]

Ed Barry, another guard in the room, was seated with his back to Hodo and the registration window and was unaware of the developing situation. When he stood and turned to ask Hodo a question, he noticed the funny blank look on Hodo's face, then the reason for it in Ricky's hands. The guards were unarmed.

Ricky didn't say a word. He just stood there, Hodo recalled, with "that dumb grin on his face." Greenawalt rose from his typewriter and moved quickly to the window to take another sawed-off shotgun and a pistol that Ricky passed in to him. Greenawalt made Hodo and Barry lie on the floor before he pressed the button to open the door for Ricky and Donny to enter the office. Then he pressed another switch to open the inner door to the visitation area. Gary had already walked casually over to the door. When it opened, Donny handed him a pistol, which he concealed quickly beneath his shirt. Then he returned outside, where two unsuspecting guards stood talking in the shade. Within a few minutes, seven on-duty guards, as well as six visitors, had been quietly and efficiently rounded up in the control room, where they were forced to join Hodo and Barry on the floor. At this point, Gary took charge and gave all the orders. Hodo, who had known Tison for most of his time in prison, remembered that "he had us. He knew it and he wasn't nervous a bit."[2]

While all this was going on, the eighth on-duty guard, Lieutenant George Goswick, was in the rest room a short distance down the hall, reading the Sunday newspaper. Gary noticed the rest room door was closed, and when he tried it, Goswick grumbled that he would be out in a minute. Gary waited quietly until he heard the flush and then eased back against the wall beside the rest room door. When Goswick stepped out, Gary pushed a pistol into his midsection, saying softly, "You make one false move and you're a dead man." There was no "lieutenant" or "sir" this time from the normally courteous Tison as he pushed Goswick toward the control room. When Goswick saw the others lying face-down on the floor, he hesitated. Tison pushed the barrel of the gun deeper into Goswick's gut and, leaning closer, added, "If you don't believe it, Goswick, just try me."[3]

The thought never entered the lieutenant's mind. Gary had killed a prison guard and had a long history of escape attempts. There wasn't an inmate in the prison who didn't know and respect his reputation as a very tough customer. People who crossed him got hurt. And everybody, even the powerful prison gangs — from the "blood in, blood out" Aryan Brotherhood through the Mexican Mafia to the Muslims — left him alone. "Nobody messed around with him," Goswick said later, "no inmate, nobody. He was not someone you would want to cross." Goswick meekly joined the others on the floor.

As they were lying there, both Goswick and Hodo noticed that Greenawalt, who had not uttered a word since Gary arrived, was trembling and looking very pale. Sweat was streaming down his face and dripping off his nose and chin. The sawed-off shotgun shook in his hands. It looked like he was losing it, and both guards knew that when he did someone would get hurt. "Randy, don't get nervous with that shotgun," Goswick stammered. "You got us covered. There's nobody going to try to jump you. It's okay. We're cool."

Greenawalt just looked at him blankly and then down at the shotgun in his hands, as if he couldn't comprehend what was happening or what he should do next. Goswick kept chattering away about being cool and not doing anything stupid. But the more he talked, the more nervous Greenawalt became. He began to move his head from side to side like a cornered animal looking for a way out. Finally, Gary, whose attention had been on the captives, noticed him. He reached over and took the shotgun out of Greenawalt's hands. At first the inmate seemed startled, as if he had just awakened from a trance, but he didn't resist at all. Then a look of relief flickered across his ashen face. The captives on the floor were equally relieved.

While attention was focused on Goswick and then Greenawalt, Ed Barry carefully reached down to the radio on his belt. His hope was that the guard in the tower closest to the Annex would hear what was happening. Tison saw Barry easing his arm away and swung around, taking aim at the guard's head. Barry cringed and shut his eyes. He thought it was all over. Unaware that the radio was already on, Gary said, "Barry, if you touch that radio, you *all* are dead. I'll blow you all away." He said it very slowly and deliberately. For a moment the only sound was the heavy irregular breathing of very frightened people. Gary's boys glanced at each other and watched their dad. Finally he said, "Okay, unbuckle them duty belts, all of you, and don't try anything. If anyone tries to key a radio again, everybody dies." He told the boys to gather up the belts and radios and put them in the Salem box.

Before they did, Gary pulled two changes of clothes from the box. He handed a pair of pants and a shirt to Greenawalt and told him to change. Randy nodded and moved into the hallway, out of sight of the women. Gary followed while the boys stood guard. He returned in denims and a western shirt, then sat down on a chair to pull on his cowboy boots. The boots were his trademark, a symbol of his influence within the prison. He was the only inmate permitted to wear them; everyone else was required to wear low-cut shoes. Tison had been given special permission to wear the boots for "medical" reasons — ankle support. Nobody believed it.

When Greenawalt had changed, Gary positioned himself at the entrance to the hall. "Okay, you guys get up one at a time," he said to the captives. "Real slow. Don't make no quick moves. If one of you goes, all of you goes. I'm going to take you across here and lock you in the storeroom. Now come out here, one at a time."

When the fourteen captives had shuffled nervously into the storage room, the shotguns were exchanged for pistols and placed back into the Salem box with the duty belts and radios and covered with the tablecloth. After issuing a final warning about remaining quiet and in place, Gary locked the door with the keys he had taken from Goswick. He stuffed a western-style Colt .45 under his belt, covered it with his shirt, and told the others to do the same with their weapons. Greenawalt, shaking and perspiring again, had trouble getting his pistol into his belt because his pants were too tight. "Come on, Randy, goddammit," Gary said impatiently. Then, "Okay, let's go. Walk slow and act like nothin's wrong."

Ray and Donny carried the Salem box and an ice chest as they walked out, squinting in the bright morning sunlight. None of them dared to look up at the guard tower, whose shadow extended almost to the car parked across the road at the far edge of the visitors' lot. It seemed like a long walk. Daniel Gustafson was on duty in the tower. He had heard some muffled sounds coming from the Annex over the intercom but since the noise stopped without any further transmission, he'd assumed that an inmate was being searched and someone had accidentally keyed a transmitter. Now he noticed five men leave the Annex, two of them carrying containers of some kind, but he thought little of it, or of the fact that visitors would be leaving so early. There was nothing unusual about a group of people leaving the Annex together on a weekend, on Sundays especially. And they didn't act suspicious. Why, one of them had a big smile on his face and was twirling a set of keys as the men walked across the lot toward the car. It was approximately 9:20 A.M. when the Galaxie pulled out and headed west on the prison road to Florence. In less than twenty minutes after the guns had first been drawn, Gary Tison and Randy Greenawalt were on the loose.

When the sun had risen over the Superstition Mountains that morning with the glare and hot intensity of a laser beam, at their house at 2221 North Sixty-first Drive on the west side of Phoenix, the three Tison boys were already up. So was their mother. Dorothy had known she wouldn't be able to sleep, so she hadn't gone to bed. Instead, she sat up in the living room in front of a television she wasn't really watching. The ashtray on the endtable beside her filled up with cigarette butts. Ricky and Ray sat up with her until they both fell asleep, one on the floor, the other on the couch.

They slept like that until Donny got home well after midnight, smelling like a brewery and pretty well loaded. Dorothy had been worried that he wouldn't show up at all, despite the assurances of his brothers. She knew that Donny didn't really want to go through with their plan. It wasn't that he was afraid or didn't love his dad, he had told her. He just thought it was a dumb, unworkable idea and somebody was going to get hurt. She was scared, herself, she said, and understood his reservations, but there didn't seem to be any other way to get Gary out of prison. Lord knows, she had tried everything she could think of over the last ten years. Besides, it was too late to turn back now, after all the months of preparation they had put into this. Now Donny was rambling on about the family sticking together and, by God, nobody had to worry about him doing his share. Dorothy made fresh coffee to sober him up, and she and her three boys sat around waiting for daylight.

It was awkward and uncomfortable, like waiting at an airport for a flight to leave after all the goodbyes have been said. For eight or nine months, they had talked endlessly about what they were going to do, through all the permutations of the constantly changing plans. Dorothy wasn't much for speeches anyway. At about six-thirty Ray walked into the kitchen and turned on the radio to see what the weather was going to be like — as if no one could guess what the weather would be like in Arizona in July — but he couldn't find a station at that hour that didn't have some preacher with a nasal Texas accent droning on about sin and damnation. When it got close to the time for the boys to leave, Dorothy said again what she had said all along: that they were doing this for their dad because there was no other way. And, Donny added, for you, Mom.

Around 7:00 A.M. the three brothers kissed her goodbye, and she hugged each one tightly and whispered, "Be careful and call when you can." She blew kisses as they drove away in her Galaxie 500 and watched the car until it turned the corner at the end of the block. Then she went back inside to look for her cigarettes.

They headed for Bob Adams's place through the early-morning stillness of the residential and industrial areas that define the west side of Phoenix. Adams lived across town in a mobile home park at 815 North. A rough-looking man, six foot four, with a ragged scar extending across his cheek and a weakness for young boys, Adams had shared a cell at the Arizona State Prison with their father, and had remained in contact with Gary since his release. During the last several months, he had visited his old cellmate nearly every week. He was one of Gary's main connections to the outside and had been in on the escape plans from the beginning.

Adams heard the car on the gravel drive and pulled the edge of his closed curtains aside. The Galaxie parked next to a fenced area used to store recreational vehicles and boats. One of the boys got out and walked over to a white 1969 Lincoln Continental with New Mexico plates. The car had been parked there among the RVs and boats since February. Ray and Ricky had been there the evening before to check things out and add a few items to a trunk already crammed with food, supplies, camping equipment, and weapons. They had done all kinds of work on the car over the months to get it ready, but the battery had weakened from sitting unused for so long, and last night they couldn't get the damn thing started. They'd had to jump start it, using Adams's car.

Adams hadn't said much because he knew it would get back to Gary, but he thought the whole plan was crazy from the beginning. He knew they'd be able to get out of the Annex — everyone knew security there was a joke — but, sure as hell, there would be shooting once they were outside, and he didn't think they'd make it out the access road. It might have worked if Gary had been able to get the professionals he'd wanted in the first place, when he'd dreamed up this whole deal, but not with three amateur kids running the show for him. All this commando bullshit, he thought, and the battery goes dead.

This morning there was no reason for him to leave his trailer, so he just stood at the window and watched as Donny unlocked the car door and eased himself in. The big engine roared to life. Donny gassed it a few times, let it idle for a minute. Then together the two cars pulled out and turned back west on Van Buren. The boys then followed a route down the Hohokam Expressway, through a corridor of billboard clutter and the stale odor of the morning's brown inversion layer, until it merged with Interstate 10. They continued traveling south, into the dazzling ozone glare, as they followed the Interstate for another half hour to Exit 185. Then they turned east for the remaining twenty miles to Florence. It was a familiar hour-long trip they had made often.

The first announcement that you are approaching the town of Florence is the whitewashed "F" on a small pyramid-shaped hill of

burned-looking rocks. The second is about a mile down the road, a
tall water tower with FLORENCE painted in black letters on its side.
Located between these two landmarks is the Pinal General Hospital, a small, ninety-one-bed facility built of concrete block painted
white.

The two cars turned into the asphalt parking lot in front of the
main entrance. Donny parked and locked the Lincoln, and then he
climbed into the front seat of the Ford after Ray moved to the back.
Together, the three brothers drove across town to the prison.

The Galaxie sagged under the extra five hundred pounds of Gary
Tison and Randy Greenawalt as Donny Tison cautiously wheeled it
out of the parking area and retraced the route he and his brothers
had taken across town less than an hour earlier. He couldn't believe
they were getting away with it as the guard towers receded in the
rear view mirror. Across town, they pulled into the hospital parking
lot and quickly changed cars, leaving the Galaxie locked. It would
remain undiscovered for nearly two weeks.

The big Lincoln roared north on Attaway Road to the Hunt Highway, passing cotton fields and desert. At the southern edge of the
town of Chandler, the car turned west onto Williams Field Road,
crossing over Interstate 10 before heading south again on a narrow
two-lane road, which cuts through the Gila River Indian Reservation
and into the farming community of Maricopa. There the Lincoln
turned west on a dirt road paralleling the Southern Pacific Railroad
tracks and continued on to Gila Bend, a tiny sun-faded community
of discount gas stations and run-down motels, jokingly referred to
as the nation's fan-belt capital because of its record-setting high temperatures. The fugitives avoided Gila Bend's only paved street by
taking dirt roads through the citrus orchards and cotton fields at its
edges. A graded road west of town skirted the Painted Rock Mountains
and took the men north across a bridge over the Gila River to their
destination, the isolated settlement of Hyder. They were about 137
miles and three hours away from Florence when they stopped.

Hyder consists of a few dilapidated houses and mobile homes, scattered along a quarter mile of the northern spur of the Southern
Pacific linking Phoenix and Yuma. Most of the houses are deserted,
except when seasonally occupied by Mexican migrants who work on
the big irrigated farms to the west, near Dateland. The handful of

permanent residents live in the mobile homes close to the tracks. A wide, flat, gravel road runs south about a mile through a particularly barren stretch of desert before curving up over a small rise. On the other side is the small cluster of native stone houses and mobile homes of Agua Caliente — a kind of low-rent spa, catering to counterculture Californians and arthritics who come in the winter to soak their stiff joints in the warm natural springs that bubble to the surface of the desert near the banks of the sometimes flowing Gila River. In summer, the place has the same abandoned look that beach houses have in the winter. This was no place to be in July — which was precisely why the Tisons had picked it. Nothing but empty desert in all directions and a good place to land a plane you didn't want anybody to see.

Mexico is only fifty air miles to the south of Agua Caliente, but it's impossible to drive, and it's one hell of a walk. An area of shifting sand covers about forty-five square miles and a hiker will sink into his calves walking through it. Daytime temperatures in the summer often exceed 120 degrees and it's hard to tell where an Air Force bombing range begins and ends in this tortured landscape. The Border Patrol regularly finds bodies of illegal aliens who die trying to cross the treacherous terrain; officials estimate there are many more whose remains have been carried away by vultures and coyotes or buried by sandstorms. The Cabeza Prieta is the unchallenged domain of scorpions and sidewinder rattlesnakes.

The Lincoln turned off the road at Hyder and pulled in beside an abandoned house set off from the others. A quarter mile behind the house, the settlement's only landmark, a barren mesa of black volcanic rock, seemed to mark the edge of the property and perhaps a past owner's dream. The paint on the three-room, wood-frame house had been faded and flaked away by the sun and blowing sand. The door was open, hanging from one hinge. Except for the rhythmic clatter and receding whistles of passing Southern Pacific freights, and the rattling of the rusted tin on the roof when the wind blew hard, it was quiet. It seemed lifeless except for a few lizards that scurried here and there and disappeared through cracks in the plank floor. The leathery remains of a lizard and a rodent that had drowned a long time ago floated in a corrugated metal water-storage tank that stood on a tilting platform of two-by-fours outside the back door.

A dilapidated shed of corrugated tin, with part of a roof and a chicken-wire enclosure, stood near the house. The five men cleared away enough debris to get the Lincoln inside, out of sight. Gary had planned the escape as a paramilitary operation, and now he changed clothes accordingly. They had brought along dark green army surplus fatigues, and Gary put on a big-pocketed cotton shirt over his T-shirt, despite the heat, like an overweight Fidel Castro. Gary was in command — there was never any question about that — but it seemed clear that he also wanted to look like a commander, though he still wore his cherished cowboy boots. For their part, the boys stayed with T-shirts and jeans.

After checking out the house they brought in some food and drinks from the car. It was empty except for a half dozen or so bunk bed springs resting on adobe bricks in each corner. In what had been the kitchen, a pile of plaster remained where the sink had been torn from the wall. A toilet rested on its side in a closet off the kitchen next to a hole in the floor where trash had been thrown. Tecate beer cans were scattered around in all the rooms, probably the leftovers of migrant workers.

The men sat on the bedsprings and sprawled on the floor, eating chili and beef stew directly from the cans, washing it down with beer and soft drinks from the several ice chests they had brought in. The afternoon temperature had climbed to 107 degrees in Phoenix. That meant it must be 110 or more in Hyder.

That first evening of freedom in Hyder was to be the high point of the whole adventure. And it was probably the high point in the lives of Donny, Ricky, and Ray Tison. The boys were elated by the ease with which they had carried out the escape, and most of the conversation revolved around that. Ricky laughed as he recounted the story, who knows how many times: You should've seen the look on ol' Hodo's face when he looked into the muzzle of that .16 gauge. That bastard like to shit his pants. And how about ol' Goswick when Dad grabbed him coming out of the shitter? And then him standing there with that who-shit-in-my-Easter-basket look like he expected Barry or someone to get up off the floor and do something. Christ, you could bust a gut just thinking about it.

What a day it had been. Everything had gone just the way it was supposed to. It would have been perfect if it had ended right then, right there, in Hyder.

Gary smiled and bragged a little with the others, and he seemed to enjoy it when he explained, using a lot of military terms, how they each would be taking turns standing watch during the night. But the heat was bothering him, and his good mood didn't last long. He started to get restless, as he had been for the first few hours on the road. It wasn't over — they still had a long way to go. They couldn't spend the rest of their lives in Hyder. They had to get out of the country one way or another. Pretty soon everyone's mood changed, too, and it got quiet.

Dorothy knew approximately where they were. The plans had been changing from week to week since earlier in the spring, then from day to day, and for the past few days, almost from hour to hour. When the day finally came, the elaborate plans for an escape flight to Mexico had been reduced to simply getting to Hyder with the hope that, in a day or so, Dorothy could find a pilot and a plane to pick them up. Originally, the plan had been to meet a plane that Gary's brother Joe was to have waiting at a landing strip near the prison. Then they were to make the one-hour flight south across the border to a ranch near Caborca, where they could hide out for a while until the pressure eased off. Then they'd continue south, possibly to Costa Rica, where Dorothy would join them. But that plan fell through when Joe was arrested on drug charges and something happened to the plane. Joe said it crashed, but who could believe Joe? Anyway, there was no plane unless Dorothy could somehow manage to get one in less than the twenty-four hours Gary figured they could stay in any one place. The wide and level graded road to Agua Caliente was a perfect, and well-known, landing strip for dope smugglers like Joe, who made such flights in and out of Mexico over the Cabeza Prieta on a regular basis. That part of the border was the emptiest, least-secure area between Tucson and San Diego. By this time tomorrow, Gary told the boys later that evening, they would know whether their mother had been successful.

That night they listened to reports of the escape on a portable radio and observed what appeared to be helicopters with searchlights near a mountain far to the east. But the choppers came no closer,[4] and despite the uncertainty about what would happen next, it seemed even to Gary that the hardest part was behind them.

The tense and, initially, buoyant mood of that first afternoon of freedom soon translated into heavy consumption of food and drink. The next morning, empty cans and wrappers were scattered everywhere; they would have to replenish their supplies. Gary told Ricky and Ray to take the car and look for a store at one of the Interstate exits. They found one about twenty miles away in Dateland, a tiny stop on the Interstate west of Sentinel. They got some beer and pop, but had to settle for potato chips, pretzels, and stale packaged pastries. They filled up with gas and started back to Hyder with the supplies. On the way, they noticed the car swaying a little, then riding funny, and decided to stop and take a look. Sure enough, one tire was ballooning out on the bottom and was slowly going flat. The heavy load and high speeds on rough roads the day before were beginning to take their toll. Back in Hyder they pulled the car back in the shed, out of the sun, and changed the tire. Gary hadn't slept much in the heat of the night and had been on edge when they left. Now he was really angry, asking why in the hell they hadn't brought an extra spare. In all the months of careful planning, and with all the survival equipment they had bought, no one had thought about something as obvious as extra tires.[5] Not even Gary. But no one said that.

The day wore on and no plane appeared, and the temperature again edged past 110 degrees. The good spirits and optimism of the night before continued to drain away. Tensions started to build. The heat was getting to Gary. He couldn't get comfortable on the floor, and the bunk springs wouldn't hold him or Randy without sagging almost to the ground and they cut into his back. He paced back and forth, making everyone else nervous. No one knew what to say, so it was quiet except when Gary would curse the heat or mutter something about a plane or his brother Joe. And, of course, he smoked. He must have smoked five packs of Pall Malls since they had left the prison. One after another. Half the time he didn't even take them out to exhale, but just let them dangle from one side of his mouth, the eye above half closed as the smoke curled up toward it. You could sometimes tell his moods by how quickly the two thick streams of smoke poured from his nostrils. He must have had lungs made of leather. He smoked that way as effortlessly as most people breathe.

They continued to monitor the reports on Phoenix radio stations for clues to what the police were doing and thinking. But the newscasts didn't say much more than they had the previous day — only that two convicted murderers, Tison and Greenawalt, had escaped from the state prison with the assistance of Tison's three sons. Later that afternoon, they heard that the state's director of corrections, Ellis

MacDougall, had said he believed the escapees posed no danger to the general public.[6] Can't argue with that, Donny said with a sigh, looking over at his dad. Gary wasn't listening.

By late afternoon, Gary announced that if the plane didn't arrive at Hyder by nightfall, they were going to leave. The question was where to go. He believed that their chances of remaining undetected until they escaped by plane were better if they remained in the rugged, largely uninhabited area between Tonopah to the north and Ajo to the south.[7] Their present hideout was about equidistant between these two points. But there were no connecting roads through the rugged Hassayampa back country, at least none that a conventional vehicle like the Lincoln could use. Gary cursed about that, saying they should've had a four-by-four like he wanted.

They spread maps out on the floor. After poring over them for a half hour or so, the choice became pretty obvious. The Interstate was not a viable option. One radio report they'd heard the evening before speculated that they might be heading for San Diego, so cops would be crawling all along the California border from Needles to Yuma. The only option was to continue west from Hyder on the graded road that followed the Southern Pacific tracks to Yuma. But what then? Gary decided that they would drive west toward Yuma, then this side of Yuma they would turn north on Route 95 and circle back east to the small town of Williams, near Flagstaff, where Gary's youngest brother, Larry, lived. Gary wasn't close to Larry, hardly knew him in fact. He had never been around home much when Larry was young, and he had been in prison most of the time since then. But Larry was family and it was worth a try. Maybe Larry would be able to get a plane for them, he said. There were plenty of landing strips on ranches in the area, and Larry had contacts, and it still wouldn't be that far to the border. Less than a three-hour flight, he figured, even in a light plane. How five heavy men were to fit into a light plane was a question no one raised.

By dusk, they knew Dorothy hadn't been able to pull it off. They all had been counting on their long-shot plan more than they realized, or maybe wanted to admit, because it was five increasingly tense men who squeezed back into the Lincoln and headed west into a twilight sky and a disturbingly uncertain future. They made a heavy load, five big men and all that equipment, and the springs on the big car flattened out low on the axles as they sped along the dusty road.

They knew they were in a precarious position until they could get that tire fixed, possibly when they got to Quartzsite, the next town they would reach that might have a gas station open late. But Quartzsite was over two hundred miles away.

About two hours later, after dark, just outside the little cotton farming community of Roll, they were relieved to get on a paved road, which zigzagged around the fields that checkerboard the Dome Valley area east of Yuma. It was after eleven when they finally turned north at a fork in the road onto U.S. Route 95. At eleven-thirty, just as they passed the gravel turnoff to Palm Canyon in the Kofa Mountains, there was a loud report, and the overloaded car sank sharply on its flattened right rear tire, waking the three brothers dozing in the back seat. Greenawalt, who was driving, joined the chorus of *goddammit to hells* and *mother-fucking sonsabitches,* pounding the steering wheel in frustration. He forced the Lincoln to keep going until the tire began to peel from the wheel and thump loudly against the fender. Then Gary screamed at him to stop, and everyone else suddenly got quiet. Greenawalt immediately pulled off onto the shoulder. As the others stood by, Ray and Ricky pulled the torn tread from the tire and tried to drive on the bare wheel. It was no use. The bumper and rear end of the car dragged on the pavement. Gary was beside himself with frustration and rage.

It was additional stress in an already stressful situation: no spare, another thirty miles to the nearest gas station, every lawman in the state looking for them. And it was hot. It felt close to a hundred degrees, with the heat still radiating off the asphalt highway and up your pantlegs five hours after sunset. No one said much except Gary, who hadn't stopped cursing. He struggled to control his rage enough to decide what to do next. Okay, here's what we're going to do, he said at last. We gotta get another car before daylight or we're done. Get that hood up, and Ray, you try to flag down any cars that come by. There won't be too many, so make it look good. Donny, you and Ricky get over there in those bushes on the other side of the road. Me and Randy'll hide on this side nearest the car. When someone stops, we'll jump them, but me and Randy will make the first move.[8]

The night was still and moonless. Only the faint glow of Yuma, some sixty miles to the south, defined the horizon. It was shortly after midnight when they saw the first set of headlights approaching in the distance.

I

Fugitives

1

"Okies"

In 1937, Gary Tison's father, a thin, raw-boned young man, stood with bowed head before a judge in the drab Bryan County Courthouse in Durant, Oklahoma. He was about to hear his sentence after pleading guilty to a string of armed robberies. The first was in Texarkana, Arkansas, on the Texas border, and the second was in McAlester, Oklahoma. The third was a serious mistake: he held up a store in his hometown of Durant and was quickly identified and arrested. It was an incredibly stupid thing to do in a town as small as Durant. His pregnant wife sat behind him now, a tiny woman, tears streaming from dark-circled eyes. A blond toddler squirmed on her lap as the judge spoke. It was the first of many trips the young man, Ruben Curtis Tison, and his son, Gary Gene, would make to courtrooms and prisons.

The scene was a familiar one in Oklahoma during the "dirty thirties," in the depths of the Great Depression. The eastern third of the state, where Durant is located and where the Tisons lived, was particularly hard hit by the weather. Accustomed to more rainfall than the western part of the state, the so-called green counties had turned brown in the drought. Decades of intensive cotton and grain farming, and a disregard for the land, had leached the nutrients from the topsoil, leaving it powdery and lifeless.[1] Conditions were bad throughout the state and, indeed, throughout the Midwest. By 1935, the drought and wind had cut a giant brown swath of suffering and desolation from the Canadian plains all the way south along the eastern slopes of the Rocky Mountains to the Mexican border. On April 14, 1935 — "Black Sunday," they've called it ever since — a storm of rolling dust swept across the flat, grassless prairies of Beaver County, Oklahoma:

"It was like a tornado running sideways, a boiling wall of dirt, horizon to horizon and several thousand feet high," Ed Calhoon recalled. "It overran a house and came rolling on. Birds were flying before it, looking desperate. Then it was on me. Cold, total darkness; static electricity played all over our old Tin Lizzie. I sat there for forty minutes. For days afterward I heard stories of chickens going to roost and drunkards praying for redemption . . ."[2]

The farms and hopes of countless families were blown away with the topsoil. Like the carrion birds that awaited the deaths of bare-ribbed cattle on the prairie, bankers watched and waited, foreclosure notices in hand, and, with grim finality, took everything a farmer had to have to make a living.

People were desperate; many were doing things they never would have considered doing under normal circumstances. Some notorious Oklahomans, like "Pretty Boy" Floyd, Bonnie Parker, and Clyde Barrow, turned to crime. Questions of right and wrong were fairly tricky when the banks being robbed were accumulating land and making money off everyone else's misery — or so it seemed to Curt Tison and many others like him at that time, in that ravaged state. People grasped at whatever means they could find to hold on to what little they had, and they followed the successes of Floyd, Parker, and Barrow with amusement and some satisfaction, just as people like them had followed the careers of the James and Younger brothers a half century before across the border in Missouri. The villains were the same: the big-money boys, who wore rings and neckties and owned the banks and railroads. To the farmers in Oklahoma it seemed that God and the banks were in cahoots, and a fair number turned from the law and conventional morality in an attempt to survive. It was easy to believe that God sent the wind and withheld the rain, and the bankers did the rest.

But others, like Curt Tison's wife, Mary, turned *to* religion in their time of need. However, these poverty-stricken farmers didn't turn to the starched-shirt-and-tie, high-toned religion of the Presbyterian and Methodist bankers they hated. Those fancy religions, they knew, were easy to live with, but tough to die by. They needed the emotional, handclapping faiths peddled by itinerant preachers in revival meetings that moved from one small town to another, assembling in abandoned Grange halls and empty barns, or, for that matter, anyplace out of the wind.

Varying themes of Pentecostal mysticism were preached by these evangelists, who in most cases were themselves only a pulpit away from the economic hardships of the people who crowded in to hear them. But these shabbily dressed men, with their dusty shoes, somber expressions, and worn Bibles, promised hope in a land stripped of hope. Hope was in the hymns they sang and the sermons they preached. They offered, as one old hymn expressed it, "a shelter in the time of storm."

Their messages were often drawn from the Sermon on the Mount and Jesus' promise of redemption in the hereafter: "Blessed are the poor in spirit; for theirs is the kingdom of heaven. Blessed are they that mourn; for they shall be comforted. Blessed are the meek; for they shall inherit the earth." In short, they offered not only hope but the promise of salvation — and it was free for the taking. To be "saved" and "heaven bound," one had only to confess his sins and to "invite Christ Jee'sus into your heart." Mary Tison did, and she prayed that her husband would find Jesus, too.

But there was a darker side to these sermons of hope, heaven, and Jesus' love: they also promised the unrepentant sinner eternal damnation. The feverish homiletics that characterized those emotional services left the listener with an especially lurid conception of damnation. Guilt and fear deepened within one's soul like storm clouds. During the altar calls that closed every service, warnings and appeals from the pulpit mixed with the morbid tones of invitational hymns and the weeping confessions of those who had gone forward, creating an unnerving dread of approaching doom:

> Almost persuaded, harvest is past!
> Almost persuaded, doom comes at last!
> Almost cannot avail,
> Almost is but to fail,
> Sad, sad, that bitter wail;
> Almost — but lost!"[3]

After a few experiences like that, a person didn't ever sin easily again.

But the same forces that drove some, like Mary Tison, toward religion pushed others, like her husband, in another direction.

Acknowledging the desperate conditions that prevailed, the judge gave the twenty-eight-year-old Curt Tison a lighter sentence than he might have otherwise, but lectured him at length about his obligations to his pregnant wife, the example he should set for his towheaded little boy, and the need to find a job so he could support them. It would be difficult for a young man to make a living in Oklahoma the way things were, the judge observed, and he suggested that after Tison served his time, he should go west to look for work. Then the judge warned Tison that he didn't want to see him in his courtroom again.

It seemed like good advice. After serving a couple of years in the state prison, with time off for good behavior, Curt Tison was released in 1939. Mary had had their second child in 1938. It was another little boy; they named him Joe Lee. Her husband hadn't been home very long after his release when she learned she was pregnant again. She had their third child, a daughter, Martha, in 1940. With three young children to feed, no job, and now a prison record, Curt decided to move his family to California, as the judge had suggested. Everyone said there was work and money to be made out there in the broad, irrigated fields and rich soil of the Central Valley. People were calling it the Promised Land. To the Tisons, it sounded too good to be true.

Like nearly everyone else they knew, the Tisons left without much planning. Not much was required when a family could pack up everything they owned in an hour or so. They would load up all their belongings, say a few goodbyes, and be gone the next morning, leaving only rusty machinery they couldn't afford to fix and empty buildings scoured gray by the grit. They left in old jalopies, disappearing in plumes of dust down the rutted dirt road that followed the Red River Valley west toward the Texas Panhandle.

No one who made the trip forgot it, and their stories are much the same — like pages from John Steinbeck's *The Grapes of Wrath*. Elzia Elliott, like Gary Tison, was just a youngster when his family moved west a few years before the Tisons:

"No one really wanted to leave," he said, "but things finally just got so bad we had to. We lived on a little farm near Lexington. I can remember helping my dad load everything we could on an old half-ton truck with spoked wheels. We let a neighbor take what was left; we just didn't have much then. We tied a tarp over it, and then used it to sleep under at night along the road.

"I remember my mother was feeling bad and worried about one thing and another, you know, with us young kids. It wasn't like taking a trip nowadays. It was just a two-lane road and the paving ended just outside of town, and it was rough dirt from there on to the next town, and pretty soon we started running out of towns. Real dusty, too. Had to keep a wet handkerchief over your face a lot of the time.

"I remember the day we left, and my dad telling me that we didn't have room to take the dogs — just a couple of old hounds, nothing special, mind you — but I sure didn't want to leave them behind; and I was bawling and everything . . .

"Well, anyway, that old truck, loaded down like it was on that rough road, wouldn't go more than about fifteen miles an hour, or it would heat up and boil over; and, you know, those skinny old dogs followed us that whole first day! I just kept watching them from the back of the truck. Sometimes they'd drop way behind and I'd think they were gone and I'd start bawling again, then we'd stop to fix the load or something and here they'd come just a-wagging their tails and licking my face. . . .

"We stopped that first evening at my aunt's house, and they were still with us. The next morning we started out again and . . . well, they just couldn't keep up. They just kept falling farther and farther behind 'til they were out of sight. I don't mind telling you, I cried myself to sleep that night; it still makes me sad to think about it. I sure loved those dogs."[4]

Years later a sick and mellowing Curt Tison told Elliott that experiences like that made most folks sad, but with Gary, he said, it just seemed to make him mean, "like a dog that's been mistreated."

"He told me that," Elliott said, "when I sat with him at Gary's trial for killing that prison guard."[5]

The roads west from Oklahoma angle through flat, featureless country to Amarillo, in the Texas Panhandle. West of Amarillo, the land begins to fall away into a mosaic of broad, irregular valleys laced with dry stream beds. Rocky escarpments, carved out of the soil by wind and rain, rise abruptly at their edges, revealing the fossilized remains of ancient seas. A suddenly irregular horizon of distant mesas and buttes jolts the senses; instead of twenty miles away, as it had been on the plains, the horizon might be seventy, or eighty, or a hundred. Distances free the imagination, become deceiving in the multidimensional glow of early-morning and late-afternoon light. Indians believed the long shadows cast by the backlit angular terrain reached out beyond the universe.

The vastness of the great Southwest can fill a person with an exhilarating, almost mystical feeling of freedom — a feeling that can fade quickly into a foreboding sense of isolation. Shades of pink and yellow, lavender and blue, appear and begin to blend into the monotonous browns and tans of the Panhandle. And through it, old U.S. Route 66, a narrow brown ribbon of dirt and concrete, stretches out toward the Rio Grande Valley, and on beyond to the Promised Land.

In the 1940s, some, like the Tisons, took the southern route from Amarillo, following Route 60 as it cut a southwesterly course through the towns of Hereford and Friona before crossing into New Mexico at Clovis. At Clovis, it was common to take a shortcut down through Roswell and over through the Bonito Valley in Lincoln County to the chiefly Mexican town of Socorro before joining Route 60 again.

A long, empty stretch of road climbed from the rock and cactus of Socorro, New Mexico, through the piñon pine and juniper country to Springerville, Arizona. Travelers were advised to carry extra gas (at 15 cents a gallon) and provisions because you couldn't count on finding anything but jackrabbits and coyotes along that road. Springerville was like a different country. Because of its higher elevation, it was usually the first town on the long trip to offer some relief from the desert heat. In the summer, travelers commonly rested a day or two there. Show Low, about thirty miles farther west on Route 60, was another popular rest spot. From Show Low, it was a rugged, winding drive down through the mountains to Globe. The most challenging stretch was the precipitous, twisting descent into the Salt River Canyon and the steep climb back up the mountain on the other side of the river. It took the better part of a day to get up over the top. Engines boiled over from the strain of the pull. Men helped each other push the hissing and steaming jalopies, as women and children walked alongside carrying as much as they could to lighten the loads. The remaining two days to Phoenix seemed easy after that.[6]

Curt Tison found a job in what was then the largely agricultural Phoenix area, and the family remained there until 1942, when they pushed on to California and the promise of more work and a better life. They settled in the farm community of Arvin in Kern County, south of Bakersfield, one of many such places in the San Joaquin Valley known for poor housing, hard work, and low wages. Arvin looked much the way Oklahoma had before it stopped raining and the wind started to blow. The soil was light and sandy, but the irrigation that flooded the surrounding fields turned it a rich and fertile brown. Acres of vegetables grew thick in the dry sunshine, producing several crops a year and creating demand for armies of pickers and pruners. The growers were making money in Kern County. But for the pickers and pruners and their families, Arvin was just one of any number of grim agricultural encampments scattered across the Central Valley.

The town wasn't too pleased about the arrival of these newcomers. By 1940, some 180,000 migrants had relocated in the San Joaquin Valley, most of them in Kern County, where the population had increased 70 percent between 1935 and 1940. The migrants were urged to move on. Armed patrols roamed the borders of the ramshackle collections of shacks and tents. These crowded, filthy camps, without plumbing or an adequate water supply, were dubbed "Hoovervilles" by their inhabitants, making a not-so-funny joke about an indifferent president they had little use for. With equal sarcasm, the "Okie croppers" gave the name "Hoover hogs" to the scrawny jackrabbits they frequently ate in stews cooked over open fires. Too often, it was eat rabbit or not eat meat at all; chicken was a luxury, and pork and beef were rarities during those bleak years.

Gary Tison came of age in Kern County, working in the fields, attending school, enduring the special scorn natives directed at the children of Okie migrants. Gary was a precocious, strong-willed kid, who soon learned to use his muscular physique and fists to good advantage when his more respectable classmates ridiculed him for wearing shoes without socks and hand-me-down trousers held up by planter's twine. Aggression became his primary response to the frustrations of a life lived on the squalid margins of an affluent society. He never forgave those early humiliations. Years later, long after childhood memories begin to fade for most people, he vowed in prison that he would return to Kern County and even the score.

But Gary's schoolyard toughness didn't work at home. As he approached adolescence, he began to run into trouble with his equally

strong-willed father. It seemed as though Curt Tison was never satisfied with anything Gary did. At the age of twelve, after a bitter dispute
with his father, Gary ran away. But after he had stayed with an aunt
for a while, his mother persuaded him to return home.

"The old man was high-tempered," Gary explained years later,
"and he drank too much back then . . . He tried to make me and
my brothers do a man's work from the time we were seven on, and
I couldn't take it . . . I knew he was just using us and, by that time,
I was rebellious to him and everything."[7]

In 1951, Gary quit school in the tenth grade. He always maintained
that he was smarter than either his classmates or his teachers. "Hell,
I had more money than the teachers had," he bragged. "I had excellent
grades and I was considered the most promising student." Then he
added with a wink and a grin, "But I was always a pretty good
promoter."[8] His hot temper and quick fists regularly got him into
trouble with teachers and school administrators, however. Kern
County discipline was too harsh for Gary, and he didn't see the need
to accept it anymore. There wasn't a person around he was afraid
of. "Hell, I was kicked off the football team for unnecessary roughness,"
he boasted. He liked to tell people that: too tough even for football.

The Tison family had grown every few years. In addition to Gary,
his brother Joe, and sister Martha, there was now a third brother,
Larry, and three more sisters: Kay, Linda, and a new baby, Carol,
born that year. Things were getting crowded, emotionally as well as
physically, in the tiny field worker's house they rented. The conflict
within the family had gotten worse as Gary continued to challenge
his father's domineering authority. Then he was arrested for breaking
into a store.

"A drummed-up charge," Gary said. "They didn't know who did
it, but they had it in for me."

Because he was a juvenile, and the burglary was his first offense,
he was placed on six months' probation.

It was at this time that Gary tried to talk his mother into taking
the younger children and leaving his father. Curt Tison had been
wandering back and forth between Arvin and Casa Grande, Arizona,
trying to find better work — or so he said. Curt never saw himself
merely as a field hand; he believed he had the ability to manage his
own business; all he needed was a little money, he said, to get established. He was always trying to borrow money, and he regularly appro-

priated money from Gary, or anyone else in the family. Gary believed his father was just squandering what little money they had on various questionable "business operations," as Curt called them, inspired by his get-rich-quick imagination and an unfounded optimism. Curt Tison's problem was that other people were a lot smarter than he thought they were. The family fell further and further into debt and emotional disarray.

Mary Tison was already sick with worry about how they could manage when Curt was injured in a farm accident. Not long after his father was hospitalized, Gary managed to get a job operating one of the big tractors used for plowing and cultivating. Driving a tractor paid much better than ordinary stoop labor, and Gary worked long hours. By the time his father had recuperated, Gary claimed that he, alone, had paid off most of the family's debts.

Curt Tison was pleased, although he didn't say much about it to Gary. Within a week he went out and traded in the old family jalopy on an almost new 1951 Ford sedan, plunging the family back into debt once again. Gary was enraged. He recalled later that his father always liked to appear successful, even when he wasn't. "And people that didn't know him as well as I did," Gary said, shaking his head, "thought he was friendly and real likable."[9]

Driving a tractor to pay off the family debts appears to have been the last sustained legitimate work Gary Tison ever did. At that point, like his father, he, too, got interested in easy money. Over the next few years he was involved in a series of armed robberies in California and Arizona. In 1954, Gary, with his brother Joe and a friend, stole a brand-new Chrysler from a car lot in Arvin and headed for Arizona. "It was just a joyride," he said with a laugh. "Nothin' serious." Outside Bakersfield, they held up a gas station, taking $39 from the cash register, a .25-caliber pistol, and a tank of gas. The next day they arrived in Casa Grande and stole Arizona license plates from a parked car, figuring that would throw the cops. It did, but two days later they robbed $234 from a grocery store in the tiny copper-smelting town of Mammoth. The Pinal County Sheriff's Office got the report, and the car was spotted. After a fast chase up the San Pedro Valley, the three robbers were forced off the road in a cloud of dust and arrested near the town of Winkleman.[10]

Gary and his sidekick were given seven-to-fifteen-year sentences in the Arizona State Prison. Joe Tison, who at age sixteen was still a juvenile, was given probation. Shortly after Gary was sentenced, his mother persuaded Curt to move the family to Casa Grande. She didn't especially want to leave California, but she was worried about Gary. He was so young to be in so much trouble, she said, only nineteen. He was her prodigal son, as she saw it, and they needed to be closer so they could visit him in prison. They weren't in Casa Grande long before she began to write letters to the parole board pleading for her son's release. A letter she wrote to a board member in October 1955 is typical of the many she sent in her son's behalf during this period:

Dear Reverend Hoffman:
   My husband and I would like an appointment to talk with you about Gary, our son. It seems my husband can't find any work here that he can do. We would like very much to go back to California, but I hope you will understand why we can't go back home and leave Gary. We feel we should stand by him and help him for he is very young. He can make a decent life for himself and help others. That is why we feel like standing by him. Don't you feel like giving him another chance? We could put both our girls in high school if we were in California. We lived there the last twelve years. So when you can see us, would you let us know? We would appreciate it very much.

                                                    Mr. and Mrs. R. C. Tison[11]

The appeals worked. Within the year, Gary's sentence was commuted. On September 18, 1956, he was released, after serving twenty-five months of his original sentence. As a condition of his parole, Gary went to work on a cotton farm under his father's supervision. By that time, Curt Tison was trying to farm some leased land outside Casa Grande. It was an unhappy arrangement and lasted only a week.

"I worked the first week," Gary said, "dawn to dusk for seven straight days. Then when I asked for my pay, he handed me a check for fifty-four fucking dollars and eighty-seven cents."

Gary never forgot the amount of that check. He tore it up and threw it in his father's face.

Curt Tison was about the same height as his oldest son, about five foot ten, and, at forty-six, weighed about 150 pounds. By that time Gary, at twenty, was a muscular 175 pounds. When Gary threw the check in his face, Curt looked like he was going to swing. Then he hesitated. For the first time in their lives, he decided just to let it ride. Gary never took him too seriously after that.

• • •

Gary said he thought about going back to California after the confrontation with his father, but there was a problem: her name was Dorothy.
Gary had known girls, but his relationships with them had amounted
to nothing more than sweaty, quick sex. Dorothy was another story.

After the move to Casa Grande, Mary Tison and her four daughters
had begun attending services at the Glad Tidings Pentecostal Church
of God. It wasn't long before Mary's faithfulness was recognized and
she was asked to do something she always wanted to do, teach a
Sunday school class. It was at church that her oldest daughter, Martha,
met a new friend, Dorothy Stanford. Dorothy was also in Martha's
class at Casa Grande Union High School.

Martha Tison was very fond of Gary. She regularly made the forty-
mile round-trip to the prison to visit him on weekends. On one of
those visits, she invited Dorothy to go along to meet her brother.
Dorothy had smiled and rolled her eyes when Martha had first shown
her a wallet photo of her handsome older brother. When Dorothy
asked her parents about it, they were concerned, but agreed she could
go when Dorothy convinced them that she might be able to help
Martha lead Gary to Christ.

Gary was struck with this pretty, petite brunette. In fact, he thought
she was the prettiest girl he had ever known. And smart. He told
Martha to be sure to bring her back.

Dorothy was equally impressed with Gary's boyish handsomeness
and broad shoulders; he didn't look like a criminal at all. And he
certainly didn't act like one. He was smart, friendly, polite, and self-
assured. And he looked you right in the eye when he talked. What
impressed her most? "Most of all," she said, "it was his beautiful
personality that I liked."

Dorothy Charleen Stanford was a shy, quiet, very proper young
woman. Her parents had moved to Casa Grande from Mathis, Texas,
not long after she was born in 1939. Like the Tisons, the Stanfords
moved west to find work during the Great Depression. Dorothy was
the fourth of six children born to Robert and Valle Mae Stanford —
three boys and three girls. Her father, a kind, soft-spoken, hard-
working man, opened a small two-pump gas station on North Trekell
Road. A shade-tree mechanic without a shade tree, he once said.
They raised their family next door in a small stucco bungalow.

"Good people," according to George McBride, a neighbor. "Folks
in Casa Grande always referred to the Stanfords as 'Mr.' and 'Mrs.'

Not because they were stuffy," he explained, "they were just nice, respectable people and the Mr. and Mrs. just seemed the right thing to call them."[12]

Dorothy had a loving but strict upbringing in a close-knit family. "I had the best parents in the world," she said once, "but they definitely were not broadminded about things." Her parents and the rest of the congregation at the Glad Tidings church did not believe in "worldliness." That meant one did not drink, smoke, play cards, dance, go to movies, listen to rock 'n' roll, or, for that matter, listen to anything but church services on the radio on Sunday. They also believed that "born-again Christian" women did not wear lipstick or rouge, earrings, or revealing clothes like slacks or shorts. Dorothy's mother wouldn't even let her wear shorts in high school gym classes.

Social life in the 1950s for the born-again teenager in Casa Grande revolved around church activities, and, for Dorothy, it was dull. Very dull. At Casa Grande Union High, the Pentecostals were thought to be a little strange, and they bore the brunt of a lot of high school humor: Why aren't Pentecostals allowed to have sex standing up? went one joke. They're afraid somebody might think they were dancing.

Dorothy was embarrassed by the jokes, but she obediently followed all the rules of the faith, even though her cloistered and regulated social life was making her feel increasingly left out. She went along with it all because she didn't want to hurt her parents; it was also the easiest thing to do. But she was restless and bored in her senior year of high school. Her impressive grades no longer were satisfying. She needed some excitement.

Meeting Gary was the most important event in Dorothy Stanford's life. In her restrained, proper way, she told her curious friends at the church that Martha's brother was just "a very nice, kind person." But then, after a while, she couldn't conceal her delight and sense of good fortune any longer. Gary Tison was the most attractive and exciting man she had ever known. It all seemed too good to be true. "He's just great," she would bubble.[13] Dorothy Stanford and Gary Tison fell madly in love in the visitation yard at the Arizona State Prison.

When Gary was released on parole in September 1956, an ecstatic Dorothy agreed at once to marry him. But her worried parents objected and forbade her even to date him. Dorothy became bitter and very withdrawn, then refused to attend church. For the first time in her life, she challenged her parents' authority: she continued to see Gary whenever and wherever she could. Less than a year later, on October 25, 1957, Gary and Dorothy, now nearly seven months pregnant, were married in Casa Grande.

On New Year's Day, 1958, their son Donny was born. The following December, a second son, Ricky, was born. By the time their third son, Raymond, arrived, eleven months after that, the loan company was threatening to repossess the car and new furniture Gary had bought, and Dorothy's parents were helping to pay their rent and mounting food bills.

Gary's difficulties with authority had resumed almost immediately after his release from prison. He got a job with Gilbert Pump, a company that built and repaired irrigation systems, but before long he had a dispute with his boss. Gary was not good at taking orders. He was a good worker, but he liked to do things his way and didn't like anyone telling him what to do. "I started having trouble with the man and one thing led to another," he explained. "I quit when they was ready to can me."

He got another job with another pump company in the neighboring town of Coolidge, but that didn't last long either. The week before Christmas, 1960, he had an argument with his boss about his wages and quit that job, too. "He was cheating me on my pay," Gary said. "He done nothing but lie to me."

It was at this point in his life, Gary said, that he began thinking seriously again about alternatives to bosses and an eight-hour day. But there never had been more than one: "Except for Dorothy's feelings," he said during a prison interview, "I had no intention of ever giving up crime. I needed a few thousand dollars real fast, and I thought to myself, Go for a bank."[14]

Instead, he went, once again, for a small grocery store, and instead of a few thousand, he got two hundred. It was March 24, 1961, and it was the first of a series of armed robberies and thefts he was to commit in and around Casa Grande. His spree ended only two weeks later when he was arrested after stealing weapons from the local national guard armory. He had planned to sell the weapons in Mexico in what he had hoped would be the beginning of a lucrative smuggling operation. Like his father nearly a quarter century earlier in Oklahoma, he didn't seem to realize that his hometown was an incredibly stupid place to launch his criminal career.

On September 1, while awaiting trial, Gary escaped from the Pinal

County Jail, stole a car, burglarized another grocery store in Casa Grande, and was back in jail within forty-eight hours. He was apprehended in the Casa Grande theater, where he ran after officers spotted him on the street.

"Luckily for you, I didn't get my hands on a gun," he said when he was locked up, "or I wouldn't be here now."[15]

On October 5, psychiatrist William B. McGrath examined Gary Tison at the request of the Pinal County Attorney's Office. McGrath had this to say:

"Mr. Tison is a powerfully built, rather florid looking man . . . He wears blond sideburns and a rather thin blond mustache. These two features, along with his pouty expression, remind one of Elvis Presley . . . His attitude toward the examiner is polite but not deferential, or apologetic, or defensive . . . His speech is rapid and he employs a good deal of penitentiary slang such as 'pulling hard time' . . . He never conveys any statement of self-blame or chagrin, except for having been apprehended. To a fairly large extent he rather seems to feel sorry for himself and to blame others for his difficulties . . .

"At one point during the neurological examination, he more or less smilingly admits that it has occurred to him to attack us, so that he might escape. However, he adds that he gave up the notion when he saw the shadows of attending guards in the waiting room and hall outside my office."[16]

McGrath noted that Tison thought he was smarter and tougher than anyone he knew, and he was proud of it:

"My IQ is damned near double the guards' over there," Gary boasted. "If I'm sent up [to prison]," he threatened, "I don't have a damn thing to live for. I almost cracked up in jail. When I get that way, I don't care. I've never seen a man yet that was too big to tangle with. So far it's very fortunate I've never killed a man."[17]

McGrath believed him. "Mr. Tison," he concluded in his evaluation, "is impressed with being dangerous. His self-image is that he is dangerous . . . and his judgement has not been at all in keeping with his intelligence." He diagnosed Gary Tison as a sociopathic personality whose abiding rage and poor judgment made him capable of, in his words, "pronounced moral perversity [and] criminality." The prognosis for change, he noted, was "rather unfavorable."[18]

On January 2, 1962, Gary Gene Tison stood, erect and still defiant, before a judge in the newly constructed Pinal County Courthouse. His wife sat behind him. Thin and pale, tears rolling down her cheeks, she seemed dazed as her mother and sister tried to console her and control the three restless little boys who squirmed for her attention. When the judge gave Gary a twenty-five-to-thirty-year sentence, she broke down and wept. Sensing their mother's sorrow, the two youngest boys, Ricky and Ray, began to cry also. The oldest, Donny, who had just turned four the day before, buried his face in his mother's lap and squeezed her as his father was led handcuffed out of the courtroom. Sixteen years later, Ricky and Ray would stand trial in the same courtroom for breaking their father out of the state prison in the most daring escape in Arizona history.

2

Quartzsite:
July 31–August 1, 1978

When you start up U.S. Route 95, the infrequently traveled link between Yuma and Quartzsite to the north, you'd better check your gas gauge first, especially in the summer, and especially at night. You'd think that there would be something along the way, maybe a rock shop with a gas pump or two out front, or one of those turquoise jewelry stands that can be found in even the most remote areas of the Southwest, but there isn't. Not enough traffic, and the cars you do see seem to be speeding like hell to get out of there and back to civilization. It's just a flat, straight stretch of empty highway through cactus and creosote scrub. With the isolation and the heat, an empty gas tank or car trouble can be deadly. In the summer it would be impossible to make it very far on foot without water.

Near midnight, when John Lyons saw a young man up ahead in the glow of his headlights, standing beside a car waving his hand for help, that thought probably ran through his mind. Otherwise he might not have stopped. He slowed down as he approached and then drove by, but he would have seen the guy was young, and the car was sitting tilted funny to one side. He hit his brakes once and coasted on a little farther, and then apparently reconsidered and slowed almost to a stop, swinging wide to his right to make a U-turn. His wife, Donna, probably was urging him not to stop — at night in an isolated area with his family along. He kidded her sometimes about her fear of strangers when they traveled, but he knew she was right — that's why he had the .38 in the glove compartment. But this guy didn't look like a drifter — they follow the well-traveled routes — or some drug-crazed fugitive from the Manson family. He was driving a Lincoln Continental, probably on his way to Vegas. He just looked like an ordinary guy who needed a hand. Besides, he was alone.

Only an hour before, the Lyonses had backed out of their driveway in Yuma to begin the long drive to Omaha, Nebraska. They thought that it would be the next to the last time they would have to make that hot, grueling trip. Just the return trip to Yuma to await his discharge from the Marine Corps, and then they could return home to Omaha for good. It was Monday, July 31, 1978.

Yuma is situated on the banks of the Colorado River, about one hundred miles west of Hyder, where the river curves sharply to the west and then to the south as it flows toward Mexico. By the time the Colorado reaches the Gulf of California, it is little more than a trickle. Its water has been redirected into a huge network of irrigation canals that extends west to the vast agricultural expanses of the Imperial Valley and east to the more than 100,000 acres of citrus groves and produce fields surrounding Yuma. A person need only look beyond the lush cultivation to the bleak mountains and the gray and brown hues of the scorched desert scrub to appreciate the importance of the Colorado. Without the river, Yuma would be unlivable.

One night in Yuma is enough for most people, and two years had been more than enough for the Lyonses. Like many western cities, Yuma has no downtown to speak of, only a four-lane strip of commercial development that stretches five miles from one end of town to the other, offering a glitzy gauntlet of motels, fast-food restaurants, and gas stations to hot, thirsty travelers on the way to San Diego or Tucson on Interstate 8. Especially trying are the summer months, when Yuma's near sea-level elevation and humidity combine with the intense desert sun to produce sweltering, enervating heat. Yuma and a handful of other river towns to its north and east — Blythe, Needles, Bullhead City, and Gila Bend — lie in the hottest, driest, most unforgiving terrain north of the Baja peninsula. The Lyonses were anxious to get back home to Nebraska.

While stationed at the Marine Corps Air Station, John Lyons had been taking classes at Arizona Western College and hoped someday to practice law. He was planning to enroll at Creighton University when they moved back to Omaha. Donna was excited about his plans, too, but she was also looking forward to going home and being nearer relatives and friends, especially since none of their family had yet seen twenty-three-month-old Christopher.[1]

The Lyonses had made the best of John's tour of duty in Yuma. Not long after Christopher was born, and John was promoted to sergeant, they moved from a tiny apartment near the strip to an attractive white stucco bungalow on one of Yuma's prettiest streets. With a neatly fenced lawn and two mulberry trees for shade, the little house at 2070 East La Mesa Drive made a big difference. When John bought a new orange Mazda, Donna was concerned about the payments on top of the higher rent they now had to pay, even with the extra money she made as a K-Mart cashier. But she was won over by his argument that in their new neighborhood they couldn't have an old beat-up car in their carport. Besides, he told her, they needed a good car for the trip home. Their old wreck might not have made it as far as Quartzsite, he said. It wasn't safe to try it.

Earlier that day, while the Tisons were hiding out at the shack in Hyder, the Lyonses were busily preparing for their big trip. John's fifteen-year-old niece, Terri Jo Tyson, had been visiting them from Las Vegas, and both John and Donna wanted her to make the trip to Omaha with them. That Monday, they were awaiting final approval from her parents. If they said she couldn't go, the Lyonses would have to detour up to Las Vegas to drop her off.

Terri Jo was a straight-A honor student at Rancho High School in Las Vegas and considered a sure bet for admission to the Air Force Academy — not bad, her father thought, for an air force staff sergeant's daughter. Though she was a top student, she was still a typical teenager who babysat for extra money, liked rock 'n' roll, and had just started to date her first boyfriend, Eddie Carroll, a nice boy her own age she had met at church. In May, Eddie had taken her to the spring prom. A photograph taken that evening shows a skinny young kid with a fresh haircut, wearing a rented tuxedo with a snap-on bow tie tilting to one side. He is standing stiffly next to a beautiful young woman with thick brown hair that falls below her shoulders and a soft smile on her lips. Eddie was mad about her.

By Monday afternoon, the temperature had climbed to 107 degrees.

Donna and Terri Jo had spent the hot day doing laundry, packing, and cleaning the house. A friend of John's from the base, Nick Volpicelli, was going to housesit. After getting Christopher to sleep that evening, Donna had showered and changed into a sleeveless yellow top and a pair of tan-and-yellow plaid slacks. Terri Jo had dressed for the weather in blue denim cutoffs and a blue-and-white tank top. They both wore sandals.

John, who had gone to Los Angeles the day before, returned home about 10:00 A.M., took a quick shower, and changed into a fresh pair of red athletic shorts, a dark T-shirt, and his usual white socks and running shoes. He and Donna loaded the car while Terri Jo got a sleepy Christopher up, diapered, and dressed. Despite the late hour, their decision to avoid the worst heat by leaving at night seemed a prudent one. So did John's decision to take along a pistol on a trip that would take them through some pretty isolated country.

John liked guns, collected them, and never took a trip without one. He wasn't a person to take chances, especially with his family. His interest in self-defense went beyond his gun collection. As the only Japanese-American kid growing up in a racially mixed neighborhood in Omaha, he had learned to use his fists early. In the marines, he kept his trim, muscular body in shape with regular workouts at the base gym. He liked to punch a bag, and he was skilled in karate. He was a confident, self-assured young man.

This trip he took two pistols along. As he and Donna loaded the trunk, he tucked an antique .45 he had just purchased, carefully wrapped in a soft cotton cloth, on top of the suitcases, between layers of clothing so it wouldn't bounce around. The other pistol, an elegant little airweight Colt .38 automatic, he placed in the glove compartment.

No one is sure whether the orange Mazda was headed for Las Vegas or Omaha that night. Terri Jo's father had not called earlier, but it seems unlikely that the Lyonses would have taken her to Omaha without her father's say-so. In either case, the first ninety miles is the same: north through the desert on a dark and lonely highway.

John Lyons was the kind of guy who would stop and help someone if he thought they needed it. As his commanding officer said later, that's just the way he was. When the Mazda's brake lights flashed again, Ray Tison said, "He's stopping."[2]

John made a U-turn and returned, making another to pull in behind the disabled car on the gravel shoulder of the road. He left the engine running and the headlights on when he got out and walked over to where Ray was standing by the trunk of the Lincoln in the glare of the lights. "What's the problem?" he said as he approached. Actually, it was fairly obvious. He could see parts of the shredded tire on the ground, and the right rear bumper was only an inch or two off the gravel. "We had a blowout and don't have a spare," Ray replied, forgetting that he was supposed to be alone. John didn't seem to notice as he squatted down beside the bent rim, examining the damage and commenting on what they could do about it. But Ray really wasn't listening as he remained standing just behind, casting furtive glances over toward the shadows on either side of the road where the others hid. He could see that there were other people in the small imported car that had stopped, but he couldn't tell how many because the headlights were too bright and he didn't want to stare. He was hoping it wouldn't be a problem as he tried to keep up his end of the discussion about the tire. "We were having a real cordial conversation," Ray said later, describing his encounter with John Lyons, when his partners emerged from the shadows on either side of the road with guns drawn.

Actually he heard his dad's voice coming from behind the bright headlights before he saw them. They had already surrounded the Lyonses' Mazda when Ray heard Gary and immediately drew the pistol concealed beneath his shirt. His dad had the door open on the driver's side and was leaning over talking to someone inside. Ray could see that he was gesturing with his pistol-grip shotgun when the door on the passenger side opened and a woman in slacks got out. "Just stand right where you are and take it easy and no one will get hurt," Ray said to John, who had risen to his feet speechless with surprise. He could see that Randy and the others had formed a semicircle around the car with their weapons drawn while Gary was doing all the talking. Oh Christ, Ray thought, as he stepped away from the glare and, squinting toward the car, saw a young girl in the back seat holding a baby.

When Donna Lyons got out, she looked over at John standing helpless by the disabled car, then turned to face Gary. "Okay, lady," Gary said to her, waving the shotgun in her direction, "just walk over there by your man."

"I'm not going anywhere without my baby," she shot back as she started to walk in the opposite direction toward the Mazda, where Christopher had awakened and was beginning to cry. Gary sidestepped into her path and stood there in his army fatigues, legs slightly apart, holding the shotgun at waist level with one hand, aiming it upward at her face. But Donna Lyons kept walking right past, stepping around him to get to the Mazda, where she leaned in and lifted Christopher, who was reaching for her, from her niece's arms. *"Now* what do you want us to do?" she asked coldly as she turned back to face Gary. Gary hadn't said a word. He just looked at her for a moment as if he was suddenly undecided about what to do next. The confused little boy looked up at the scowling stranger, then turned away, burying his face in his mother's neck. "All of you get into the back seat of that Lincoln up there," Gary said finally, in thick, rasping tones. "You, too, sister," he said, waving the shotgun toward Terri Jo, who had climbed out of the back seat cradling the Lyonses' Chihuahua in her arms. But he said it without taking his eyes off Donna, who returned his stare. Gary wasn't used to that.

Randy Greenawalt moved closer to herd the two young women the short distance to the other car. "Okay, get moving," he said, trying to make his preadolescent voice sound as gruff as he could. He didn't seem as nervous as he had been at the prison during the breakout. You could tell he was enjoying this.

The three brothers all noticed that the two women were young and very pretty, but that's as far as their thoughts went in that direction. The whole situation made them feel awkward and embarrassed. Acting this way with a couple of women and a baby was a lot different from a confrontation with a bunch of thick-necked prison guards. This wasn't part of the plan, that's for sure.

John Lyons was still standing beside the Lincoln as Donna approached with Christopher, and Terri Jo followed close behind, carrying the dog. "Look, we don't want any trouble," he was saying to Ray, and then to Gary, when he walked closer. "Take the car, you can have our money, or whatever you want. Look there's a thirty-eight in the glove compartment and a forty-five in the trunk. Take them. Just don't hurt anyone. There's no reason to. Hey, we stopped to help you guys. We'll stay here after you're gone. We won't go anywhere until you tell us. You'll be long gone by that time. Just leave us some water and we'll stay here. Please don't hurt anyone. We have a baby."

"Okay, everybody in the back seat" was Gary's reply. John got in first and moved across to make room for the others. Donna followed with the baby, sitting in the middle, and Terri Jo sat next to her by the other window. Randy pushed the door closed behind them. Gary told Donny to drive and told Ray to ride with him in the front to keep the family covered. "Turn left onto that gravel road by the signs a little ways back. We'll switch cars back in there off the road," he said, adding that he, Ricky, and Randy would follow in the Mazda. He warned the Lyonses not to try anything.

They turned the cars around and drove back south less than a mile before turning left on the road to Palm Canyon. The Lincoln scraped and dragged seven tenths of a mile on the gravel road to where it intersected with a rutted dirt road that followed along an underground gas line. They turned south on the gas line road, drove a few hundred yards, and stopped. Gary yelled out to park the two cars trunk to trunk. He said to leave the engines running and the headlights on. By the time they stopped, the flat tire had twisted itself completely off the rim.

Gary was the first out of the cars. "Outside," he said as he jerked open the rear door of the Lincoln. "Up here," he ordered, beckoning with the shotgun to the front of the car as they climbed out. The bewildered family huddled together, squinting and shielding their eyes from the bright headlights. It seemed as though Gary was everywhere at once, giving orders. "Donny, you stand here and keep them covered. The rest of you dump the stuff in their trunk and start putting our stuff in the Mazda," he said. While Gary smoked and watched and paced back and forth between the cars, Ray, Ricky, and Randy began to unload the trunks, exchanging the contents of the Lincoln and the Mazda. As they unloaded the Mazda trunk, they sifted through the Lyonses' belongings for valuables. They found nothing but the .45 John had told them about. Everything else was piled on the ground. Someone had already removed the .38 from the glove compartment back on the highway. Gary walked to the front of the Lincoln, where the captives were standing, and told them to hand over their wallets and purses and any identification they had on them. Donny dropped everything into a large cloth purse they had taken from Donna. Then Gary yelled impatiently at the others milling around between the two cars. "What's taking so long?" he demanded. "Just get all that goddamn stuff together and into the fucking Mazda and don't worry about it right at the moment. We ain't got all night to fuck around."

Moments later, when the transfer was complete, Gary walked off into the shadows a short distance and called for Ray to pull the Lincoln over to where he stood in a clear area among the creosote near a large saguaro cactus. Donny herded the Lyonses out of the way as Ray pulled the Lincoln ahead and then angled it back toward his father, the sagging rear bumper tearing out bushes and leaving a furrow behind. "Okay, that's good," Gary yelled as the sand began to churn up from the rear wheels. "Just leave it running and get those plates off it." Ray left the headlights on so he and Ricky could see as they removed the New Mexico plates with a pair of pliers and a screwdriver.

As the two brothers were on their way back to the Mazda with the plates, Gary walked over and stood about ten feet in front of the Lincoln. Suddenly shots rang out as he began blasting the radiator and headlights with his .16-gauge shotgun. The noise was deafening and came so unexpectedly that no one can remember exactly how many shots he fired. He got the headlights easily in the first volley, but it took quite a few more before steam and coolant began hissing from the radiator. He kept firing, the sawed-off shotgun snapping upward with each shot, until the big engine began to chug erratically. Then it shuddered and gasped, like some blinded and helpless metallic monster, before dying.

Everyone, even Greenawalt, was shocked by the noise and suddenness of Tison's bizarre action. When the shooting stopped, Christopher was sobbing hysterically and trying to hold his ears and cling to his mother at the same time. Donna had his head pressed against her, covering his exposed ear with her hand, and whispering to him. Numb with fear, Terri Jo stood motionless next to her, head down, her lips pressed against the head of the trembling little dog she held tightly against her chest. John was distraught, turning first to Donny and then to the others, asking, "What's he doing? What's going on? What are you going to do with us?" as the sound of the shots began to fade. No one answered. All eyes, like John's now, were still on Gary as he turned and started walking toward them in the darkness. "Lincolns are hard to kill," he mumbled as he stepped into the light where they waited, and shook out another cigarette.

The three brothers assumed that their hostages would be left unharmed with the car. Why else would their father have bothered to shoot out the radiator and headlights except to make sure the car wouldn't run and the headlights couldn't be used to signal for help? It would be daylight before they could notify the police. Or would it? It was the answer to that question that was bothering Gary. They weren't that far from the highway. Only about a mile. They really didn't need the car to get out of here. Nothing would prevent these people from walking that short distance. And who wouldn't stop along the road to help a young family with a baby? There were bound to be cars passing before dawn. That wasn't enough time.

"Okay, Donny, let's get them people over to the Lincoln. I want them all in the car," Gary said after lighting the cigarette. As they walked the short distance to the car, John Lyons pleaded with Gary to spare their lives. Gary continued to ignore him.

John was the only one talking in the grim little procession through the cacti. Even Christopher was quiet except for an occasional sob. The three brothers felt kind of sorry for this stranger, but they thought he should've figured out that they were just going to leave them there. It wasn't as if their dad was going to shoot a whole family and a baby, for Christ's sake, the way he blasted that Lincoln. The two women seemed pretty calm, as though they had figured it out, but the guy was really shook up.

"Please don't hurt my family," John Lyons pleaded. "If you just tell us what you want us to do, we'll just sit here until midafternoon. We won't tell anyone . . . Give us some water, that's all we ask for . . . Just leave us out here and you all go home . . . Jesus, don't kill me."

Ricky said later that he couldn't remember the exact words John used as he pleaded for mercy. "We were standing in front of [the Lincoln]. Mr. Lyons made a statement that he . . . he ask him . . . He said something to do with 'Jesus, don't kill me.' I don't remember the exact words he used . . . It [the plea] was just . . . I would say more or less directed at everyone . . . Dad said he was thinking about what to do with those people. He said something like, 'I'm thinking about it,' and he *was* thinking about it real hard — if he wants to do this or not — and at that time he said to Donny, 'Go back and get some water.' Dad was pretty upset at that time."

"I looked at my dad," Ray said, "and he was, you know, he was like in conflict with himself, you know. What it was, I think, was the baby being there and all that, and he wasn't sure what to do. That's what I think about it *now*," Ray added significantly, months later.

But at the time, neither Ray nor his brothers were sure what their father was thinking about, because outside those prison walls Gary's personality had changed. He was a different person.

"He thought about it just for a few seconds," Ray continued, "and sent us boys down to the Mazda to get a water jug." When Gary asked for the water, Donny turned and walked back alone to the Mazda to get it. The command came as a big relief, Ricky explained, "because . . . Mr. Lyons at that time just said, 'Leave us some water.' Okay? So my dad . . . that is the reason he sent back one of us to get the water. He said, 'Go get the water,' and Donny went back [to get it]."

Things seemed to be getting a little strange when their father had started blasting the front end of that car without saying a word. What was Gary going to do next? It was hard to tell what he was thinking; he didn't discuss anything or explain. They'd kind of had a plan before and now he just seemed to be making things up as he went along. And he was getting mean about everything — yelling, ordering everyone around. He had really changed. His moods and actions were difficult to anticipate. It was almost as if he had become a stranger.

While Donny was gone, Ricky and Ray looked on from where they were standing, a short distance in front and to the side of the Lincoln, between it and the Mazda, as Gary herded the Lyonses and Terri Jo into the back seat.

"These people were escorted into the Lincoln and [got] inside," Ricky explained. "They went, more or less, between us . . . We were still out in our positions and Dad kind of put them in . . . opened the doors and told them to get in."

Randy stood silently off to their left, by the front passenger door, holding a sawed-off .20-gauge shotgun across his belly. Randy never said much, and you could never tell what he was thinking, either. They knew nothing about him, or his past, other than that he must have done *something* wrong to be in prison. He just did whatever Gary told him to do.

Everybody was jumpy and the tension seemed to be getting worse; you could feel it like electricity in the hot, still air. Suddenly Gary looked back toward the Mazda and yelled angrily, "Where the hell's that water? What's takin' so long?"

"Donny was having problems finding the water jug," Ricky said, "because the back of the Mazda was pretty full with stuff. So that's when me and Ray went back and tried to help him get the water, because Dad called back again, you know — this time a little higher tone — wanting to know where the water is."

When Ricky and Ray got to the Mazda, Donny was frantically rummaging through the crowded trunk. "We had to unload everything to get to the water jug," Ray said. Believing that they were going to leave water with the family, the three boys poured some from one of the five-gallon storage containers they had into a smaller jug, since they couldn't afford to leave one of their large containers behind.

There is some confusion about what happened next. Ray recalls remaining at the Mazda to help Donny repack as Ricky started back to the Lincoln with the water. But Ricky remembers that he and Ray walked back to the Lincoln together. After they filled the smaller jug with water, he said, "me and Ray came back with it. At that time we were headed to the Lincoln to give it to the Lyons family, and Dad told us to come [over] to him."

As Ricky walked toward the rear of the car, Gary said, "No, bring it over here."

"I thought you wanted me to give it to them," Ricky replied, motioning toward the Lyonses.

"Just bring it here," Gary repeated impatiently without looking at him.

Gary took a long drink, tilting his head back but never taking his eyes off the people in the car. Then he wiped the water running down his chin with the back of his hand and just stood there, swishing the jug at his side, the shotgun resting across his forearm. He continued to smoke a cigarette, still watching the car and occasionally looking out toward the highway.

It was an eerie scene. No one spoke. Even John Lyons's pleas had stopped. Everybody just waited, trying to guess what Gary was going to do next. He stood there like a large, menacing animal. Everyone stood back from him, afraid to do anything because it might make things worse.

Every movement was exaggerated by the long shadows fluttering in the peripheral glow of the headlights. The only sounds were the engine of the Mazda idling some fifty feet away and the soft hiss of the coolant still draining out of the Lincoln's torn radiator. Gary inhaled deeply, then flipped the cigarette butt into the darkness and set the jug on the ground at his feet.

What's going on now? Ricky wondered. He's going to leave these people here without water? Everything had slowed down, and it was too quiet. Ricky felt like he just wanted to get away — from this place, these people, even his dad. He decided to walk back to the Mazda to help with the repacking.

When Gary took that last deep drag on his cigarette, he had made his decision, but he was going to need some help. "Randy, come over here," he called. Ricky watched as Randy lumbered over.

"Randy and Dad went to the back of the Lincoln and there they just conversed," Ricky said. "I didn't hear what they were saying, if they were saying anything. I'm sure they were. At this time they came back around to the sides of the Lincoln. My dad was on the right [driver's] side and Randy was on the left. And, at this time, I noticed the shotguns in their hands raise up and they started firing. I seen the flashes. My dad had the sixteen-gauge and Randy had a twenty-gauge. I seen flashes from each weapon, but I couldn't say exactly how many times each of them fired . . . Well, when this started, me and Ray went back to the Mazda."

Ray's mind was a blur. He had trouble remembering exactly where he was, or what he was doing, when the shooting started: "I don't remember going back [to the Lincoln with the water]," he said. "As I remember, we were [still at the Mazda], and just as we were getting a little water . . . we could have even started loading it back up . . . but that's when we started hearing the shots."

Probably eight or nine shots were fired in the first volley, which was broken only by the seconds it took the two killers to dig into their pockets, reload, and resume firing a second volley, and then a third. They fired the first shots from the waist, gangster-style. The bullets shattered the windshield and the partially open side windows, showering the victims with broken glass and deadly ricocheting pellets. One shot ripped into the front headrest, tearing out a fist-sized chunk of upholstery. Tison and Greenawalt stepped closer as the terrified victims, illuminated by the strobe-light effect of the muzzle flashes, lurched and twisted, attempting to ward off the deadly onslaught with their hands and forearms. Blood and shards of glass and torn bits of upholstery splattered the car's interior.

Donna was first hit in the chest. Christopher was standing on the floor between her legs, facing her, with his arms around her waist. Dying but still conscious, she bent over, gathering him closer in an attempt to shield him with her body. The first shot was followed by multiple others to the back of her head and shoulders. When Donna lost consciousness, she toppled sideways against Terri Jo, who was huddled in the corner, exposing the baby pressing against her stomach. Approximately sixteen shots had been fired when the shooting stopped. Gary had fired eleven of them.

The three sons had watched it all, their minds reeling in stunned disbelief as their father and Greenawalt, silhouetted by the muzzle flashes, methodically fired into the helpless victims. It was as though everything was happening in slow motion. Just when it seemed that the last shot had been fired, there would be another, and someone's head would snap back, and it just kept on like a nightmare when you think you're falling and your stomach is knotted up waiting to hit, but the horror continues as you just keep falling until you wake up screaming, and realize it was just a bad dream. But no one screamed, and there was no waking from this nightmare.

Later, when Raymond was asked how long the shooting continued, he replied, "Longer than it should have. It's hard to set a time on it. You know, my mind was just racing. I was trying to work everything out in my head as to what [was] happening . . . It was like it wasn't real . . . like what was happening really couldn't be . . ."

When it was over, Greenawalt walked back to the Mazda, resting the .20 gauge casually across his shoulder like a hunter returning from a duck blind. The brothers were stunned and silent, but Randy was excited, talkative. Flushed with some perverse sense of accomplishment, he was talking tough for the first time. Using his gruffest voice, he told the boys to "load up" and "get in the back seat." They did, as if they were in a trance. Ray, his temples pounding and feeling dizzy, had just squeezed into the corner next to the window, and Ricky was halfway in, when two more shots shattered the silence. Startled, Ricky snapped around in the direction of the shots and saw Gary leaning over next to the right rear window of the Lincoln.

"My dad was still at the Lincoln," he said, "and firing into it. But at this time I noticed he was on the other side . . . I heard a couple more shots from, you know, the Lincoln."

The two shots he heard killed Christopher Lyons. Partially protected by the back of the front seat and his mother's body, Christopher was still unharmed when the shooting stopped. Then Gary, pausing to check the grisly remains for signs of life, either saw him move or heard him sobbing. He leaned in real close. The muzzle was no more than a few feet away when he pulled the trigger. Twice.

Donny, Ricky, and Ray Tison were sitting numbly in the back seat of the Mazda when Gary walked over and lit another Pall Mall. Standing with his back toward them, he urinated for what seemed a long time, the shotgun cradled in the crook of one arm. Then he got in, squeezing his thick body uncomfortably into the small bucket seat where Donna Lyons had been sitting. "Okay, let's get outta here," he said. The sulfurous odors of gunpowder and sweating bodies blended with cigarette smoke in the suffocating darkness. Ray's head was pounding and he thought he was going to vomit, but he held it down; he knew his father wasn't in the mood to stop again. Randy drove as they headed back out the Palm Canyon road and turned north on Route 95.

Ray recalled that once they reached the highway "it got real quiet. Everybody was, I think . . . Everybody had run that through their heads — what had happened — and it took me a little while to grasp on to it, you know, because it just happened all of a sudden. You know, it just kind of set me back. It made me start thinking, you know, about those people."

"Yeah, everybody was pretty quiet," Ricky agreed. "Nobody was saying much of anything, even Dad."

The stillness they left in the desert was broken by sounds coming from the Lincoln as the critically injured John Lyons regained consciousness and struggled to open the right rear door. He was bleeding heavily from multiple wounds from his neck downward to his thighs. Flesh and muscle had been torn from his forearms as he tried to protect his face from the blasts. His wife slumped dead next to him, the mutilated body of their little boy between her legs. The back seat was slick with blood. He got the door open and staggered about twenty-five feet before he collapsed, rolling over on his back, knees drawn up toward his chest in pain, his bloody forearms held defensively in front of his face. He died in that position.

Terri Jo was sitting on the other side of Donna, next to the left rear door. When the shooting began, she turned her head and body to the left, pressing her face against the partition that separated the rear and side windows of the car. With her body, she sheltered the little dog she had held since the abduction. When Donna died, she fell over against Terri's back, her body absorbing the shots intended for Terri Jo. Miraculously, Terri Jo was hit only once in the right hip, but the wound was deep and bleeding badly. She had remained motionless when the shooting stopped, resisting the impulse to reach for Christopher, who was stirring beside her, because she could still hear someone walking around the car. Then came the deafening concussion of those last two shots and she knew Christopher was dead. Like John, as soon as she heard the car drive off, she struggled to get out. He was on one side, she on the other. As the door swung open, she rolled to the ground, unable to stand, pushing the uninjured dog out ahead of her. The door closed loosely behind as she started to crawl, dragging herself down a dry wash into the darkness toward Route 95.

She had crawled about a thousand feet before she became too weak to continue. Then she did an extraordinary thing. Aware that she was dying and that she had no identification without her wallet, she removed the small leather collar from the dog and fastened it around her left ankle. The identification tag on the collar had John Lyons's name and address on it. Then Terri Jo Tyson began to lose consciousness. She died lying on her side, her head resting on her hands, her legs drawn up as if she were sleeping, the frightened little Chihuahua pushed tight against the hollow of her stomach. It remained there, dying of exposure, as Donna had always feared it would.

That night, over two hundred miles to the north, in Las Vegas, Jo Ann Tyson — John Lyons's sister and Terri Jo's mother — was awakened from a restless sleep and bad dreams of a darkened desert:

"I heard one of my kids call 'Mommy,'" she said, "and I went and looked in the rooms and they were all sound asleep. I walked back into our bedroom and said to my husband, 'Harry, wake up, something's wrong.' He said, 'What do you mean?' And I said again, 'I know there's something wrong with Terri Jo. I heard her call me.'"

Unable to sleep, Jo Ann went to the phone and called her mother in Nebraska to see if she had heard from John and his family. Her mother said that she hadn't. "When she told me that," Jo Ann said, "I just knew something bad had happened."[3]

It had been a rough two days for prison officials. On the morning of the escape, Warden Harold Cardwell was playing golf in Florence with the prison chaplain, Father Alex Machain, and three other prison officials. As he was lining up a shot on the sixteenth green, a car from the prison skidded into the gravel parking lot and an officer leaped out and jogged across as the warden looked up from his putt. Cardwell cursed when he heard the news. The captive guards had chopped their way through the ceiling of the locked storage room and crawled across the rafters to a point over the hallway where they kicked out another hole, dropped to the floor, and sounded the alarm before unlocking the door to release the others. This was accomplished in less than ten minutes after the escapees had driven away. Still cursing and fuming, Cardwell drove immediately to the prison. He had more than the usual reasons for concern.

Standard procedures were followed as teletypes rattled out an alert to police across the state. In Pinal County, the site of the escape, roadblocks were placed on all major roads leading out of the Florence area, but it was nearly an hour before they were in operation. Helicopters and spotter planes from the Department of Public Safety fanned out from the prison, scanning the highways and backroads for a two-tone green Ford Galaxie, then, a little later, a Lincoln Continental. But there were problems coordinating the search, the major one being that there was no common radio frequency linking the various agencies involved in the manhunt. The prison, state police, and county sheriff's departments realized belatedly that each had an independent frequency, and so the Lincoln sped unnoticed across the desert in the midst of a communications vacuum.

In contrast, a detailed and curiously informed dispatch replaced the initial alert not long after the warden arrived. It read as follows:

> All Arizona stations. Prison escapee plan. Armed and extremely dangerous. Will not be taken alive. Escapees may switch vehicles to an off-white Continental with a New Mexico license unknown and proceed southwest through the Cimarron Mountains to Ventana, Tracy, and Ajo and northwest to the Gila Bend Mountains and hide out one week. Final destination may be a ranch near Arlington or Gillespie Dam which has a cropduster strip and aircraft waiting. One aircraft and several sheds in the area are stashed with numerous weapons. If possible they will fly to San Diego, or south to Mexico to Arden Lee Smith's ranch. Smith is known in Mexico as Freddi Llama and is in prison at this date. They will sell weapons in Mexico if possible. There may be an aircraft near Ventana awaiting them if they are being pushed by officers. It appears that this escape is well planned and caution is urged to all.[4]

3

Close Calls:
August 1–6, 1978

When Nick Volpicelli arrived at the Lyonses' house after midnight, it was dark except for the light left on in the carport. At that hour, 160 miles to the north, an orange Mazda with five men inside pulled into the dirt parking lot of the Arrowhead Bar in the little town of Congress, about 80 miles northeast of Quartzsite. It was closing time, and the bartender, Barbara Prosen, recalls that a young man walked in alone and bought a sixpack of beer. She remembered because it was an odd purchase.

"He asked for three Schlitzes and three Coors," she explained, "and I don't like breaking up sixpacks. And there was something else: hardly anyone around Congress drinks Schlitz."[1]

Cold beers in hand, the Tisons and Greenawalt continued north out of the low desert, climbing pine-forested slopes into the cooler temperatures of the Sierra Prieta. They followed their northerly course through Prescott on Route 89, across the yucca-studded high range lands of the Kaibab Plateau to Ash Fork. It was nearly dawn on August 1 when they turned east on old Route 66 to Williams. The sun was just rising as the overloaded Mazda rocked and scraped over a rough U.S. Forest Service road and pulled up to a deserted sheepherder's cabin in a secluded wooded area just outside of town. There was a small pond nearby. It was a familiar spot to the Tison boys. They had gone swimming in that pond summers before when they visited their Uncle Larry at his house a short distance away.

The five weary men unpacked their gear and, in the process, collected the wallets of their victims. Gary took the money, then instructed the others to put the wallets, driver's licenses, and other identifying materials in one of the purses. "Here, let me see that," he said, taking the purse from Ricky. He picked up a handful of rocks, put them in the purse, and zipped it closed. "No one's going to find it there," he said as he tossed the purse into the middle of the pond. When Ray was asked later if he had looked through the wallets to see who their victims were, he replied, "I never did look at anything, really, because I didn't want to be reminded of it."

But the others did look. There were photographs of Christopher in Donna's wallet: Christopher as a chubby newborn; Christopher standing in his crib; a recent studio portrait of him dressed in a little outfit with a collared shirt, his blond hair parted neatly and his mouth in a big grin. Next came a smiling photograph of John, all dressed up in a sport coat and tie, that Donna had taken before the party they had gone to the previous New Year's Eve. You could see her smiling reflection in a mirror behind him. John had one of her in his wallet, taken the same evening. Donna looked very demure and pretty in a new black cocktail dress she had bought for the occasion. "Sexy" was the way John described it to his sister Jo Ann. Terri Jo's wallet was stuffed with photographs: her parents, her four brothers and sisters, an Irish setter puppy, Eddie and herself at the prom. But the thing that pulled them up short was a membership card she carried. Without a word, Donny handed the card to Ricky. The girl's last name was Tyson. Could she have been a relative? they wondered.

"No way," Gary said impatiently when he looked at the card. "Joe's the only one that spells it that way, with a *Y*. No one else does." (None of them was aware at the time that the murders they had just committed were at a site just east of a dry river bed called Tyson Wash.)

It was an awkward moment for Gary, confronted once more, in the presence of his sons, with the vicious and obscene reality of what he had done. He had to offer some explanation. Of the three boys, Ricky was the most gullible. Gary took him aside.

"Dad made the comment to me," Ricky said, "that Randy — you know, I couldn't tell you the exact words he used, but he said it was Randy that wanted to kill those people real bad. He said that's why he went along with it."[2]

So Gary told his sons that it was Randy's idea — not his — to kill a young family that had stopped to help them. It was a lie his sons — with the sound of those last two shots still ringing in their heads — could not believe, not even Ricky.

After a restless couple of hours, Gary suddenly announced a change in plans. It was too risky to try to contact his brother, he said. Lawmen were bound to be watching his house. (He was wrong, in fact, but it was a reasonable assumption.) Instead, he said, they would rest until sundown and then drive on to Flagstaff. Randy said that he had a friend there who had promised, in letters she had written to him in prison, to help him if ever she could. It was risky, but all their options were risky. At the moment, Gary was less concerned about getting an airplane than he was about getting a larger vehicle; the Mazda was much too small. They needed a van or a truck, preferably one with four-wheel drive, he said. The ride from Quartzsite had been miserable. They'd had to sit on lumpy sleeping bags, their knees pushed up under their chins, holding in their laps leaking ice chests and water containers that wouldn't fit into the small trunk. The rear window shelf was so stuffed with clothing that it blocked the view behind. The car was riding on flattened springs that groaned and threatened to snap on every bump, and the goddamn thing wouldn't go more than fifty on the level, and they would soon have mountains to climb in every direction. It would be too conspicuous grinding along like that.

While the others napped on and off, Gary, still too agitated to sleep, paced and smoked a chain of cigarettes, waiting for nightfall. Every hour he would go to the car, punch on the radio, listen to the news, then resume his restless routine. The news reports on the jailbreak contained no new information and seemed less frequent. Maybe things were settling down. But it was what the newscasts didn't say that was important to Gary: there was no mention of bodies found near Quartzsite. Gary knew that soon all hell was going to break loose. They had to get out of the country quick, and he had to figure out how.

No one talked much, too absorbed in memories of the night before. They were all numb with fatigue, but only Randy was able to sleep for any length of time, and his soft snoring annoyed the others. After a while, Gary, who was sitting off by himself on a sleeping bag he had folded up against a tree, suddenly rolled to his feet, blurting out, "That orange is too noticeable." It took everyone a couple of seconds to figure out what he was talking about. It was getting to be a pattern. He was thinking all the time, but you never knew what about. Then, abruptly, he would give an order and everybody jumped. It might be something simple like "change the station on the radio" or, now, an announcement that they were going to paint the car. But it was always an order; never a question, except to ask why something was taking so long. It was making everyone nervous wondering what he was going to say or do next. And no one dared make him mad.

Gary told Donny and Ray to drive into Williams to buy spray paint at a hardware store they had seen earlier. "Primer paint. It'll probably take a dozen cans to cover it," he said. They also needed more cigarettes and groceries. Gary was anxious to get moving. He said nothing about the bodies — that was a subject no one would mention again — but he knew it wouldn't be long before someone became curious about that Lincoln Continental parked out there by itself in the middle of the desert.

The hardware store was in the town of Williams, Arizona, a cluster of small businesses around the railroad overpass of the Atchison, Topeka, and Santa Fe on old U.S. 66, right where Route 64 cuts north following the unused spur of the railroad through Red Lake and on up to the Grand Canyon. Situated too close to Flagstaff and too far from the Grand Canyon, the town stopped growing when the trains up to the canyon stopped running; it became downright quiet when Interstate 40 replaced old Route 66. Before that the old highway had funneled the cross-country traffic right through town, and in those days all sorts of people stopped there. But nowadays, storekeepers can remember all the sales made in a day and, sometimes, even in a week. By nine o'clock most evenings, a person can look along the main street to a vacant intersection where the only movement is a stoplight shifting silently through a monotonous and unnecessary sequence.

The clerks remember Donny and Ray. The brothers bought groceries and cigarettes at the general store, then walked across the street to the hardware store, where they purchased twelve cans of gray primer spray paint. They paid in cash, mumbled thank you, and left.

Back at the campsite, the car was given a crude but reasonably effective paint job that just about covered the original bright orange that John Lyons had liked. The Tisons and Greenawalt spent the

rest of the afternoon napping and eating. At dusk, they left. The
peculiar gray Mazda, looking splotchy and dull and riding a good
six inches lower than it should have, splashed along the wet backroads
of the Kaibab National Forest, eastward some thirty-five miles to the
outskirts of Flagstaff. It was dark when it pulled up to a phone booth
in the parking lot of a convenience store near the Slayton Ranch
Road about eighteen miles northeast of town.

On the day of the prison escape, Tom Brawley had just returned
from Washington after attending a seminar at the FBI Academy.
He had arrived in Phoenix on a night flight early that morning,
and by the time he completed the two-and-a-half-hour drive to Flagstaff, he was exhausted and flopped into bed.

Brawley, thirty-six, had been in law enforcement since he joined
a police auxiliary in high school. In 1978, he became a lieutenant
with the Coconino County Sheriff's Department. Brawley had probably investigated more murders than any man in the state.

"Route Sixty-six and now Interstate Forty go right through Coconino
County," Brawley said. "That means practically every psychopath on
his way to L.A. stops here for gas and a cup of coffee. A good number
don't have enough money so they rob someone then kill them so
they can't be identified. We're always finding bodies around here.
In other places, homicides usually involve people who know each
other. Not here. Strangers kill strangers. That's what makes the investi-
gations tougher. You always have to start from scratch. Most of the
time we don't even know who the victim is except for a physical
description — you know, it's a male or female about a certain height,
age, and so on. Sometimes it's been a while — like they've been out
there all winter and we don't find them until the snow melts — and
all we have is a skeleton."[3]

The adopted son of two Mormon schoolteachers, Brawley was raised
in the tiny ranching community of St. Johns, Arizona, at the edge
of the Navajo Reservation. Good manners, a neat appearance, and
an easy southwestern drawl provide clues to his background. But
the Mormonism didn't quite take. Tom likes a shot of good whiskey
once in a while, and twenty years of drinking strong black coffee
and a three-pack-a-day habit have given him the husky voice of a
country western singer. "I guess that makes me a Jack-Mormon,"
he says with a grin.

. . .

Tom Brawley probably knows Randy Greenawalt better than anyone else does — even Randy's family. Maybe *understands* him is more accurate. No one is quite sure why Greenawalt went wrong. His family background is what psychiatrists describe as "unremarkable." Randy was born in Hannibal, Missouri, in 1949 and grew up in that area. The second of four children, he had an older sister and two younger brothers. His sister and youngest brother turned out fine, but Randy and his brother Jim turned into killers and broke their parents' hearts. His parents, James and Betty Greenawalt, have no idea what happened to those two boys.

Randy doesn't blame his parents. He believes that he had a "close" relationship with them both, although it seemed to him that his father was always a little more open and honest than his mother. The only resentment he seems to carry is that they didn't give him a middle name.

After graduating from high school in 1967, Randy said, he was "saved and baptized." He spent the following year as a student at Missouri Baptist College with an eye on the ministry. But then, he said, "I let Satan lead me down every rotten, filthy path he could find, and I broke Jesus' heart."[4]

He dropped out of college and joined the navy. Within the next two years, Randy was married and divorced twice, and court-martialed twice for stealing. The navy released him with an administrative discharge in 1971. Randy blamed his difficulties on a "mental breakdown" brought on by Satan and his wives' infidelities.

The difficulties continued. Three years later, in 1974, when he met Tom Brawley, he was drinking heavily and still stealing, but by then he was killing his victims. One cold January night, Randy and his brother Jim stopped outside Flagstaff at a rest area along Interstate 40. They were low on money and looking for a trucker to rob. They found one sleeping in the cab of his truck. Randy approached the truck quietly and looked in. Then, estimating the distance and the angle, he drew an *X* on the dusty side door, marking the spot where the sleeping man's head rested before returning to the car where his brother waited with a .243-caliber rifle. A single shot shattered the winter stillness and the man's skull. Randy described what happened next:

"I went to the wing window and broke into the truck to rob the man. His head was all torn up, but he was still groaning and moving, maybe by nerves. There's no way a person could live with their head blown all over the place, and I thought he was alive and suffering. I felt real sorry for him, so I shot him again under his chin."[5]

When an investigator asked Randy's brother Jim why they did it, he replied, "I don't know. Randy just feels good when he kills."[6]

There is no doubt in Tom Brawley's mind about that. When Brawley talks about Greenawalt, it's always in a thoughtful, matter-of-fact tone, but you notice the undercurrent of contempt that surfaces from time to time:

"Yeah, ol' Randy, I talked with him often in the Coconino County Jail after he killed that trucker," Brawley drawled. "He likes to talk, if he thinks you know what you're talking about — and he's got nothing to lose. He and I got along real well. He's very, very pleasant, and real smart — very high IQ, around one-forty. He'd sit down and talk with me like an old friend, trying to please me, always trying to please me. He reminds you of a little puppy dog, all friendly and polite. He'd act real interested in anything you brought up. And he enjoyed doing little things for you, like he'd always get up and pour me new coffee when I was out. I'd call him Randy and he'd call me Tom, you know, real friendly like. Randy really liked to talk about what he'd done — after, of course, he knew we had the goods on him anyway.

"A lot of killers are like that," Brawley said, exhaling a stream of blue smoke. "They enjoy bragging about what they did — they're proud of it. It builds their egos, and I'd always take advantage of that to get information, just playing their egos, like I did Randy's. Actually, it was hard to shut Randy up — almost impossible at times. He used to request to see me, saying he had something important to tell me. Sometimes he did drop leads on purpose so I'd bring him down to my office, pour him a cup of coffee, and let him smoke my cigarettes. He liked that. Yeah, ol' Randy would talk with me even when his attorneys told him not to. They'd get kind of upset about it.

"Yes, sir, he was real easy to get along with in jail," Brawley said. "Real sociable, enjoys people, all that. But on the street, he's a cold-blooded killer — the worst I've ever seen. I worked eight homicides on that sonofabitch. At least eight innocent people died because of him; that's why I'm going to attend his execution. I never had any desire to see one before, but I think his will be worthwhile and give me some peace of mind. Kind of like the culmination of all my efforts. And then knowing he's not going to hurt anyone again — ever — when I finally see him die. That's important. Funny, but you know with all his brains, I don't think that bastard ever figured out how much I despised him."[7]

Brawley had just fallen asleep when the phone rang. It was the Coconino County Sheriff's Office. There had been a prison escape at Florence and one of the escapees was someone Brawley had worked hard to put behind those walls — Randy Greenawalt.

"That sonofabitch," Brawley said into the phone. "Well, he's gonna kill somebody, so we better find him right away."

There wasn't much to do right off but be on the alert in case the escapees headed up toward Flagstaff. The escape itself was out of his jurisdiction, two hundred miles away, but he had a hunch that that might change.

"I just had a feeling," he said, "that ol' Randy would show up in Flagstaff, even though everyone had them heading south for the border."

Brawley knew one thing for sure: he wasn't going to be able to go back to sleep. He lit a cigarette and got dressed, his mind methodically clicking over what he remembered about Randy.

As more information began to filter in, he learned that the other escapee, Gary Gene Tison, had a brother living nearby in Williams. He decided to drive over there and have a talk with him. Larry Tison and his wife were upset when he arrived and flashed his badge at the door.

"I thought you'd be comin'," Larry said, "but we don't know nothin' about it. We haven't heard from him, or anyone else, and we don't know where he's at."

"That's the truth," his wife said. "We didn't know nothing about the escape until I heard it on the radio and told Larry."

Brawley thought they might be telling the truth, but he had their house placed under surveillance that night just the same. The officer given the assignment arrived later that evening, just a few hours after the fugitives, undetected, had left their hideout at the sheepherder's cabin in the woods not far from Larry's house.

The next morning, Wednesday, August 2, Brawley came into the office early. He was reviewing information on the escapees' prison records when he noticed that Greenawalt had a woman by the name of Trout on his visitors' list at Florence. She had a rural Flagstaff address.

"Hey, Terry," he called to a sergeant in the next office. "Do you know anything about a woman named Trout who lives here and knows Randy? There's a woman by that name with a Flagstaff P.O. box on his visitors' list at Florence."

"Trout? I don't know anyone by that name around here," Sergeant Terry Kenny called back. "I bet they got it wrong. There was an older woman, Eric Mageary's mother, by the name of Ehrmentraut who used to visit Randy when he and Mageary were in jail here. I bet that's who they mean. Let me check."

He came back a moment later. "Here it is. Kathy's her name — Kathy E–h–r–m–e–n–t–r–a–u–t," he said, spelling the last name. "Yeah, Mageary's mother. Sixty-three years old, lives out in Doney Park."

"We better have a talk with her," Brawley said.

That afternoon, Kathy Ehrmentraut was busy, as she was every afternoon, delivering newspapers to her rural customers scattered along the backroads of Coconino County. It was about three o'clock when a small foreign car with a bad silvery paint job and two young men inside pulled up in front of her red Datsun truck as she sat parked along the road in front of a line of mail boxes. One of them, a person she didn't recognize, called her name.[8]

"Are you Kathy Ehrmentraut?" he asked as he walked up to the truck.

"That's what they call me," she said without looking up.

"Could I talk with you a minute?" he asked politely.

"I didn't think much of it," she explained later. "People stop me along the road like that all the time because about three-fourths of Flagstaff owes me money. So I wasn't surprised when this young fella got out. I just figured he was another customer."

"Well, how much money do you owe me and which mailbox are you?" she asked, again without lifting her eyes from her work.

Donny Tison replied that he wasn't a customer. "I'm a friend of Randy's," he said. "Randy Greenawalt. He asked me to see you."

She looked up when he said that. "Who are you?" she asked.

Donny explained that Randy wanted to see her. It was important, he said. Kathy said she could read the newspapers she delivered and imagined that it was.

"What does he want?" she asked.

"He just wants to see you," he said. "He'll explain later."

Kathy agreed to meet Randy at her mobile home at nine that evening. "You better tell him that my three little grandsons are staying with me," she yelled as Donny was getting back into the Mazda. As yet, no one knew about the bodies in the desert near Palm Canyon.

Kathy had first met Randy Greenawalt four years earlier, in 1974, when Randy was in the Coconino County Jail standing trial for killing his third, or possibly fourth, truck driver. He had the cell next to her son, Eric Mageary, who was awaiting trial for armed robbery. She liked Randy. His soft, teddy-bear qualities, his shy little smile, and his eagerness to please appealed to this twice-married widow. Behind bars, Randy was a charmer. The poor boy had just made a mistake. He said it was his brother who killed that trucker, not him. Unaware of the dead truckers before this one, Kathy believed him. Kathy couldn't imagine Randy wanting to hurt anyone. He was lonely and depressed and she felt sorry for him.

"No one else did," she explained. "I was trying to show him that someone out there did care."

After his conviction, Randy was taken to the Arizona State Prison, where, unless paroled, he was to spend the rest of his life. He and Kathy began to correspond immediately, and their friendship deepened. When her son Eric was convicted and also transferred to Florence, she began to make the long weekend trip to visit them both whenever she could. She and Randy had never been lovers in a physical sense, but she was flattered by Randy's increasingly romantic attentions. In Randy's mind, at least, the platonic relationship seemed to be blossoming into much more. At first it was a little embarrassing, but then she found herself looking forward to his "Dearest Sweetheart" letters with the delicate little hearts and X's and O's decorating the envelopes and his closings.[9] Randy's letters made her feel good.

"I didn't see any harm in it," Kathy said later. "With me being so much older, I thought when he got out I'd be dead — or at least he'd see how old I was by that time, and that would be it."[10]

At sixty-three, Kathy Ehrmentraut hardly fit the image of the mysterious *femme fatale* some reporters later dreamed up. Her tastes in fashion ran to baggy denim jeans and flannel shirts, and mud caked her thick-soled shoes from feeding the nineteen hogs and fifty-eight piglets she was raising behind her trailer. Her hair was so short that only a few quick strokes with a comb were required in the morning, and her strong hands were callused from heaving bales of newspaper in and out of her truck every afternoon. To neighbors like Bonnie Van Arsdale, underneath the denim, calluses, and blunt language, Kathy Ehrmentraut was the kind of person you could turn to for help. "She's like nails on the outside," Bonnie said, "but inside, she's a marshmallow. She'd help anyone."[11] One Christmas, Bonnie recalled, she and her husband were down on their luck and Kathy took out a loan and gave them the money to buy presents for their children. She was always lending money to friends and extending too much credit to her newspaper customers. A trusting and unsophisticated woman, she was too busy to bother with close accounting or to keep track of bad checks.

About nine o'clock that evening, Kathy's big Doberman began barking as headlights turned into her driveway. Her mobile home was set off from the others tucked into the woods and clearings along Velvet Valley Road, a two-lane blacktop that winds through Doney Park. Assorted building materials, discarded toys, and rusted machine parts were scattered around it. She didn't throw things away; never could tell when they might come in handy, she claimed. When she saw the car stop, she walked outside to quiet the snarling dog, whose lunges were threatening to break the chain. A door opened and closed and the car backed out and left. As her eyes were adjusting once again to the darkness, a tentative voice said, "Kathy?" and she could see Randy's broad form in the driveway. There was an awkward embrace, a few words, and they went inside.

There wasn't much small talk. Randy was nervous.

"We have to sit there," he said, motioning toward the large picture window, "and leave the drapes open and the light on. They're watching us and I can only stay forty minutes."

He got right to the point. They needed her four-wheel-drive Dodge pickup, parked back by the hog pens. They couldn't make it in the Mazda. "It's way too small," he said, "and the cops'll probably be looking for it soon." He didn't explain why.

She told him the truck wasn't hers, it was her son's, and besides it wasn't running. "Needs a new transmission and who knows what else," she said. "It'll take at least two or three days to get the parts and fix it — if you got the tools and know-how, and I sure don't."

Later Kathy claimed that she tried to talk him into giving himself up.

"I can't," he replied.

"Why not? They're going to get you sometime, and if you turn yourself in they'll be easier on you and maybe you'll still have a chance to be paroled."

"It's no use. I can't. Don't ask me why."

"Why?"

"Something terrible has happened, that's all. It's best that you don't know."

"He never did say what it was," Kathy said later. "But I believed him when he said it was bad, so I just didn't say any more about it."

Exactly forty minutes later, headlights and the barking dog announced the return of the car.

"We have to have a truck, or a van, or something, or we're dead meat, Kathy," Randy said as he got up to leave. "We can't make it in that damn little car. I'll have to go back and talk to the boss about what to do." He gave her a self-conscious hug and left.

Daylight was just beginning to outline the dark pines behind her trailer on Thursday morning when she was awakened by the barking Doberman. Moments later, there was a knock on the door. When she opened it, Randy and Donny Tison stepped inside quickly, pulling the door closed behind as someone drove away in the car. She could see that both were armed.

They sat down in the kitchen, and once again Randy got right to the point. He told her that they wanted her to buy a truck for them in Flagstaff. With what? she asked, and explained that she didn't have the cash. Randy asked if she could get a bank loan, assuring her that she would be paid back. Kathy thought a moment and then said she probably could get a loan at the Valley National Bank, where she had a small savings account. "But it better not be for more than two thousand dollars," she said, "or you'll be here till Christmas waiting on them to approve it. I pay my bills, but they know I don't make much money." She got up to make coffee.

The fugitives didn't have time to spare, and two thousand was better than nothing. Donny, who was more familiar with truck prices than Randy, thought that with a little luck they might be able to find something at that price.

They also asked about weapons. We need more guns, Randy said, asking if she had any in the house. Kathy showed them what she had, a half dozen or so firearms owned by her late husband. While they were examining the array of weapons, she went out to feed her dog and pigs. When she returned, they had selected a Smith and Wesson .357 Magnum pistol and a Winchester .264 rifle.

Just then, her three small, pajama-clad grandsons walked sleepy-eyed into the kitchen, surprising the two jumpy visitors. The oldest, Eric, whom Kathy referred to as "my son," was ten and lived with her regularly, but because his mother, Kathy's daughter-in-law, was undergoing breast surgery, Kathy was also taking care of his two little brothers temporarily. While she was making toast and frying eggs and bacon for her grandsons and her two hungry visitors, she told Randy if they expected her to do all this in town, she couldn't do it with three children in tow and be able to finish in time to deliver newspapers that afternoon.

"I'll have to leave the two little ones with you," she said to Randy.

Randy paused, then shrugged, "Okay, but tell them they can't go outside while you're gone. I can't be chasing them around outside."

"Did you hear that?" she asked the two little boys, who were looking warily at the fat, surly-looking stranger sitting across the table. "If you play in your room and are good boys," she said, "I'll bring home a surprise."

After finishing their breakfasts, they gave Randy another look, then scampered off to their room, slamming the door behind them. Kathy said she wasn't concerned about leaving the children with Randy because he had never done anything to give her any reason to worry.

Gary had told Donny to select the truck, one with a camper shell and four-wheel drive, or maybe a van. Kathy, Donny, and Eric squeezed into the small cab of her Datsun truck, the boy in the middle, straddling the stick shift, and Kathy at the wheel. It was about a half-hour drive into Flagstaff, but it seemed longer this trip. A naturally friendly person, Kathy tried to make conversation, but Donny only grunted occasionally and stared straight ahead, never looking at her. It wasn't hard to tell that behind the dark sunglasses and surliness, he was a very edgy and distracted young man. She left him alone and talked with Eric until they got to town.

As they drove along the commercial strip on old Route 66 as it enters Flagstaff, Kathy pointed out the pros and cons of the various used-car dealerships they approached. They made several stops, and Donny started to get nervous. Everything that met his dad's specifications was too expensive. He couldn't pay attention to the salesmen because he was watching for cars pulling into the lot or police cars going by. As he became more tense, he began to turn to Kathy for guidance or reassurance to ease the strain. Gradually he started to ask her questions and finally to confide in her to a limited extent. It was difficult, he said, to find a good used truck so quickly. There was no way to be sure about what he was buying, no time to check the trucks out, and the ones that he liked were too expensive. It was obvious to Kathy that he was uncomfortable with the responsibility. It was also clear that he was worried about displeasing his father.

Finally, at Gus' Used Autos on Switzer Canyon Road he found almost what he was looking for at a price Kathy could afford — or rather, what a Valley National Bank loan officer would approve without any delays — a half-ton 1970 Chevrolet pickup, with four-wheel drive. The front grille was missing and it didn't have a camper shell, but it sounded okay. He hadn't seen anything better for the money — $1,995 — and they were running out of time. Terms were discussed — hard cash, Kathy told the salesman, a man she knew as "Crazy Al." Then they drove over to the Valley National on West Birch Avenue. Donny waited in the Datsun with Eric while Kathy went inside to arrange a $2,175 loan to cover the purchase. When they got back to the used-car lot, the salesman explained that it would take another half hour or so to process the remaining paperwork for the transfer of title, registration, and license plates. While they waited, Kathy walked over to K.B.'s sporting goods store and purchased more ammunition, as Randy had told her to do. Donny smoked, chewed gum, and tried to appear inconspicuous as he sat in the truck with Eric while she was gone.

It was past noon when she returned to the lot. The paperwork still wasn't finished: the phone had been ringing and other customers were on the lot. Now Kathy, too, was becoming nervous and impatient about the delay. She was worried about leaving her two grandchildren at home so long with someone they didn't know, and she had only a couple of hours left to pick up and deliver an afternoon's load of newspapers. She would have angry customers calling or, worse yet, stopping by to get their papers.

By this time Donny was convinced that everybody who passed by was staring at him. Each time someone made a phone call inside the office he watched intently to see if the caller looked over at him. Does he recognize me? Is he calling the police? Finally Kathy came into the office and said that she couldn't wait any longer, explaining that they could return later, after she delivered her newspapers, to get the truck.

Donny finally had to agree to leave, though he was reluctant. He knew that his father expected him to have a truck when he returned; he also had learned how hot-tempered his father was. He and his brothers had never seen that side of Gary when they visited him at the prison. Demanding, sure, but never mean the way he was now. If he returned empty handed, he didn't know what Gary would do. And he didn't want to find out. He had never been afraid of his father before, but he was now. Or was he just anxious that Gary might be disappointed in him?

The afternoon papers they picked up carried a story about the escape on the front page. The article dealt mainly with the controversy at the prison surrounding the breakout, and it was accompanied with photographs of all five fugitives. Donny read the story as Kathy drove, commenting, with a slight smile, that his photograph — one of the few he had ever had taken — didn't look much like him. He showed it to Kathy. She looked at the newspaper, then at him, and agreed.

Kathy insisted on stopping at the trailer to check on her two grandsons. When they arrived, she was relieved to find that the children and Randy had gotten along without any difficulties. The two youngsters jumped around her, chanting for the surprise she had promised, and told her that they had only left their room once, to go to the bathroom. They feigned pouts when Kathy told them she hadn't had time to get their surprise, but she assured them she would as soon as she finished with the papers. Their smiles returned.

But Randy wasn't smiling. When the commotion subsided, Kathy noticed the full ashtrays and the scowl on his face. "What took you so long?" he demanded. And then to Donny, "Where the hell's the truck?" Without waiting for answers, he said, "Some goddamn salesman was just here pounding away on the fucking door."

After Randy calmed down, Kathy, the two men, and all three children piled into the Datsun. First they were going to drop off Randy near the campsite; then Kathy, Donny, and the children would deliver the newspapers before going back into town to get the truck. They turned north at the Mountain View Market and dropped Randy off in a forested area about four miles farther down the road. As he got out, Donny told him to be sure to explain to his father the reason for the delay.

Randy nodded. "Okay, but you know he's still going to be hot under the collar."

A couple of hours later, the newspapers delivered, Kathy and Donny, with the children in back, drove back into Flagstaff to get the truck. On the way, Donny began to loosen up even more. Now he initiated the conversation, but Kathy wasn't sure whether he was speaking to her or talking to himself because he mumbled a lot and didn't look at her when he spoke. She could tell that he was deeply disturbed. "It's turned into a horrible mess," he mumbled. "I'm very, very, tired. I'd just like to rest."

They drove on a little farther in silence, then, looking out toward the high peaks of the San Francisco Mountains, Donny cleared his throat and spoke more clearly. "You know, when Dad — when we got Dad out — well, he has changed completely. Before, he was, you know" — he paused a moment — "like our dad. Now he has a knife at our throats all the time." He paused again. "I wish there was some way to . . ." He didn't complete the sentence.

When Kathy had signed the papers for the used truck, a dark blue Chevy pickup, Crazy Al handed her the keys, a receipt, and the title, and Donny finally drove away. Kathy stopped at another sporting goods store, where she purchased more ammunition for her .357 and the .264. Then she dashed into Ralph's Liquors for the treat she had promised her grandsons — three cans of pop — before heading home. Altogether, she had spent about eighty dollars of her own money on ammunition. Randy had offered her some money that morning but she'd refused it.

About two o'clock that afternoon, Ron Mead was working at the Mountain View Market, outside Flagstaff, when he noticed a badly painted Mazda pull in and stop near the phone booth at the far edge of the parking lot. The Mountain View sells rudimentary groceries, beer, ice, and gasoline. Most of Ron Mead's customers, largely determined by the store's isolated location away from the main highway, are people like Kathy Ehrmentraut who live in the area. He knows them all, and everybody is friendly. He had never seen the odd-looking Mazda before, or the three strangers in it. He thought they were acting suspicious when they just sat there in the car for a minute, looking all around, before getting out. And they definitely weren't friendly. Two of them entered and walked past without speaking. That's unusual, he thought, watching them in the overhead mirror, browsing around, casting wary glances in his direction. Shoplifters? They sure look familiar, he thought.

Ricky and Ray Tison filled two shopping baskets with assorted luncheon meats, canned goods, sandwich spread, several loaves of bread, potato chips, and soft drinks and beer. The bill came to $46.68. It was an unusual purchase, Mead thought, still trying to recall where he had seen those familiar faces as they stood by the cash register. When people buy in that quantity they usually go to a supermarket, where the prices are a lot cheaper.

Mead noticed that the other stranger, an older, very heavy man dressed in army fatigues and wearing aviator sunglasses, was making a call from the phone booth across the parking lot.

Finally they drove off, but members of the group returned to the store several more times that afternoon and evening to buy gas, Coleman fuel, paper plates, cigarettes, and more food. Ron Mead found their shopping patterns and furtive behavior odd. By this time, he was convinced that he had seen them somewhere before.

When Gary and the two boys saw the strange pickup truck back at their hideout, they hesitated until they saw Donny standing beside it. Gary looked it over, asking about the missing grille above the front bumper. You could tell he wasn't pleased.

"Couldn't you find one with a camper shell, or a van?" he asked impatiently. "How in the hell are we all going to ride in this goddamn thing without being seen, for Chrissakes?"

Donny explained it was the best he could do with the money they had. "You said you wanted a four-by-four," he said. "It was the only four-by-four in Flagstaff we could afford. I looked all over." Then he walked away and sat down by himself and lit a cigarette. "We can take the seats out of the Mazda," he sighed wearily.

And that's what they did. As Gary watched, Ricky and Ray took wrenches and began to unbolt the two bucket seats from the Mazda. They also decided to remove the radio and take it with them. They lifted the seats into the rear of the truck and secured them facing the rear. Then they dug wheel-width trenches in front of the stripped-down car and pushed it in to rest on its frame. They covered it with pine and manzanita boughs, and dusted it with soil and grass. They did a good job: it was hard to find.

It is quite possible that plainclothes detective Bill Pribil passed Kathy and Donny on one of their several trips in and out of Flagstaff that Wednesday afternoon. When he pulled into Kathy's drive, he said, there was nothing but an old truck on blocks in the back and the dog, which barked loudly enough to make someone come out, but no one did. He knocked on the door, unaware that nothing but an inch of fiberboard separated him from eternity: Greenawalt was observing him from behind drawn curtains with a .357 Magnum in his hand. Thinking Pribil was a salesman, Randy just waited. "If I had known that motherfucker was a cop," he said later, "I'd have blown his fucking head off."[12] As it turned out, Pribil returned to Flagstaff alive with nothing to report.

Even so, Tom Brawley was certain the fugitives were in the area. "At that point," he recalled, "I don't know why, but I was convinced the Tisons and Greenawalt were close by . . . I had no *evidence* that they were in the area, but I *felt* they were there. Intuition and experience led me to believe — no, I *knew* — they were there. I had been working around the clock on this case. I was the only one doing that, and I knew Randy, and I could just sense that they were going to go to Ehrmentraut's. I talked with the sheriff and told him, 'I feel they're here . . . and, if I'm right, they're going to head for Ehrmentraut's.' We had her place under surveillance but I told him that we needed more men."

Sheriff Joe Richards wasn't so sure. There was no evidence to support Brawley's hunch, and he was reluctant to call in additional men and equipment on the basis of a feeling he did not share. Brawley wanted 150 officers, including at least two SWAT teams, plus a couple of helicopters and access to an airplane, if needed. It was a major commitment of money, manpower, and equipment, and the possibility of professional embarrassment, if they were wrong, loomed large. The press was already questioning the competence of the prison officials responsible for the escape. It was not hard for Sheriff Richards to imagine headlines reading "FUGITIVES OUTSMART POLICE AGAIN" if the plan failed.

"The sheriff was very leery," Brawley recalled. "So I told him, 'Hey, if I'm wrong, I'll resign, no problem.' "

Because of Brawley's insistence, Richards agreed to summon additional officers and equipment from the state Department of Public Safety to supplement his own men and the Flagstaff police, and to set a trap. Additional officers filtered into Flagstaff throughout Thursday evening. At 3:00 A.M. Friday, August 4, a briefing was held. The plan was to hit Kathy's house at dawn. Heavily armed officers and equipment were stationed at assigned locations in the Doney Park strike area. SWAT teams surrounded the mobile home. Roadblocks were positioned on all roads leading out of the area.[13]

Earlier that same Thursday evening, shortly after dark, Kathy left Eric to watch his two younger brothers and, following Randy's instructions, drove back out to the spot on Slayton Ranch Road where she had dropped him off that afternoon. Apparently her house was not yet under surveillance, or else the surveillance was poor. No one saw her leave, nor did anyone follow her. She would have led them directly to the fugitives.

As she approached the spot, she could see a pickup truck parked along the opposite side of the road facing her, and she slowed down. It was hard to tell in the dark, but it looked like the truck she had bought that day. Her guess was confirmed when it blinked its headlights. She pulled over on the shoulder, and turned her headlights off. She remained inside for only a minute or so, but it seemed a long time before a door opened and closed and Randy's thick form approached cautiously across the road.

She gave Randy the ammunition and they were "just chatting" when a raspy voice called from the blackness, "Okay, it's time to go." All she could see was the red glow of a cigarette in the darkness behind the windshield. They were still lingering over parting assurances and promises when their chat was again interrupted. Randy nervously continued his whispered endearments as he walked backward toward the other truck. When the voice yelled, "Goddammit, Randy, I said it's time to go," Greenawalt turned so quickly he stumbled. "You better go now, Kathy," he stammered over his shoulder. Kathy knew he couldn't see her, but she waved goodbye anyway when she heard the door close.

That was the last contact Kathy had with Randy and the Tisons. She remembered Randy smelled bad. His odor floated in the fresh mountain air that night like the scent of a farm animal.

As Kathy's taillights flickered out of sight, the Chevy engine roared to life, gears scraped, and the pickup lurched forward. Now the fugitives headed east along back roads across the San Francisco Wash toward the villages of Sunrise and Leupp on the Navajo Reservation. Few cars used these partially paved, partially graded, and frequently washed-out roads across the vast expanse of the reservation. Gary drove, and Randy sat with him in the front. The three brothers, riding in the back of the truck, tried to get comfortable, taking turns in the bucket seats from the Mazda and stretching out in the truck bed on sleeping bags and blankets. It was a clear, starlit night. In the high desert country, a clear sky after sunset can mean a quick thirty-degree drop in temperature. It dropped to 47 degrees that night, and it was much colder than that in the back of the truck. The journey was becoming increasingly uncomfortable. As they bounced across the rutted reservation roads, the fugitives had no idea that their journey had very nearly come to an end outside Flagstaff.

Just before daylight on Friday morning, as police took up positions and leveled their weapons at Kathy Ehrmentraut's trailer, the blue Chevy pickup was passing through St. Johns, Arizona — Tom Brawley's hometown. The morning sun promised welcome relief to the chilled and cramped occupants riding in the back. At the fork of the road in Alpine, they turned left off Route 666, following Route 180 south into New Mexico's scenic Gila National Forest and through little towns like Luna and Buckhorn to Silver City — Billy the Kid's home. Legend has it that Billy, at the age of twelve, killed the first of his twenty-one victims in Silver City. The man died for insulting Billy's mother.

Gary knew the story, and he knew the area. In 1958, he had worked briefly at the Old Heart Mine in the mountains about twelve miles south of town. He sometimes drank beer in Silver City, where there were lots of Billy the Kid stories.[14] The mine he worked in was owned and named after Reverend Heart, a grizzled old preacher Gary's mother had known. On Sundays, the story goes, Heart loved to preach about the riches that awaited the faithful in heaven, where the streets were paved with gold. But old Heart himself didn't want to wait that long for his share. He had "gold fever." He'd preach long enough to build up a little stake from the collection trays, then he'd be off, chasing down every rumor he heard about silver or gold here on earth. People laughed at him, but Gary said that he made more sense than a lot of preachers, even if he never did get rich.

· · ·

At first light on Friday morning, a voice on a bullhorn broke the stillness outside Kathy Ehrmentraut's trailer.

"This is the police. You are surrounded. There is no chance to get away. Come out with your hands on your head."

Startled, Kathy Ehrmentraut rolled out of bed and looked out the window, gathering her frightened grandsons close to her side. The announcement boomed out again. A perimeter of police cars blocking access to the road were visible in the gray light. She opened the door and shouted that there was no one there but herself and her three grandsons. At that moment, two helicopters swooped in and hovered on either side of the trailer, their blades whumping loudly, whipping up dust and pine needles. Kathy and her frightened grandsons came away from the house at the police's instructions and a SWAT team moved in to search the inside. A few minutes later, an all-clear was signaled and Tom Brawley approached with Kathy Ehrmentraut in tow. Together, they entered the trailer.

At first Kathy denied any knowledge of the fugitives, but Brawley didn't believe her. "Don't give me that bullshit, Kathy," he said. "I know they were here." Brawley wasn't in the mood for delaying games. His credibility, his professional reputation, and his job were riding on his hunch. Kathy hesitated a moment, then said, "Okay, okay . . . Yeah, they were here, but they're long gone. They left last night."

I knew it, Brawley thought to himself. He was both disappointed and relieved. It may have been just dumb luck that they got away, but at least his hunch had been correct. Kathy told him that, as far as she knew, the fugitives were unaware that a trap was being prepared — an impression confirmed later by Greenawalt.

"Randy told me that they had no idea at all that we were on to them," Brawley said. "It was just a damned coincidence — and a damn shame — that they left when they did, or we would have had them right there."[15]

Unfortunately, Kathy didn't know where they were going.

Everyone in the Doney Park area was startled by the noise and commotion. Helicopters were circling low over the countryside and police cars seemed to be racing everywhere. It wasn't long before everyone knew who they were looking for, including Ron Mead at the Mountain View Market. That's it, Ron Mead thought to himself, that was the Tisons coming in and out of the store. He called the sheriff's office, and later that morning he positively identified photographs of Ricky and Raymond Tison. The photograph of Donny was so poor, he couldn't be sure. But he said he was fairly certain the older man he saw at the phone booth the day before was Gary.

On the assumption that the fugitives might still be in the area, the search continued for days in the rugged back country north to the Grand Canyon and south along the Mogollon Rim. Deputies on horseback followed tracking dogs through the brush and timber. Helicopters skimmed the treetops along Forest Service roads looking for a badly painted gray import, a two-tone green Ford Galaxie, or possibly a cream-colored Lincoln Continental. Ron Mead had described the Mazda, but the police still had no idea of its significance. It remained camouflaged and unnoticed for over a week in the forest a few miles from Kathy's trailer.

Palm Canyon cuts back into the shadows of the Kofa Mountains' rocky escarpments. It is an area of special interest to ecologists because the only natural stand of palm trees in Arizona grows within its protective walls. The drainage from seasonal rains transforms recesses on its floor into clear, rock-strewn pools that attract a wide variety of birds and animals. Occasionally it is possible to catch a glimpse of a mountain lion drinking or a herd of majestic and elusive bighorn sheep climbing the steep talus slopes above the canyon rim.

On Sunday, August 6, game warden Tom Peeples drove out to make a routine check on conditions in the area. He was driving in the graded access road when he noticed a car parked off in the desert scrub. It was about three o'clock in the afternoon — the hottest part of an August day, when both the ground and the air are superheated, and everything looks bleached out, and even drawing a breath is hard work. Peeples thought it odd that a car had been backed off the road in this heat, miles from any shade or obvious point of interest, and decided to take a look. As he approached, he noticed that the right rear door was open but there didn't appear to be anyone around. He turned off on the gas line road and parked his pickup truck. When he stepped out of its air-conditioned cab, the heat hit him like a board across the chest. He was prepared for that; but he wasn't prepared for the stench.

As he approached the Lincoln, he noticed the headlights were smashed and the grille and radiator screen had been damaged by what appeared to be gunshots. Glass from the shattered side windows sparkled incongruously like ice crystals among the parched creosote and rabbitbush. Then he saw an eerie figure sitting upright, slumped slightly to one side, in the back seat. As he drew closer, he saw that it was a bloated and partially decomposed corpse. Peeples thought it was a woman because of the long hair, but he couldn't be sure, and he didn't want to go any closer. Only the sound of flies broke the stillness. Clouds of nausea floated up and caught in his throat. He felt lightheaded.

As he turned to go back to his truck, he noticed another body in the brush near the car. It was a man dressed in red athletic shorts and a dark T-shirt. The body was lying on its back with its legs drawn up to the chest; the forearms extended stiffly upward, fists clenched like a boxer, covering the face and what was left of the eyes. Peeples radioed the Yuma County Sheriff's Office and reported what he had found.[16]

Within an hour sheriff's deputies arrived. What they observed was grisly even by the standards of men accustomed to scenes of violent death. They spoke in hushed tones as they began to measure, photograph, and gather the evidence. The shattered windshield and side windows, and the blast-shredded headrest of the front seat, indicated that the victims had had endless moments to hear, and to see, and to contemplate, the horror of what was happening to them. A closer examination of the car's interior revealed a third body, an infant. Barely visible, it had been tightly enclosed between the legs and under the right arm of the adult. Only fragments of skull and tissue remained of its head.

The area was scoured for evidence. Imprints and measurements were taken of tire tracks and footprints; the Lincoln was dusted for fingerprints; eighteen empty yellow and purple shotgun shells, scattered around the car, were diagrammed and placed in labeled plastic bags; a couple of cigarette butts were picked up and similarly bagged — Pall Malls.[17] No identification was found on the three victims. The investigators did not yet know that there was a fourth, Terri Jo Tyson, lying unnoticed a thousand feet away.

The long shadows of late afternoon had faded in the afterglow of a sunset that seemed to extend halfway across the heaven when men with rubber gloves and surgical masks finally placed the bodies awkwardly into thick plastic bags and lifted them into an ambulance. As they removed the infant's body, a small plastic medicine container was discovered clenched in its fist. The name "Christopher Lyons" and "MCAS" were on the prescription label. The prescription had been filled at the Marine Corps Air Station dispensary. Without that clue, it would have been days before the family could have been identified. The prescription was for phenobarbital. The bottle was empty. Apparently Donna Lyons had given Christopher the sedative when he started to cry as Gary blasted the front of the car.[18]

Captain Cecil Crowe of the Yuma County Sheriff's Office said the next day that the murders were the worst he had seen in twenty-seven years of police work.[19] Radio and television newscasts were the first to announce the discovery, stirring the first ripples of outrage that were to swell and roll like a riptide across the state. By Tuesday morning, August 8, there seemed to be little doubt who had committed the ghastly crime. "ESCAPEES TIED TO SHOTGUN SLAYING OF FAMILY" was spread across the front page of the *Arizona Republic*. The story announced Governor Bruce Babbitt's authorization of a $10,000 reward for information leading to the capture and conviction of the killers. It went on to describe the horrible manner in which the young couple and their baby had died.[20] Babbitt, a buttoned-down and bespectacled liberal Democrat (sometimes referred to as the only preppie in Arizona), was emotional as he spoke to the press: "This is a classic illustration of why we must have the death penalty, and why we must apply it."

Public outrage over the slayings, fueled by recurring reports of corruption and incompetence within the Department of Corrections, quickly increased the political pressure already bearing on prison officials. The escapees had to be apprehended first; then those responsible for the escape would be dealt with. While the largest manhunt in the state's history accelerated, prison officials began to jockey for position in their attempts to deny responsibility for what had happened on July 30, 1978, and thirty-six hours later in the Quartzsite desert.

On the same Sunday, August 6, that Tom Peeples discovered the bodies in Quartzsite, some fifteen hundred miles away in Fremont, Nebraska, Donna Lyons's brother, Paul Chadwick, phoned Francis Lyons, John's uncle, to inquire whether his sister and her family had arrived yet. He hadn't heard from Donna since she'd called last week, he said, and the trip shouldn't take that long unless they had stopped somewhere. Do you know if they took John's niece back to Las Vegas? he asked. No, they didn't, Francis Lyons replied. In fact, he said, Terri Jo's mother had called just the other night to ask if they were in Omaha, or if anyone had heard from them.

If Paul had been concerned, now he was worried. He couldn't get to sleep that night. Early the next morning he called John's uncle again to see if they had arrived during the night. They hadn't. He skipped breakfast and made the short drive to the Washington County Sheriff's Office, where he worked as a deputy. It was his day off, and the dispatcher was surprised to see him when he walked in about seven o'clock. Paul explained that he was worried about his sister and her family and wanted to send out a missing persons bulletin.

The dispatcher told him that the teletype had been down a couple of hours before he arrived, so there was a backlog of messages that had to clear before he could use the machine. Paul poured a cup of coffee and wrote down in pencil the essentials of the message he wanted to send out. As he was waiting with the dispatcher, idly watching the messages roll off the machine, a "BOL" designation caught his eye. It was a western states alert to "Be On the Lookout" for the Tisons and Greenawalt, who were now wanted in connection with a triple homicide and possible kidnaping. (Terri Jo Tyson's body had not yet been found.) He had heard about the prison escape but not about any murder. The killers were last seen near Flagstaff, the bulletin said. The teletype clattered on. Then Chadwick sucked in his breath and grew faint: in horror he read that the fugitives were thought to be driving the victims' car, a 1977 orange or gray Mazda with Arizona license number VEV-432 — the same plate number Chadwick held in his hand.[21]

II

Corruption:
1976–1978

4

Fathers and Sons

The three Tison brothers were known as "nice boys" in Casa Grande. No one could remember any of them having been involved even in a schoolyard scuffle when they were growing up. "It just wasn't their nature," a neighbor said. The worst thing anyone could remember was their stealing a case of beer from behind a Casa Grande saloon. A boyish prank — nothing more — and a good-natured justice of the peace had sentenced them to a day picking up litter along the highway.

Except for the fact that both Donny and Ricky bore a marked physical resemblance to Gary, the three boys seemed to be very different from their father. None of them displayed much anger or aggression, and no one had ever observed sociopathic tendencies in them. Donny was a good-natured, gregarious young man, who enjoyed an active and normal social life. Ricky and Ray were quieter and more withdrawn, but still pleasant and agreeable. There was no record of any disciplinary difficulties or problems in dealing with authority. Nonetheless, the mark of Gary's influence — and Dorothy's — was indelibly, and tragically, etched on their personalities. During the thirteen days they spent with their father after the prison break, they were extremely docile. In response to his violent behavior, they remained passive and compliant to Gary's wishes. It was their deference to authority, their desire to please, that kept them from making the independent judgments required to break free from their father's powerful and destructive influence.

The Tison brothers were reared in a psychological environment very different from that of their father — and from that of most children. The antagonism and conflicting values that molded Gary's aggressive and rebellious personality were not part of their upbringing. They had no overt conflict with either parent — partly, no doubt, because their father was in prison throughout most of their formative years. Although they had to contend with the stigma of Gary's bad reputation, life was never as difficult for them as it had been for their father growing up in Kern County during the Great Depression. Indeed, all three boys had pleasant memories of a lazy, Huckleberry Finn kind of childhood, "plinking" jackrabbits for fun, whiling away hot afternoons at the town swimming pool, skinny-dipping in an irrigation canal, playing "three flies you're up" baseball with neighborhood kids in the empty lot next to their grandparents' house. Their maternal grandparents, with whom they spent much of their time, had been very loving, and they could take reassurance from their own parents' love of them, who were separated unfairly, their mother told them, by their father's imprisonment for a crime he didn't commit.

But the shadow of Gary Tison's imprisonment cut across those sunny memories. The sense of loss and overwhelming injustice that accompanied it was stirred anew at the end of each weekend visit as they hugged their father goodbye — often, guards noticed, with tears welling up in their eyes. Throughout those long years, the boys attempted to reconcile the image of Gary's reputation — a hardened criminal, a convicted killer — with the strong, wonderful man they visited on weekends.

Gary's boys never forgot their mother's tears on that gloomy January morning in 1961 when their father was led, handcuffed, off to prison. Dorothy didn't let them forget. It was so unfair, she continually reminded them, to take their daddy away when they all needed him so badly. She never did explain to her sons *why* Gary had been sent to prison, she only insisted that it was unfair. And so the myth of Gary Tison as society's victim was planted and nourished in the minds of his three young sons.

After Gary's imprisonment in 1961, Dorothy remained in Casa Grande, living near her parents and Carol Stanford, her brother's wife. Both her mother and Carol helped with the children while Dorothy continued to work as a secretary at a local business. It was a difficult time for Dorothy, and the strain showed. All the energy and vitality of her youth were visibly drained from her slight frame by the responsibilities she had to bear alone. She had few emotional reserves left to deal with normal but unanticipated events. Ordinary things — childhood illnesses, cars that wouldn't start — became crises. And every weekend, when she might have gotten some rest, she and her three little sons instead faithfully made the trip to see Gary at the state prison, for it was important, she believed, for boys to grow up with a father's influence.

Although Dorothy remained friendly with Gary's two older sisters, Martha and Kay, she did not stay close to his mother and father; as a result, the three boys didn't see much of them even though they lived nearby. Dorothy thought their grandfather, Curt Tison, would be a bad influence on his grandsons. Gary had told her how his father had made him and his younger brothers, Joe and Larry, help him in a number of illegal activities, including armed robberies. Giving Raymond the middle name of Curtis was as far as Dorothy intended to go in encouraging a relationship with Gary's father.

Dorothy knew Gary's stories about his father were true. When Gary was sent to prison, his brother Joe replaced Gary as Curt's partner in crime. Shortly after Dorothy met Gary and he was paroled the first time in 1956, Curt had moved the rest of the family back to California. They settled in Oxnard. Curt was between jobs as usual, in debt, and low on money when he and Joe, then sixteen, walked into a small grocery store, each brandishing a .32-caliber pistol. The clerk didn't resist, and emptied the contents of the cash register into a paper bag. As the thieves drove away, the clerk wrote down the inept pair's license plate number. Within an hour, police were knocking on the door of the little house the Tisons were renting, and Mary answered. She lied, telling the police that Curt and Joe had gone to Arvin for the day. But Mary Tison was not a good liar, and the police asked if they could search the house. Flustered, she agreed. They found Curt kneeling in a closet, trying to cover himself (and the $547 he and Joe had stolen) with old newspapers. Joe was in another closet, squatting behind some hanging clothes with a sheepish grin on his face.

A few months after their arrest, Ruben Curtis Tison, still thin but now turning gray, once again stood with bowed head before a judge, this one in California. His wife sat behind him. The judge asked him if he had anything to say before sentence was passed.

"Judge," he replied softly, "I made a great mistake when I went in to take the man's money. I been taught different than that." Then, his voice gaining strength, he continued, "But God has forgiven me and I intend to live for the Lord the rest of my life. When I get out, I intend to go straight and live for the Lord."

Curt Tison had uttered the same sentiments, in almost the same words, twenty-one years before in a dingy Oklahoma courtroom. This judge was no more moved than the first one. It was bad enough, he said, to rob a man at gunpoint. But to involve a young son in a crime was an awful thing to do. His sons would do better without him, he said, and he gave Curt Tison a sentence of five years to life for armed robbery.

Dorothy could never understand Gary's mother, Mary. For all her Sunday school–teacher self-righteousness, she just stood by while her no-good husband forced their sons into crime. Every time he was arrested, Curt Tison would go into his getting-back-to-God routine, and Mary would buy it. Why she continued to believe he was truly repentant was beyond Dorothy's comprehension. Dorothy and everyone else knew that Curt Tison was a liar and thief, and he hadn't changed in over twenty years.

In one respect, Dorothy Tison was like Gary's mother: despite the warnings of relatives and friends, she refused to recognize her husband's true nature. Like Mary, she just couldn't believe that it would be better for her and the children if she left her husband. He was a wonderful person, she insisted, he'd just had some bad breaks. He'd gotten off to a bad start because of his father. But he wasn't at all like Curt, she would tell her sister-in-law Carol. For one thing, Gary was very intelligent. He was as smart as anyone she'd ever known, and, unlike his father, he had the potential to do anything he set his mind to. He'd learned his lesson, and, most importantly, he wanted to change. And he would, she said, because Gary loved the boys and would never do to them what his own father had done to him. Even in prison, he helped her raise those boys. He was interested in what they did; he listened to their problems; he kept track of their report cards; and he always encouraged them to be the best at whatever they did. The boys loved him and he was a good influence on them. Carol would look at her and shake her head, for she could see that Gary was obviously a younger version of his father.

But Dorothy knew how important her own father had been to

her, and she wanted her sons to have a father like hers. Given another chance, she believed, Gary would be that kind of father to Donny, Ricky, and Ray. He had promised her that, and she had faith in him.

Except for a ten-month interlude in 1966–67 when Gary was on parole, the Tison boys never knew their father outside prison walls. Nearly all their knowledge of him came from those bittersweet weekend visits in a tightly controlled institutional setting. These contrived visits, combined with their mother's complete devotion to a man she spoke of only as a benign and heroic figure, molded their idealized view of their father. Dorothy's sadness, and the migraine headaches that hit her when they returned home, defined his importance to their family.

Dorothy Tison was obsessed with the desire to have her husband back again. That obsession, and the wildly unrealistic idealization of Gary that grew from it, became the two overriding, and ultimately destructive, influences in her life — and in the lives of her three sons.

Donny, Ricky, and Ray Tison always thought of Casa Grande, Arizona, as home. Even after Dorothy got a job in Phoenix and they moved to the city, their hearts remained in Casa Grande, and they spent their weekends there.

At night the little town is just a splotch of flickering lights in an empty desert west of Interstate 10, midway between Tucson and Phoenix. At sunset, when the town's radio station, KPIN, goes off the air, it departs from its country-western format to play an orchestral "We Believe in America." That's just about the hour you begin to notice the lights from the interstate, and the town itself.

During the day, this low-slung western community fades into the shimmering glare and haze of the desert and cotton fields that surround it. Interstate 8 passes by a few miles to the south and strings out for some 170 desolate miles to Yuma, with nothing but a truckstop or two in between. This dusty little agricultural community of around ten thousand inhabitants does not lie on the way to anywhere. Except for a scattering of fast-food restaurants and a couple of chain supermarkets along the main drag, Casa Grande hadn't changed much since the early 1940s, when the Tisons and Stanfords began filtering through from Oklahoma and Texas looking for work.

The south side of town, where the Tisons lived, is modest. Faded stucco bungalows are separated by empty lots strewn with tumble-weeds. To the north, the stucco houses are a little larger, the paint on the houses and the pickups in the driveways a little fresher, and there are more trees and struggling lawns of Bermuda grass. But as a rule people with money don't live in Casa Grande. The real money is out on the big ranches and cotton farms that surround it.

As little boys, Donny, Ricky, and Ray attended Sunday school at the tiny Glad Tidings Pentecostal Church of God at the corner of Fifth and Lincoln, a short walk from their Grandma and Grandpa Stanford's. Shirley Elliott attended the church and taught a Sunday school class at that time.

"I remember those three cute little boys coming to Sunday school every Sunday with their Grandma Stanford," Mrs. Elliott recalls. "When Gary went to prison, Dorothy's mother would bring them to church with her. It seemed like after Dorothy married Gary she started to backslide and stopped coming to church on a regular basis, but the boys came with her mother. Then after Sunday school, Dorothy would take them with her to visit their dad. It was so sad because every Sunday when it came time for prayer requests, one of those cute little fellas — and it wasn't always the same one — would request prayer for their dad: 'Please pray for our daddy,' they would say, 'so he will get out of prison.' Those words still ring in my ears today — those dear little boys requesting prayer for their dad. Poor little fellas, how they wanted him back home."[1]

Just like their mother. But Dorothy was intent on doing more than praying about it. Throughout Gary's confinement, he and Dorothy worked together to coordinate their appeals for his release. Gary read all the legal books he could get his hands on, memorized statutes and cases, and took a typing course. His cell was a constant clutter of legal books from the prison library. He spent much of his spare time hunched over a small portable typewriter Dorothy had bought him, working on briefs, letters, and appeals. Guards remember how he resented cell inspections because it meant that he had to rearrange all his material before he could begin working again. He also had been caught hiding contraband *Playboy* magazines on a couple of occasions.

On August 3, 1965, Gary applied for a commutation of his sentence. The form he had to fill out included the question: "Why do you feel you are entitled to a reduction in sentence?" Gary typed the following explanation of his past and his plans for the future:

On April 1, 1961, I was arrested for committing numerous crimes. In the months before sentencing I made a nuisance of myself in the eyes of the law [Tison had been a passively belligerent and uncooperative prisoner]. I can't undo the trouble I've put them through and the only possible excuse I can offer is that I was inadequate, immature, and not willing to face the responsibility I created by my marriage. After arriving here, I began to take a good look at the position I was in and the reason for my being here. To understand fully the reasons it was necessary for me to read and do a lot of research in psychology. The space on this request doesn't permit me to explain my findings as I'd like to. I can say that my desire was for monetary wealth and notoriety gained through illegal means. After realizing this, I began to realize the possibilities that life offered me by not being a criminal. I have a wife who loves me and has no desire to be wealthy; three wonderful sons who need and want me as a father. I have also discovered that the better things in life do not require a great deal of money. I'm physically and mentally able to earn a living for myself and my family and know that I will enjoy doing so for them as well as for myself. I ask for this consideration for an early release because I feel that I am prepared for life as I should have lived all along.[2]

A few days after Gary's application had been submitted, Dorothy persuaded a family friend, Luther Leonard, to offer Gary a job upon his release. Leonard reluctantly agreed, in spite of Gary's dismal employment history, because he felt sorry for her and respected her parents. She also asked him to inform the parole board of his offer. A few days after Gary's application arrived, the parole board received Leonard's letter:

> Dear Sir:
> I am superintendent of Casa Grande Cotton Oil Mill. I have promised Gary Tison a job when he is free to accept it. I have known Gary Tison for several years and know him to be a hard-working man. He loves his home and family and anything you might do for him would be greatly appreciated by me.[3]

Dorothy also wrote regularly to the parole board. Her letter of May 2, 1966, was typical of her many pleading letters requesting her husband's release:

> Dear Mr. Hoffman:
> I am writing to ask you to please let Gary come home. I won't be very logical because I am under quite a strain right now. Our youngest son is in the hospital and I have been staying with him. I could sure use Gary's good strong shoulder to lean on. It is not

serious, and I believe the worst is over, but he has an allergy and these have a way of recurring, and it is especially bad when the kidneys are affected. It is very hard on the mind when one of your children are in the hospital and you know they have to be very sick or they wouldn't be there, and it can be quite expensive, too. Today I worked and I wanted so bad to be with my son. It seems that working is one of those necessary evils, though, especially in my case. Gary could not help little Ray any more than I can, but at least he'd be with me and give me a little reassurance. Right now I feel that after five years I am reaching the point of collapse. I'll need him next April, but I need him so much more right now. So won't you please let him come home. The time Gary has spent in prison has served its purpose. It has given Gary and myself time to think things through and to reach a better understanding of each other and to realize just what we want out of life. We have it in each other and in our three wonderful sons. We don't want to be separated again and, that alone, will make Gary stop and think twice. Also, I do plan to continue working as long as is necessary after Gary gets home so it will alleviate some of the financial worry. But only as long as necessary because I want to be home and enjoy my sons before they are grown and gone. This has been hard on them and they are looking forward to their Daddy being home before next Christmas, so please don't disappoint them.[4]

The letter closed with "Sincerely," and there was no question that it was heartfelt.

Dorothy also asked others to write to the parole board, and a few did, urging Gary's early release — always, like Luther Leonard, more out of sympathy for Dorothy and the children than from confidence in Gary. Eventually Dorothy's tireless efforts succeeded, and on July 1, 1966, Gary was paroled after serving five years of his twenty-five-to-thirty-year sentence. It was the happiest Fourth of July celebration Dorothy and the boys ever had, and hopes rose for a new and normal life together.

By this time Donny was nine years old. Ricky and Ray were eight and seven respectively. Child psychologists agree that these are critical ages in the psychological and emotional development of little boys, when they are especially sensitive and attentive to the dominant male in their lives. They look to such a person — a role model — for cues to appropriate male behavior. This was especially true for the Tison boys because Gary was not only their father, he was also, more than most fathers ever become, a heroic figure, a product of their mother's stories and those artificially idyllic weekly visits to the prison.

Gary's return home on parole was like the arrival of a sports hero or a movie star. His sons adored him. They had waited all their young lives to spend time with their dad, and they thrived on his attention. They loved his masculine cowboy ways, the boots he wore, the horseback rides he took them on in the desert. On warm Saturday afternoons, Gary might buy them milkshakes or ice cream cones at the Dairy Queen downtown. Then they would walk across the street to the town park and sit in the shade of the tall cottonwoods and talk. The three curious little boys wanted to know everything about this man they had missed so badly, and he and the boys tried to make up for all the years they had lost.

Stories were one way to recapture lost time. Gary was a wonderful storyteller, and Gary Tison was the hero of every adventure. They were always colorful and exciting: there was the one about the bully he had beaten up for insulting his sister in the schoolyard over in Kern County; there were the touchdowns he had scored on the Arvin High School football team — or was it Bakersfield? Sometimes he got mixed up, but it didn't matter. They listened enthralled to bogus tales about how the government had trained him for secret commando missions during the Korean War. Their mother had told them what a smart man their father was, and his stories convinced them that he wasn't afraid of anything.

Prison? Well, boys, he said, I was framed and sent up for something I didn't do. In spite of my war record, he added. Yes, prison was tough. You had to be tough to survive. He told them of bad men he had "called out" and beaten in fair fights, and he told them how stupid and corrupt the prison guards were. It seemed like everyone was weaker, dumber, and less courageous than their dad. The seeds of idealization their mother had sown in bedtime stories when Gary was in prison were now brought to full bloom by Gary himself. Gary was everything their mother had promised he was. He was the one person they never wanted to disappoint.

Gary Tison had a commanding and manipulative personality. Prison officials, inmates, politicians — even, later, reporters — were impressed by him. To Donny, Ricky, and Ray he was the smartest, bravest person around. And he was always right. They could not remember their mother ever disagreeing, in an important way, with anything he ever said. Gary never had to raise his voice, nor did he ever have to spank his children.

The ten months of Gary's parole remains a cherished memory in the lives of the Tisons. That Christmas was the only one the boys could remember spending with their father outside of prison; it was the happiest Christmas they ever had. Gary had bought them a model race car track, and he sprawled out on the floor with them to play with the set. They laughed and yelled, and the boys romped all over his broad back like happy puppies. It didn't matter that Gary operated the controls more than they did, they were just glad to have him there. Dorothy had told them that their dad was the best Christmas gift she could ever give them. As she watched them together on the floor, she was so happy it made her eyes sting.

"Dad always wanted to be the hero, and he was to us," Ray recalled years later with a rueful smile. "He had a great personality and he was a smart man. And you could tell that people who knew him respected him a lot. The time we had with him back then was a very good time. We loved him very much. In some ways, I think, we idolized him."[5]

"Yeah, it was a very happy time," Ricky agreed. "Me and Dad were pretty tight. There were a lot of good feelings and I only saw him mad once during that whole time. He was good to our mother, and he never hit his sons."

"It was just more exciting, more complete to have Dad with us," Ray added. "There was more of a fullness . . . But then, that's all we ever wanted, a family life with all of us together."[5] It was the first time they could remember their mother smiling and happy.

But it didn't last long. The holidays passed, and the Christmas bills began to pile up on top of the regular expenses, and by February, only seven months after his parole, Gary was broke and out of work. Once again, he was unable to keep a job for any length of time. He just couldn't work *for* anyone. He had to be in charge, and it was tough to find an employer who could accept those terms. So while Dorothy continued to do secretarial work, he stayed home and began to explore other ways to make money.

In February, Gary was arrested for passing a bad check at the Casa Grande Truck Stop. It was an incredibly stupid — or self-incriminating — thing for a man on parole to do. Doug Ballard, the manager at the truck stop, had known Gary and Dorothy for seven or eight years. He couldn't imagine why Gary would try such a thing with an old friend. The fifty-dollar check had been made out to Dorothy, and she had endorsed it even though she must have known it was no good. At Gary's arraignment, Dorothy was by his side, with the boys in tow. She looked thin and worried, her eyes red from crying. Gary accepted all the blame and denied that his wife knew anything about the check. He seemed contrite as he told the judge that he would make good on the money he owed Ballard. He only did it, he explained, because of the pressure of unpaid bills and the need to feed three children. My family needs me at home, he said. I'm no good to them back in prison.

Doug Ballard was "damn mad" about the check, but he wasn't about to wreck someone's life for fifty bucks. He felt bad about the situation and said that if Gary returned the money, he wouldn't press charges. It seemed like the only reasonable thing to do, and the judge dismissed the case, giving Gary a stern lecture and warning him that his parole could have been revoked. Gary appeared chastened and genuinely sorry, nodding in agreement with everything the judge said. Then he apologized and thanked him. "You have my word, sir," he promised. "So help me God, it won't happen again." But someone saw him wink as he was leaving the courtroom.

Gary could always lie like that without apparently feeling a twinge of guilt. But, like other sociopaths, he also had a way of repeating his mistakes. Cunning as he was, he never seemed to learn from his experiences with the law. Even as Gary made that promise to the judge, he was already deeply involved in a smuggling scheme. This time it involved farm machinery. He had "thrown in," as he described it, with four men from Casa Grande who had bribed Mexican customs officials in Nogales to let them sell used tractors across the border. Arrangements had been made to unload them on a buyer in Caborca. When the deal fell through, Gary decided to keep $275 of the bribe money himself. When his partners, one of them a salesman for a farm implement business, asked him for the money, Gary denied that he had it. They knew he was lying, and they turned him in to the police. When Gary told his side of the story, they denied any knowledge of an illegal sale in Mexico. Gary said it was a classic double cross. The police, he said, were being paid off by some influential local businessmen who were involved in the scheme. But it didn't matter. For the second time in as many months he had violated the terms of his parole, and on April 28, 1967, he was arrested. Within a week, his parole had been revoked and he was back in prison to await trial.[6] Dorothy and the boys were alone again.

On September 18 of that year Gary was convicted on the embezzlement charge, and Judge E. D. McBryde sent him back to prison with a light sentence, to run concurrently with the remainder of his previous sentence for armed robbery. It meant Gary once again faced at least twenty years behind bars. As he was being led handcuffed down the hall outside the courtroom, his distraught wife rushed toward him and tried to kiss him goodbye. "I'm sorry, you can't do that," prison guard Jim Stiner said gruffly, pushing her away. On the one-mile drive back to the prison, Gary produced a pistol and ordered the startled guard to take a farm road toward Coolidge. A short time later the truck pulled off into a field and stopped under a palo verde tree that grew next to an irrigation ditch.

Tison made Stiner get out and told him to sit down on an overturned washtub. Stiner, probably trying to remain calm, offered Gary one of the cigars he carried in his shirt pocket and asked if he could smoke one himself. Tison declined the offer, but agreed to let Stiner smoke. Jim Stiner didn't know it was his last. He had taken only a couple of puffs when Gary shot him three times in the chest. Once for Dorothy, he said, once for himself, and once to make sure Stiner never pushed anyone again. The last shot was fired downward at a forty-five degree angle as Stiner tried to struggle to his feet. He toppled face down into a stagnant puddle of irrigation water.[7] Gary waited until the bubbles disappeared before he got back into the truck and drove off.

After his arrest, Tison was asked why he did it, since he could easily have left his victim handcuffed to the tree and still made good his escape.

"I was pretty sure I hit him in the heart," Gary replied, "so I just went ahead and put two more into him . . . And the amount of blood that was leaving him, I'm quite certain he was dead before I left. I would never purposely harm anyone I knew and respected, but I didn't know this man at all."[8]

After shooting Stiner, Gary immediately headed back to Casa Grande. It was a familiar pattern for him — heading for home whenever he got in trouble. He seemed each time to forget that it was the place where he was most likely to be recognized and arrested.

He stopped at an abandoned ranch house on the outskirts of town, where a change of clothes and a couple of sandwiches had been stashed. It wasn't hard to figure out by whom. He quickly changed into his cherished pair of "roughout" cowboy boots, a fresh pair of

Levi's, and a western shirt. Dorothy had even thought to leave him the wide-brimmed Stetson he liked to wear when he rode horses with the boys. It reminded her of Audie Murphy.

The next morning he was spotted in Casa Grande, driving a station wagon he had stolen at gunpoint an hour before from a woman with a baby. Aware that he had been seen, he quickly pulled into the carport of a house on Kadota Street. He jumped out and took up a position behind the patio wall. Within minutes, the house was surrounded by police. When Tison was ordered to surrender, he answered with gunfire. Lawmen could just see the top of his Stetson as he crouched behind a swimming pool pump. Officer Clem Duckwall took careful aim and put a bullet through the top of the hat, knocking it from his head. Tison immediately yelled that he was giving up and tossed his pistol over the wall. Prison Warden Frank Eyman was one of the first to grab him.

"We should've put a bullet through his head right then," Eyman said. "I wanted to shoot that bastard so bad, but we needed him to find where Jim [Stiner] was. If I had known Jim was already dead, I would've killed Tison right there. It would've been easy and something I would've enjoyed doing. I wish I could've taken Tison back in shackles to that irrigation ditch where he killed Jim. Then I would've liked to have taken a sharp knife and cut his throat an inch at a time. I mean it," Eyman emphasized, his eyes sparkling with anger. "Jim Stiner was a fine man. Gary Tison was a savage sonofabitch."[9]

Frank Eyman's assessment of Gary Tison reflected the mood in Casa Grande after the Stiner murder and the ensuing shootout, the first in the town's history. On the same day, Gary's brother Joe decided that he was going to change his name, or at least the spelling of it.

The morning their father was captured, Donny, Ricky, and Ray were in school. Identifying Gary by name, the principal announced that there would be no outside recess, explaining that there had just been a gunfight in town. A dangerous criminal had been caught after holding a woman and a baby at gunpoint. He had made the woman cook breakfast for him, then had stolen her car. Everyone would have to remain inside the school for safety's sake. That afternoon, Donny heard one of the teachers whisper to another that Gary had killed someone. Do you think he did? Ricky asked Donny later when they were walking home. I bet they're wrong, his brother reassured him. I don't think Dad would kill anyone.

Stiner's murder and the shootout on Kadota Street were the main topic of conversation in Casa Grande for the six months before Gary's trial. During the trial it got even worse. Dorothy did her best to shield the boys from the stories, but that was impossible. Not only did they miss their father terribly; now they had to endure all the awful things everyone was saying. Even in school their teachers continued to talk and answer questions in class about what had happened. Dorothy knew she had to do something to protect her children.

On March 25, 1968, Gary Tison was given two consecutive life sentences for Jim Stiner's murder, and it seemed to Dorothy like the end of the world. What was the point of this marriage now? she asked herself. She still loved Gary, but maybe she should file for divorce. Relatives and friends alike urged her to leave him. He's no good, they said. There's no future for you, think of the boys, end it while you're still young. Carol Stanford, Dorothy's sister-in-law, told her to consider what remaining in the marriage was doing to her and the boys. Carol had never liked Gary. "From the first time I met him," she said, "he always tried to play the big-shot role, always bragging about what he'd done or gotten away with. He wasn't sorry for anything he did." She also was convinced that he had cheated on Dorothy whenever he could get away with it. "No good," was the way she described him. "And especially no good for his sons."[10]

Dorothy could see no future with him, but she found it difficult to contemplate any happiness without him, and she just couldn't go through with a divorce. She quit her job, took the boys out of school, and moved to Wilmington, California. She had to get away, to take stock of her life and decide what was best for the boys.

But California was a disappointment. It was the farthest any of them had ever been from home. They all missed Dorothy's parents, and they missed Gary. Terribly. In spite of everything, he remained the most important person in their lives. And now they were too far away even to visit on weekends.

Gary wrote almost daily. He missed them badly, he said, and was very depressed. He pleaded with her not to leave him; he said he needed them as never before. Dorothy waited anxiously for his letters, then dreaded opening them. What was the point of it all? she kept thinking. And she knew there wasn't any. But it wasn't what she thought about Gary, it was what she *felt* about him that she couldn't change. He remained the love of her life.

Moving away had been perhaps the most difficult decision she had ever made. She had always been close to her family. Now they were putting pressure on her to end the marriage they had never approved of in the first place. You and the boys have to get over him, they had said, and you can't do that if you're visiting him every week. As much as we miss you, stay in California if that's what it takes.

It appears the move to California was as close as Dorothy ever came to severing her relationship with Gary. But she couldn't do it. She was lonely in California. Her migraines had gotten worse, and the pressures of trying to care for three little boys and hold down a new secretarial job at the same time were beginning to overwhelm her. Her appetite was gone and she was losing more weight, existing it seemed, on coffee and cigarettes. This is no life, she decided one night after the boys were asleep and she slumped exhausted into a chair. It wasn't fair to the boys to deprive them of their father when they loved him so much. A father even for a few hours on the weekend was better than no father at all. Within a year of leaving, she moved back to Arizona, settled in Phoenix, got a job there, and resumed her weekly visits to the prison.

Dorothy never actually acknowledged to the three boys that Gary had killed a man, even when they heard the story from others. The boys knew better than to ask questions about why their father was in prison for life. Instead of confronting the reality of their situation, Dorothy continued to hold out the hope to them that someday, some-how, in spite of everything, justice would be served and their dad would be released.

"We didn't know too much about it [the Stiner murder] — it was kept a secret — something we didn't talk about," Ricky said later. "I knew Dad escaped — I did not know about the guard and the shooting until later. I just remember Mom, Grandma, and Grandpa standing on the sidewalk talking to cowboy-dressed police and they were upset at the escape. We heard about the rest of it at school. The teachers informed us — they told the students in front of the classroom."[11]

Later, when the boys told Dorothy about the announcement in school, she was furious. Your father was framed, she said angrily. Gary didn't hold anyone hostage, and he shot that man in self-defense. She was very upset. After that, Ricky said, they just didn't talk about it again.

Years later, Ricky was asked how he felt when his father was sent back to prison. He had repressed the event so deeply, it was hard for him to remember it, let alone describe his feelings. "I don't know," he said. "It was kind of quick — it just happened all at once — I wasn't shocked, but I was surprised. Mom explained some — there was some preparation. I don't remember what I felt like. I didn't feel one way or another." Then, noting that his earliest memory of his father was visiting him at the prison when he was about three years old, he said, "I didn't feel sad — I was used to it."[12]

But he wasn't. Ricky had always been a nervous, anxious child. In June 1965, a year before Gary was paroled, Ricky's third-grade teacher made these comments in his record: "A good little worker — very nervous — afraid of failure." A year later, a month before his father was released, his teacher noted, "Still nervous, immature, tries hard — a good worker." Tests revealed his IQ to be 97, in the lower half of the normal range. By the third grade, Ricky was performing below grade level, and that pattern remained throughout his school years. Despite his learning difficulties, Ricky was never a disciplinary problem. He was always a well-mannered and obedient child — a child who made every effort to please his teachers.

The sense of loss that Ricky experienced when his father was sent back to prison in 1966 was profound. He had always had symptoms of stress. Until the age of eight, he had been what child psychologists call a "rocker"; that is, he would sit alone and silently rock back and forth as if in a trance, often until he fell asleep. When he did finally go to bed, he usually wet the sheets. There had been a noticeable improvement in these problems during the period his father was home. Now with his father gone, once again he began to wet the bed several times a week and to complain of recurring stomach pains. Dorothy was worried about him. He seemed to have lost interest in everything. He would just sit silently for long periods of time, staring blankly at the television or into space. The physical symptoms grew worse in California and continued after their return to Arizona. The abdominal pain was subsequently diagnosed as a duodenal ulcer. In addition to ulcer medication, doctors prescribed a tranquilizer.

"It was just for my nerves," Ricky explained, denying that it was also for depression. "I wasn't feeling down. I was usually just in deep thought."[13]

Ray too was having stress-related problems. Like his mother, he began to have migraine headaches after his father was returned to prison. The pain was so frequent and so severe that he began to miss school regularly. When he would feel the pain coming on, he said, "I would just start to daydream about being able to take care of my mother, and having Dad home, and everybody being happy." Then he would just get quiet and wait, and hope that the pain would go away.

In school, Ray was a better reader than Ricky, but his school record was much the same. His IQ of 106 was in the upper half of the normal range, but his achievement test scores, like Ricky's, were usually below grade level. He seemed to be trying, although he often daydreamed instead of listening or working. He was always cooperative and polite, and his teachers could tell that he had the potential to do better. Like Ricky, Ray seemed to improve when Gary came home. "A good reader in the preprimers," a teacher noted that year. "Very good concept of numbers — good writing habits." But when Gary was sent back to prison, Ray fell into the old pattern. "Somewhat immature," his teacher wrote, "but well-behaved. At times he shows the strain of having visited his father."[14]

Life without Gary was truly hard on the whole Tison family. By the time the boys had reached adolescence, the realities of Gary's criminal sociopathology had been so deeply buried under layers of myth and fantasy, and so distorted by the idyllic memories of his brief parole, that they all viewed his imprisonment as an outrageous miscarriage of justice.

Of the three boys, Donny seemed best able to handle the disappointment of Gary's return to prison. Unlike Ricky and Ray, Donny faced the loss squarely. He found relief from the stress at home in a number of close friendships, and he enjoyed a more varied social life for a boy his age than either Ricky or Ray. He was more verbal and outgoing. He was also a more capable student than either of his two younger brothers.

According to Mike McBride, one of Donny's best friends, Donny was always more independent and more inclined to follow his own instincts than his brothers were. The two younger boys spent most of their time together or with relatives, like their younger cousins Stan and Timmy Stanford. Donny, on the other hand, made new friends easily.

Donny grew into a pleasant-looking young man, with his father's broad shoulders and muscular build, and he was mature and at ease with girls. He had gotten serious about one girl, but her parents broke it up as soon as they learned who his father was.

"Yeah," Mike McBride explained, "they either broke it up, or Donny had heard that they were going to, and he ended it. I'm not sure how it happened, exactly, but it was too bad. He really liked this girl. He first met her when she came in to apply for a job at the Pizza Hut. I was the manager and he went to work for me after he got out of the marines. Ol' Donny wanted me to hire her right away because of the way she was built — you know, she had real nice boobs and all. Well, I did hire her and I'll tell you he was hitting on her continuously after that. And you could tell that she liked him, too. She gave him a monogrammed cigarette lighter for his birthday. Then he took her to a family reunion or something that the Stanfords had and her parents found out who he was. Well, that was it. They wouldn't let her see him again."[15]

In spite of such bitter experiences, Donny seemed to be slipping free of the psychological bondage that had, in fundamental ways, prevented his brothers from developing a healthier, more realistic, and less obsessive perspective on their father and his situation. Although he never was critical of Gary, Donny realized his father had made serious mistakes. He was the only one in the family to accept the fact that Gary probably deserved to be in prison. He regretted it, but he was not, like his mother and brothers, consumed with the injustice of it.

"Donny didn't talk about his dad a whole lot," Mike McBride said. "I could tell he liked him and all, and he knew his dad was a tough hombre, although he never really said why he was in prison. It was kind of common knowledge about his dad, though, with everybody living around each other all their lives. But it just wasn't brought up — unless Donny did — and that wasn't very often. And when he did, it was usually just to say that he was going to visit him. But he did tell me once, one night we were just laying on the floor drinking beer and listening to rock music at my place — and I'll always remember it — that he wanted to make sure that he never ended up like his dad."[16]

Perhaps Donny was more mature and independent because, even as a youngster, he was always the outsider in this oddly self-contained and socially insulated little family. He did not share his mother's and brothers' obsession with Gary's imprisonment. He was more involved in other things; his moods were also less dependent than his brothers' moods on his mother's. He didn't like to hang around the house watching television, as they did, waiting for Dorothy to come home and fix supper. He also never shared his brothers' interest in guns and hunting. His decision to quit school and join the marines did not represent a lack of interest in completing his education. One of the first things he did after his basic training was to study for, and pass, the high school equivalency exam. And shortly after his discharge, he enrolled at a junior college. Donny joined the marines because he just wanted to get away, to put some distance between himself and his family.

Donny loved his father, but as he grew older he saw Gary as he was and not as his mother had made him out to be. Once in exasperation, during one of their many discussions of their father's predicament, he reminded his brothers that Gary had *killed* a prison guard. *There was no way they're going to parole someone who did that.* This is not to suggest that he understood his father completely, or that he was immune to his father's manipulations. But Donny was resigned to living his life without Gary; his brothers were not.

Ray and Ricky remained remarkably immature and naïve, too closely tied to their mother. When it came to girls, the boys liked to flirt on occasion, but they weren't very good at it. It's unlikely that either one ever had a serious date, let alone a girlfriend. Ricky was shy and backward around girls his own age, despite the fact that he was the handsomest of the three boys. Maybe it was because he was self-conscious about his bad overbite. Older women found his boyish shyness, ready grin, and good manners appealing. He was the sort of boy who seemed to draw out women's maternal instincts. He always seemed younger than he was.

Ray liked girls and, more often than Ricky, made furtive efforts to date, but it never seemed to work out. He would strike up a conversation with a girl, then drop the initiative, as if he wanted to be pursued. He'd give her his mother's unlisted phone number — instead of getting hers — and that's where it would end; no one ever called.

It was as if Ray and Ricky were three or four years younger than they actually were, in actions and interests, which is probably one reason why they spent so much time with each other and with younger cousins instead of with girls. Their childhood friends seemed to out-grow them and drift away after adolescence. Unlike Donny, neither one felt comfortable around strangers. Sensitive to their father's notori-ety, they showed an unmistakable hesitancy about outsiders, male or female. They had learned from their mother that most people couldn't be trusted, and their infrequent efforts to become part of a larger social life were minimal, guarded, and almost invariably unsuc-cessful. And the more insulated they became, the more difficult it seemed to be for them to venture out.

As time passed, the obsession with Gary that Dorothy shared with her two youngest sons was reflected in a perverse sense of family pride and a kind of siege mentality that teetered over into paranoia. Anyone who criticized Gary could expect a major argument.

"When you live in a small town," Ricky said, "and you've got the school principal standing in front of the classroom making announce-ments about your old man, you learn to deal with it. The attitude is, if your father's in prison, you must be lower than dirt. Finally, you say to hell with you all. My name's Tison and I'm proud of it."[17]

Ray agreed that it was always a struggle to live with their father's reputation, but he seemed convinced that if other people could get to know his father as he and his family did, they would come to like and respect him. But since that wasn't likely to happen, he said, "the most important thing was sticking together, no matter what hap-pened."[18]

The ingrained loyalty to their father, and the notion of "sticking together" as a family in a hostile world, had the effect of siphoning off ordinary childhood resentments. That strong, almost irresistible, inclination to test the limits of parental authority was absent. It was as if the boys never reached that stage of adolescent development. "They always listened to their mother. And I mean *always*," Mike McBride said. "If she said be home at a certain time, they would be home at that time. Even Donny. Even when they were older. They never gave her any hassles that I know of."

How could they, when this frail, long-suffering woman bore the injustice of their father's imprisonment so bravely? There was little reason to rebel. Dorothy made remarkably few demands on her sons other than insisting on the weekly visits to see their father, which they wanted to do anyway. Even when, one by one, they dropped out of school, her objections were milder than might have been expected, given her own proud record of accomplishment in school and her appreciation of the importance of a high school diploma. Nor did she exert any special pressure on them to find jobs to supplement her modest income (she had risen to the level of head secretary and office manager for a small Phoenix insurance and real estate company). Only Donny became financially independent, by joining the marines when he quit school and working regularly, after his discharge, while he attended junior college. His brothers depended on their mother and occasional part-time jobs for their spending money. Neither Ricky nor Ray ever held a regular job for more than a month or two.

"Life at home was fairly lazy," Ricky admitted with a broad grin. Apart from doing occasional chores around the house and keeping their mother's car running, most days when they weren't in school (and by the time they were teenagers, both boys were "ditching" classes regularly), he and Ray would just "sit around and watch TV" until their mother got home from work and prepared supper. Sometimes they would make the one-hour drive from Phoenix back to Casa Grande to putter around their Grandpa Stanford's gas station, pumping gas or helping him work on cars, or would loaf around town, often babysitting with younger cousins.[19]

When Dorothy was asked about the "lazy" lifestyle Ricky described, she shrugged and explained that her own parents had been very strict with her. "I tried to be different with the boys," she said. "I was more liberal."[20]

So other than family loyalty and obedience, there were few parental expectations the Tison boys had to satisfy. But that loyalty sometimes was expressed in extraordinary ways, illustrating the depth of their commitment.

The Arizona State Prison did not permit conjugal visits. As a consequence, surreptitious sex was common among inmates and their wives, or girlfriends, in the visiting areas. If the participants were reasonably discreet, the guards were inclined to ignore the goings-on: such are the humiliations of prison life. More difficult to imagine, perhaps, is that Gary and Dorothy engaged in sexual acts, with some regularity, in the presence of their sons.

"Sure, it happened," said prison guard Marquis Hodo. "Lots of people knew about it. I've had inmates tell me about it, as well as other visitors, and they didn't have any reason to lie. The boys would be sitting on one side of the picnic table, facing out toward the yard, and Dorothy and Gary would be sitting on the other side, facing the other direction, toward the wall. The boys would sit there across the table with their backs to their folks, holding newspapers up like they was reading so you couldn't see Dorothy going down on Gary behind them. Yeah, it was no secret. And that went on even when the boys were older and knew what it was all about. Other visitors knew what was going on, too, but they usually didn't complain because they were either in the same boat or else they were afraid to say anything because of Gary. No one messed with Gary."[21]

For the boys the logic was familiar. Forget the stares of strangers; forget the embarrassment and the shame. If it was something their dad needed, someone had to hold the newspapers. It was that simple.

Children conditioned to participate passively in their parents' sexual activity, as the Tison boys were, are probably not well prepared emotionally to question, let alone challenge, other parental passions, like violence. They respond to it, too, numbly. Even Donny — the least conforming, the most mature, the one son who had managed to remain on the periphery of the fantasies, the myths, and the obsession that had consumed the lives of his mother and younger brothers.

5

Trusty

During the Christmas holidays in 1977, nearly eight months before the escape, Gary Tison's sister Kay Wolfe received a long letter from Gary. Receiving a letter from her brother wasn't unusual; she got one nearly every week. He wrote that he was completing a script for a movie that would be based on a history of their family and their travails since they moved west from Oklahoma. He said it would also include a final segment about what he described as his "perfect" escape from prison. The escape that Gary described did sound exciting to Kay. The way it was planned, Gary would be flown to Mexico in a plane that would be waiting at a runway not far from the prison. At first, Kay wasn't sure if he was serious or had just plugged the idea into the story to liven it up. Gary went on to say that he had instructed a friend, Johnny Rodriguez, to give her the script in the event he was killed in the attempt. That, she thought, sounded pretty serious. She recalled that Gary had introduced her to Rodriguez in Los Angeles in 1962. He was a tall Indian who dressed in western clothes, and she remembered him as a mysterious and intriguing man.[1]

That same month, Gary also wrote a letter to his brother Joe and had Ricky deliver it. In that letter, he explained the general outline of his escape plan. It also contained instructions concerning what he would need from Joe in order to pull it off successfully. He told

Joe that he wanted either a Dodge or Chevy van equipped with survival gear, automatic weapons, preferably AR-15s, and between $5,000 and $10,000 cash in denominations of five, ten, and twenty. And finally, he said that he wanted Joe to have a plane ready to fly him to Mexico. At this stage, Gary apparently envisioned hiding out in some remote area for a period of time before eventually flying to Mexico. The letter went on to restate the terms of the bargain he and Joe had agreed on. In return for Joe's help in the escape, Gary agreed to arrange the murder of an inmate who was scheduled to testify against Joe in an upcoming grand jury investigation of narcotics operations in Pinal County. That part of it would be easy; Gary had done it before.

Not long after he received the letter, Joe took a trip to Tulsa. He arrived at his sister Carol Ericcson's house in a black-over-lavender Lincoln Continental he had purchased two months before in Albuquerque for $1,250. As was his custom, he had paid with $100 bills. The color, however, was too flashy for what he had in mind, and when he got to Tulsa he made arrangements through Carol's husband, who was in the used-car business, to have it repainted. Something less conspicuous, he told John Ericcson. They decided on a solid cream color.

But Joe wasn't in town just to visit relatives and have his car painted. He was there to do business, and for Joe, that meant meeting and cutting deals with business associates in the booming narcotics trade. In particular, he wanted to interview an airplane pilot by the name of Terry Tarr. Joe had first met Tarr in 1971 when Terry was dating Carol. Terry used to take her flying. After Carol married John Ericcson and moved to Tulsa, Joe continued to keep track of Tarr. Pilots were useful people to know in his business. Joe called him to invite him over for a little party he was going to host at Carol's.[2] Tarr said that he would be happy to come. Joe threw good parties. Joe said the purpose of the visit was purely social — just old friends getting together over the holidays — but Tarr suspected that there was more to it than that. Nothing was ever purely social with Joe.

Before calling Tarr, Joe had met with a Mexican man known only as "Memo" and his wife, a Latin beauty named Maria. According to Carol, Memo and Maria were a striking pair. Extremely well-dressed, poised, and articulate in both Spanish and English, Memo, Joe told her, was a major Mexican drug dealer. And he was, Joe said, "loaded." Carol couldn't help noticing that her normally self-assured brother seemed awed by the suave Mexican; in her words, "Joe showed him a lot of respect."

The Mexican couple visited Joe at the Ericcson's home several times to discuss the terms of Joe's purchase of a large quantity of marijuana. A deal was made, and Joe then turned his attention to the problem of transporting the marijuana north across the border. That was where Terry Tarr figured into his plans.

When Tarr arrived for the party that December evening, Joe quickly got to the real purpose of the invitation. He inquired whether Tarr still had his pilot's license. When Tarr replied that he did, Joe told him there was big money to be made if he was interested in "flying weed in from Mexico." Tarr knew what he was talking about and said that he would be interested if the price was right. Joe assured him that it would be and went on to explain about the dope waiting to be picked up on a ranch near Santa Ana. Why don't you come out to Arizona and I'll show you around? Joe suggested. Tarr mentioned that he usually did business with his cousin Ed Willingham, adding that Ed also might be interested in "throwing in with them." Joe said that as far as he was concerned there was plenty of business to go around. And so an association was born.

But Tarr had an alternative plan. Before Joe returned to Arizona, Tarr and Willingham invited him to go with them to Fort Smith, Arkansas, where, Willingham said, there was a ceaseless demand for dope because of the army base there. After a few days in Arkansas, the three men drove to Florida. Terry and Ed wanted to show Joe a boat they had bought for the "business." With so many boats and waterways in Florida, they explained, there was no way the Feds could control what was brought in. They planned to dock the boat in Key West. Joe was impressed with the possibilities in Florida, but he said that he still thought that it was probably easier, safer, and more profitable to fly marijuana in from Mexico. There were thousands of miles of empty desert and countless landing areas along the virtually unpatrolled border. "Why, hell," Joe said, "out there, you could make enough money flying for me to buy yourselves an airplane, too." He told them to think about it.

A few weeks after Kay Wolfe received Gary's letter about his movie script, a curious event occurred at the Arizona State Prison. On January 18, 1978, inmate Bobby Tuzon was transferred from the main prison to the medium-security Trusty Annex across the road. It seemed like a routine transfer, and maybe it was. Tuzon was serving a twenty-year sentence for second-degree murder. That was his first offense, and his prison record was good. The Annex was much less crowded and, therefore, less dangerous than the main building. The dormitories were small, with only twelve two-man rooms, which afforded more privacy. The inmates who were housed in the Trusty Annex worked as cooks, bakers, and maintenance workers. Good assignments, if you had to do time. Tuzon had been assigned a job as a cook.

His mentor, the person who was to teach him his new job, was Gary Tison. He was also assigned a room next to Tison's. Not remarkable — except that Gary was looking for a pilot to fly his escape plane, and Bobby Tuzon was the only licensed pilot in the entire prison population. Tuzon filled one of the two critical requirements of Gary's escape plan; now all he needed was an airplane.

If Bobby Tuzon's transfer to the Annex seemed, on the surface, unremarkable, Gary's presence there was not. Tison had begun his life sentence in maximum security in 1967 for prison guard Jim Stiner's murder. He had spent a long time there in solitary confinement. Before murdering Stiner, he had made three previous escape attempts. Then, after three years of unsuccessful requests, Tison was transferred to the medium-security Trusty Annex. To people familiar with Tison's record, the transfer was astonishing.

Frank Eyman, warden of the Arizona State Prison, had been a close friend of Jim Stiner's. He despised Gary Tison. "I can tell you when I was there," Eyman said, "that sonofabitch wasn't sitting around playing 'Jesus Loves My Soul' on a mouth harp. I made damn sure that he did hard time."[3] But the evidence suggests that the clever and beguiling Tison worked hard to overcome the stigma of having killed a prison guard. There is a high rate of turnover among guards at the prison, and it wasn't long before Jim Stiner's name had begun to fade from memory. Within a couple of years, it was hardly ever mentioned. Gary's newly developed courtesy and cooperative attitude molded the newer guards' perceptions of him. In the summer of 1970, less than three years after he killed Stiner, he was transferred out of maximum security. A year after that, he was named editor of the prison newspaper. Even Eyman's attitude toward Tison seemed to soften, for Gary invariably wrote positive and constructive articles about the prison administration.[4]

After Eyman's retirement in 1972, Tison managed to ingratiate himself with the warden's temporary successor, Bud Gomes, who took over as acting warden for a year. Gomes, a pleasantly phlegmatic man, had spent most of his life working in the prison system. For Gary, the benign indifference of Gomes was a welcome contrast to Eyman's bristling contempt. Gomes was frequently invited to share last meals with inmates about to be executed. "I always enjoyed the food," he said, "because it was specially prepared. Steak, fresh bread — much better than the usual meals. Most of the time, I was the only one really eating, but you get used to that after a while . . . When you work in a prison," Gomes said, "you can't dwell on what people did to get there, because none of it is very pretty." Gomes never trusted Tison, but he bore none of the hostility toward him that his predecessor had.[5]

From the moment Tison was moved to medium security, he had been planning an escape, but he bided his time because he knew that Eyman was due to retire soon. Frank Eyman gave shoot-to-kill orders on escapees and enjoyed having himself photographed with the bodies. Gary was certain that the old man would welcome any opportunity to have him killed. Eyman had told him that himself on more than one occasion.

Not long after Eyman retired, Gary made his move. At 1:30 P.M. on September 4, 1972, Gary and fellow inmate George Warnock walked into the guards' office in the main prison yard and drew pistols they had hidden under their shirts. A third inmate, Duane Warner, stood watch outside as Tison forced the four guards to strip. They were then herded into a storage closet, where they were tied with venetian blind cord and locked in. The three inmates quickly changed into the guards' uniforms and made their way unnoticed to the adjacent industrial yard, where they hoped to scale the wall and another fenced enclosure beyond. But the wall proved too much of an obstacle, and they were discovered later that evening hiding in the prison laundry. Warner and Warnock gave up immediately when guards fired tear gas, but Tison remained inside.

"Come on out, Gary. We know you're in there," guard Roy Duer yelled. "If you don't come out, we're going to have to come in there with firepower." Gary still refused to answer. After another volley of tear gas, he finally staggered out, coughing and choking, and gave up without a struggle. The guards found a pistol hidden in the laundry. There were strong suspicions that Gary had gotten it from Dorothy.[6] Gomes immediately had Tison moved back to maximum security.

Despite Tison's violent past and his ominous reputation for repeated escape attempts, he was quick to find favor in the eyes of the new warden, Harold Cardwell, who was appointed in 1973. Cardwell had been brought in from the Ohio state prison system. Before that, he had been a marine. He liked to think that he was a tough, no-nonsense administrator who understood prisons and criminals. To Cardwell, Gary Tison was just another inmate, and Jim Stiner was little more than a name.

In March 1973, only six months after his most recent escape attempt, Tison once again applied for a transfer out of maximum security. He knew it wouldn't be approved, but he also knew it was smart to start applying early because institutional memories are short. Repeated applications, combined with good behavior, had a way of ultimately generating a sympathetic response from prison transfer committees. In August he applied again, and he continued to do so every six months.

Eventually the strategy worked. In March 1975, a lawsuit filed on behalf of inmates at the Arizona State Prison by the American Civil Liberties Union claimed that conditions at the prison constituted "cruel and unusual punishment." ACLU Attorney Frank Lewis presented evidence of crowding — two inmates confined in nine-by-five-foot cells built for one, toilets that bubbled up into the sink bowls when they were flushed, and sewage lines that leaked into the drinking water. The prison had only two physicians, of questionable competence, for more than two thousand inmates.

The evidence was overwhelming and skillfully presented. In September 1977, Federal District Judge Carl Muecke ordered that immediate action be taken to remedy the situation. As a first step, he ordered a 20 percent reduction in the inmate population in the maximum security section of the main prison.[7] Muecke also ordered a complete review of inmate security classifications by an independent committee composed of mental health professionals instead of prison officials.

Cardwell asked Deputy Warden Joseph Martinez to begin the process of screening and transferring prisoners out of maximum security by selecting seventeen inmates who could be moved to the medium-security Annex. Martinez submitted his list a few weeks later. Gary Tison's name was on it.[8]

The selection of Tison was hard to understand. In addition to his most recent escape attempt in 1972, and his 1967 murder of a prison guard and the gun battle that preceded his capture, Tison had broken out of the Pinal County Jail in 1961. Every five or six years since he had been in prison — and always in September — he would attempt to break out. Yet on September 29, 1977, Gary Tison was moved across the road to the Trusty Annex. When the warden was asked about the transfer, he offered this explanation:

> I was given a list of seventeen inmates by Martinez. Final approval of the seventeen transfers in this group was made by me. I was aware that Tison met the criteria for medium custody as approved by the Department of Corrections. I also had personal knowledge that since I had been warden he had displayed a positive attitude, refused to participate in inmate strikes, committed no aggressive acts, and had not participated in illegal gang activities. Tison also had functioned well in a dormitory setting in the main yard, had worked responsibly as editor of the inmate newspaper, *La Roca,* and was active in college-level courses.[9]

Prison officials also hinted that the "strike-breaker" reputation Tison had earned during an inmate insurrection earlier that year would have made it unsafe for him to remain in the cell block. The striking inmates had persistently called for Cardwell's removal as warden. Tison publicly condemned the strike and defended the warden's policies. Gary had, in fact, begun currying favor with Cardwell the moment he took over as warden in 1973.

Tison wrote letters to officials, made positive statements about Cardwell to the press, and spoke to official prison visitors. Informed and articulate, he gave a good interview. Although he was invariably critical of the prison system, he never criticized the warden or the director of corrections, John J. Moran. Cardwell and Moran were always described as good administrators, dealing as well as anyone could with problems they had inherited from former warden Frank Eyman. Tison never missed an opportunity to praise Harold Cardwell, especially if he knew there was a reasonable chance that Cardwell would hear about it.

Cardwell hadn't been warden very long when Tison gave a typical performance in a Phoenix television interview. It inspired this letter, dated June 4, 1974, from John J. Moran, the director of corrections:

Dear Mr. Tison:
I had an opportunity to see you on the "Arizona Today" program. You displayed a lot of good judgement and sense. Many of your thoughts were quite perceptive and I am sure your presentation

was very helpful in assisting the Department of Corrections in developing better understanding of inmates and the problems of prison and rehabilitation. You should be proud of your contribution.[10]

A copy of Moran's letter was sent to Cardwell. Tison, Cardwell was soon telling others, was a good example of a hardened criminal who had been rehabilitated.

Bud Gomes recalled that a delegation from the state legislature had made a fact-finding trip to the prison during the inmate strike and uproar in 1977. The legislators were escorted around by a prison official who answered their questions. When the group met Tison, their attention focused on him.

"Before long nobody would be listening to the guide who was escorting them around," Gomes chuckled. "They'd all be crowded around Tison, you know, asking him questions like 'How is this working?' or 'What do you think about that?' I'd watch him out of the corner of my eye and pretty soon Tison was doing all the talking and the guide would just be standing there listening to him like everyone else. He was very impressive."[11]

Cardwell thought so, too. When politicians or reporters wanted to talk with inmates about conditions at the prison, Cardwell invariably referred them to Gary. Tison was always careful to interject complimentary remarks about the warden and the fine job he was doing in a difficult situation.

A major complaint of the striking inmates was the manner in which prison officials selected those to be transferred.[12] Most inmates were convinced that too many of Cardwell's transfer decisions were based on favoritism. A related demand was that Cardwell be fired.

The *Arizona Republic* supported the inmates' charges. Major problems were found in the reclassification process at the prison. The disciplinary and work records kept on inmates consistently contained inaccurate or unconfirmed information, the paper said, and psychiatric evaluations were usually superficial and inconsistent. Prompted by the escape of a double murderer, Herbert Shockey, from a minimum-security compound, the *Republic* described the reviews done by the prison's transfer committee as "shallow and brief."[13] In summary, it concluded that the criteria used in the classification process were questionable, and there was more than a hint of favoritism in the way transfers were approved or denied.

Without any important political support in Phoenix, Cardwell was a man under siege. Governor Raul Castro strongly hinted that the warden's days were numbered.

It was in the midst of this bitter controversy that Randy Greenawalt decided to write a letter to Director of Corrections John Moran. In it he praised Cardwell and condemned his fellow inmates. The letter, dated March 18, 1977, read as follows:

> Dear Mr. Moran:
>   I just got through reading in the paper and listening to all the news about [Governor] Castro wanting power over the warden. As a prisoner here in the main yard at Arizona State Prison, I don't feel it is necessary at all.
>   Warden Cardwell has handled every situation down here with amazing awareness and fairness. I have held jobs here that permit me to view first hand some of the goings on of the operation of the prison here and I cannot see one problem that he has not handled in a proper and secure way. His methods are effective and fair at all times and he does not ever play favorites in any decision he makes which is a large problem in other institutions.

Greenawalt went on to attribute the strike to the "ignorance of a few power-hungry inmates — the blind leading the blind," as he put it. He concluded with this plea:

> To keep this short and sweet, all I ask is that Warden Cardwell be kept in his position because the thought of a weaker and "more understanding" warden replacing him is terrifying. There are some bright lads down here that feel the same about this as I do. We just don't go around spouting off til we get good and mad at what is going on.

He signed it, "Respectfully, Randy Greenawalt."[14]

Moran welcomed letters like that, especially from inmates. He sent Cardwell a copy of the letter. Cardwell was delighted. He remembered the name. It wasn't hard. Apart from Gary Tison and another inmate, Charles Schmid (later murdered), Greenawalt was the only other inmate who defended the warden.

In July, two months after the inmate strike ended in 1977, Tison wrote to Cardwell once more requesting that he be given a Trusty classification. It was an extraordinary request from an inmate with his record of attempted escapes, and who in addition was a suspect in the prison slaying of inmate Tony Serra in January. Referring to his most recent escape attempt, however, as "my last incident," Tison reminded Cardwell that he had been a model prisoner for the four years during which Cardwell had been warden. He knew his unwavering support during the recent turmoil would be fresh in Cardwell's short memory. And, given Cardwell's own hostility toward Tony Serra, who had been stabbed to death, Tison was apparently confident that his involvement in that killing would not present a major problem. He explained to Cardwell that he had attended "a few sessions with a prison psychologist . . . I was told everything concerning my behavior was OK."

His letter continued:

> Sir, I am not asking you to place me directly outside. I realize the procedure must be followed and every inmate is required to work on the trusty gang for a number of weeks. I am also aware due to my lack of physical work for a number of years the trusty gang might halfway kill me. But I do know that I need the physical work. If I survive, I will be in better shape mentally and physically than I have been for years.
>
> Warden, I am not afraid of work. In fact, I enjoy it. And I will assure you my work habits are good. I put my whole being into my job. I am a capable individual in welding, operation of heavy equipment, a fair mechanic (I've been away from it 10 years), a fair electrician, and can operate most heavy equipment. At one time or another in the last fifteen years I have worked at all of the above jobs in this prison.
>
> Sir what I am trying to say is that I am a productive person and know that the more hours I work, the faster my time goes.

Tison closed his letter with this assurance: "Warden Cardwell, you have my word of honor (if that means anything to you), I will never give you any cause to regret changing my custody status to that of Trusty."[15]

Cardwell was impressed with the letter. He knew Tison was a hard worker and he liked his sincerity. To him that meant more than Tison's three previous escape attempts and his reputation for violence within the prison.

The transfer even surprised some of Cardwell's subordinates, who were well aware of his reputation for playing favorites. Bud Gomes recalled his feelings when he first caught sight of Tison at the Annex:

"Tison, for God's sake, after killing Jim Stiner and three previous escape attempts, was able to get a transfer. What amazed me was that in a relatively short period of time, [Tison was] reassigned and transferred to an area where he could accomplish an escape. I thought,

'What brought this all about?' I don't know the classification system —
I was never involved in classification. But, personally, when I saw
Tison out there . . . well, I just thought, 'Boy, that's something.'

"But Tison could charm you. I don't know where he got it, but
I'd seen him do it to more people than Cardwell. He was very amicable,
very communicative. He would answer questions very politely when
he wanted to. And he always seemed very sincere in what he said.
He was very in command of himself. Very impressive, yes, sir. But
underneath . . . well, at least I could see, he was very strong-willed
and, of course, very dangerous. And when I saw him in that Annex,
I couldn't figure it out. I thought to myself, well he's just biding his
time."[16]

Once in the Annex, the clever and forceful Tison quickly established
himself as the straw boss of every prisoner in the facility. On January
18, 1978, the day Bobby Tuzon arrived, Tison and Dave LaBarre
welcomed him by saying that they had heard that he was a licensed
pilot; they had some things they wanted to discuss with him later.
Tuzon was very surprised when he learned just how familiar they
were with the details of his life. They knew, for example, that he
was doing time for killing his brother-in-law during a family dispute
in 1974; that he had been a student at Arizona State University major-
ing in business administration; that in 1969 he had been arrested
for landing a Cessna 150 on Paradise Lane in Phoenix to impress
his fiancée; that he had married the woman, whose name was Irma,
and that she was a beautician; and that his wife now lived with their
three small children in Mesa.

How would they get all that information? And why would they
bother? Tuzon wondered. He tried to laugh it off by asking how
much else they knew. Tison took a long, thoughtful drag on the
cigarette he was smoking before he spoke. "Bobby," he said, "we've
checked you out. We know everything about you." Tuzon noticed
that Gary's eyes had a way of "boring into you" when he spoke.[17]

Tison's information on Bobby Tuzon's background probably came
from William Bernard Anthony, a former inmate then on parole,
though Tuzon claims that he had told no one at the prison that he
had a pilot's license.[18] According to Tuzon's later testimony, Anthony,
a licensed pilot himself, was "running information and making connections for Tison on the street."

On January 22, when Bobby's wife, Irma, visited him, he discreetly pointed Gary out to her, saying, "Let me know if anyone contacts you about anything." When she asked why, he said he wasn't sure, but Tison's unusual interest in him and his family had him concerned. On January 29, the next time Irma visited, Bobby once more called her attention to Tison, who on that day was visiting with two of his sons. He's up to something, Bobby thought, but I don't know what.

On January 31, Tuzon learned that the final appeal of his murder conviction had been turned down. It was depressing news. All he could think about was twenty more years behind bars, away from his family. Tison came in from the galley. "Too bad about your appeal," he said. When Tuzon asked how he had found out about it, Tison ignored the question. "Now," he said, "it's time for us to have a little talk."

Tuzon was not much older than Gary's own sons, and Gary seemed to take a vaguely paternalistic interest in him. One day Tuzon received a letter from his wife telling him that their young daughter was very ill and had been taken to the hospital. He was very upset and wanted to call home, but prison regulations limited outgoing calls to certain prearranged times, unless it was an emergency. But it was hard to prove an emergency since so many people lied about it. When he told Gary about the situation, Gary said, "Wait here, I'll take care of it," and left. Only a few minutes passed before a guard came up to Tuzon and told him he could use the phone. Later, Tuzon tried to thank Gary, but Gary just shrugged it off and said that he was glad the little girl was going to be all right.

It was obvious to Tuzon that Gary not only had access to a lot of information but also had status and influence inside the prison. It was equally clear that Gary wanted him to know that he could either help or hurt a person very easily. Tison enjoyed extraordinary privileges. He was the only inmate permitted to wear nonregulation shoes (he wore cowboy boots). When Tuzon asked how he managed to get away with it, Gary laughed and pulled a medical prescription out of his wallet. The prescription said that the boots were needed for "ankle support."[19] Tison hated low-cut shoes, and the boots had become a cherished symbol of his recognized status within the prison hierarchy.

More astonishing, however, than the prescription boots was the rumor that Tison often carried a .22-caliber derringer inside one of his boots. Some said that guards had let him have it to protect himself during the inmate strike. Others claimed that he had an "understanding" with the guards. Tuzon said that Tison was the only prisoner who was never searched during routine Trusty shakedowns. It was another such "understanding," Bobby said, that enabled Tison to receive plastic bags of marijuana and cocaine concealed in sacks of flour that were delivered regularly to the prison galley. Although Tison was not a user himself, drug dealing provided him a significant source of income and, according to Bobby, supplemented the income of some poorly paid guards. Tuzon also had some suspicions about higher-ranking prison officials, who permitted the traffic to flourish.[20]

Tison could charm prison visitors as well as officials. Martha LaBarre recalled that whenever she brought her daughter-in-law and grandson to visit with Dave, her son, Gary would rush over to see the little boy.

"Everytime you'd see Gary," she said, "he'd just be smiling and talking with the baby, you know. And if the baby didn't go over there to him, he'd come over to us to see him. One time when Dorothy was there, they gave the baby one of their sandwiches and a cold drink. After that, the baby and Gary were just real good buddies. It was cute to see them together. Whenever we would visit, the baby would always look for Gary, and if he didn't see him, Gary would holler and the baby would run over to him."[21]

Lita Beigel was a regular Sunday visitor to the prison during this period. On one occasion, not long before the escape, she noticed Dorothy bent over Gary's lap as they sat on the back bench of a picnic table in the visiting area. Dorothy was performing fellatio as Gary cradled her head in his hands. The couple, Beigel complained, were in full view of several children. Embarrassed and angered, Beigel went over and demanded that they stop, threatening to throw hot coffee on them if they didn't. She said Dorothy covered Gary and looked up at her coldly, but said nothing. Gary was enraged. He remained seated but warned her through clenched teeth that he would take her boyfriend "behind the wall" (prison slang for a beating or worse) if she ever bothered them again. Two guards, Beigel said, witnessed the whole incident but didn't do a thing to intervene.[22] A few moments later, she looked over at Gary and Dorothy and, once again, she could see only the top of Dorothy's head. It was apparent that the guards did not bother Gary Tison.

Bobby Tuzon was well aware of that as he sat across from Gary on his bunk on that gloomy last day of January 1978 and Gary began to talk in the confidential manner he used when the subject was something important. Tison told Bobby that he and some others were planning an escape. They wanted him to come along because they needed a pilot. Tison confided that his brother Joe was going to have a plane waiting at an isolated cropduster strip, a short drive from the prison. They had already obtained maps and charts, fuel estimates, and photographs of their destination — a ranch in Mexico just south of the tiny Arizona border town of Sasabe, near Caborca, in northern Sonora. The ranch was owned by a friend of Gary's, fellow inmate Arden Lee Smith. "Smitty" was doing fifteen years for drug smuggling and had offered the isolated ranch to Gary as a sanctuary in return for a future consideration. Tison offered Bobby $25,000 for the job.

Tuzon thought Tison was joking — or crazy. Could Gary have gotten the idea from a Charles Bronson film about a guy escaping from a Mexican prison in a helicopter? He laughed self-consciously when Gary asked him what he thought. Come on, Gary, he said, be serious.

That was a mistake. Tuzon watched Gary's expression freeze. His unblinking, penetrating stare made it clear that this was no if-I-had-the-wings-of-an-angel pipe dream. Tison was dead serious. He didn't say anything for a minute, but he flushed around the neck. He lit a cigarette without taking his eyes from Tuzon's. Finally he spoke, leaning across the narrow space between the two bunks. In the same very controlled tones, he told Tuzon he was serious and that there really wasn't any choice: either Bobby went along and flew the plane, or he would leave prison feet first like Tony Serra. Tuzon had heard the rumors that Tison had set up the attack on Serra, the inmate who was stabbed to death a year before.

Tison's tough reputation as someone "no one messed with" was well established. Bobby needed time to think and he was scared. He told Gary that he would cooperate; he didn't know what else to say. When he did, Gary suddenly smiled that odd smile of his — only his lips smiling below cold, empty eyes — and reached across and patted Tuzon on the shoulder. "I thought you'd see it my way," he said.

6

Brothers and Cellmates:
1976–1978

In October 1977, Raul Castro had resigned as governor of Arizona to become President Jimmy Carter's ambassador to Argentina. In the wake of the disturbing revelations of prison corruption and mismanagement and two consecutive years of inmate strikes and violence, the new governor, former secretary of state Wesley Bolin, fired John J. Moran, the director of corrections, on November 29, 1977, naming John B. McFarland as acting director. The decision was unpopular with the legislature. The person who should have been fired, many believed, was not the director but the warden. Had Moran been willing to fire Cardwell, Moran could have kept his job. It was obvious to everyone that Cardwell was incompetent, and some thought he was corrupt.

But Moran's name, along with Cardwell's, had been linked to organized-crime activities within the prison — in particular, to the contract murder of inmate Tony Serra on January 3, 1977. Serra was the first of several inmates killed within the prison in the twenty-five beatings and stabbings that were recorded in 1977.[1] He also was numbered among a handful of recent murder victims in Maricopa County whose deaths were linked to organized crime. But Serra had been stabbed and bludgeoned to death in the prison license plate plant, whereas the others had been shot or car-bombed or had "committed suicide" in Phoenix.

Tony Serra had been convicted on land fraud charges in 1974 and was serving an eight-to-ten-year sentence. Before his conviction, he had been the sales manager for the Great Southwest Land and Cattle Company. The company was described by the *Arizona Republic* as "a crooked land firm believed by police to have been controlled by [Ned] Warren." Mafia figure Ned Warren, the paper said, was "the godfather of land swindlers."[2]

Four months before he was killed, Serra had been interviewed at the prison by attorney Atmore Baggot and a man named Richard Frost. Baggot and Frost were members of Congressman John Conlan's political campaign organization. Conlan was seeking the Republican nomination for a U.S. Senate seat vacated when Carl Hayden had died. Congressman Sam Steiger was opposing Conlan in the September Republican primary. Baggot and Frost wanted to know about Steiger's rumored connections with Ned Warren, and Serra was a likely source of information.

The race for the Republican senatorial nomination was a bitter struggle between two far-right-wing candidates competing for the same hardcore Arizona conservatives. Steiger, a transplanted city boy from New York, liked to project the image of a hard-riding, often profane cowboy from rural Yavapai County, embodying a macho conception of the West. Conlan, in contrast, cultivated the image of a clean-living, churchgoing man: his West was the land of golf and tennis in Scottsdale. Despite their divergent styles and images, both were extremely conservative, but since neither candidate's political views were in question, both campaigns sought to make their opponent's integrity the major issue. As the election approached, their tactics became dirtier.

Steiger's organization decided to challenge Conlan's moral purity and conspicuously displayed born-again Christianity. A whispering campaign was launched, in which questions were raised about Conlan's sexual preferences. Conlan's people, in turn, pursued the rumors about Steiger's real estate dealings with Ned Warren and other shady characters. At the time, Warren was appealing a 1975 conviction on two counts of extortion, and hardly a day passed without a story about him appearing in the Phoenix papers. Baggot and Frost believed that rumors of corruption could destroy Steiger in the final weeks before the primary. When they asked Serra, he told them that the rumors were true.

Serra said he knew the whereabouts of missing real estate records that would further link Steiger to Warren in fraudulent land schemes. He told them that, following Warren's instructions, he had buried the incriminating evidence in the desert near Florence, after Maricopa County attorney Moise Berger had lifted the records from the files in the district attorney's office. Earlier, Berger's office had claimed that the missing records (which included phony land sales contracts and canceled checks paid to bribe a former Arizona real estate commissioner) had been "lost."[3] Serra insisted that Berger was lying. The records, he said, were taken with Berger's knowledge and cooperation.

Serra went on to describe an abiding friendship between Warren and Steiger and Steiger's former congressional aide, Joe Patrick. According to Serra, Warren had been a "silent partner" with Steiger and Phoenix attorney Neal Roberts in acquiring land and developing the Lake Pleasant Lodge near Phoenix. Serra said that he personally had sold the lease to Steiger. In 1968, he became friendly with Steiger, Patrick, and Roberts. "We all drank at Rocky's Hideaway," he said, "and saw each other socially, you know."[4]

Serra's interview was too good to keep quiet. Baggot decided to go public with it right away. He went to the *Republic,* and the story was published on August 13, 1976, less than three weeks before the primary election. A second story followed on August 21. Baggot had assured Serra that his anonymity would be protected, but when the articles appeared they identified him by name. Baggot and Frost had issued Tony Serra's death warrant.

After the August 13 story appeared in the newspapers, Richard Frost called the prison and was routinely given permission to visit Serra again, but three hours later, Harold Cardwell called Frost and canceled the interview. Frost described Cardwell as being "very irate" on the phone. "You could get a couple of finks killed," Cardwell warned. Frost later said that he had been told by unnamed sources that "considerable political pressure ha[d] been brought against the warden to prevent an[other] interview with Serra."[5] Sam Steiger and Cardwell, they learned, were friends.

Don Bolles, an investigative reporter for the *Arizona Republic,* had long been aware of the associations Serra described. Bolles had written a number of stories about organized crime in Arizona, and the persons he wrote about didn't like what he was saying. He obviously knew too much, and there was concern that his stories would stir the curiosity of the state attorney general, a liberal Democrat with a Harvard degree by the name of Bruce Babbitt. Everybody knew that Babbitt was politically ambitious and was looking for issues and opportunities to increase his visibility. Nobody wanted to play Jimmy Hoffa to Babbitt's Bobby Kennedy.

A year before Tony Serra's story appeared in the *Republic,* Bolles was writing a series about organized crime in Arizona, particularly with regard to real estate, banking, and racetrack gambling. On June 1, 1976, a part-time tow-truck driver and greyhound breeder named John Harvey Adamson called Bolles. The reporter was well aware that Adamson was an errand boy for the people he had been writing about. Adamson told Bolles he had some information about Sam Steiger's connections with the crime-connected Emprise Corporation. Steiger had once been an outspoken critic of Emprise's operations, but the criticism had abruptly stopped. Adamson told Bolles that Steiger had been lured into a lucrative land deal by Emprise representatives. Bolles said he was interested in learning more, and the two men agreed to meet the next morning at the Clarendon Hotel in downtown Phoenix.[6]

According to Adamson, at the appointed hour the following day, he and a partner, James Robison, hid in the parking lot and watched while Bolles parked his car and entered the hotel. Adamson walked quickly to Bolles's car and attached six taped sticks of dynamite and an electronically controlled blasting cap to the frame beneath the driver's seat. Bolles returned to the car a short time later when Adamson didn't show. As soon as he slid inside and closed the door, either Adamson or Robison pressed the electronic detonator. The bomb exploded with tremendous force. Bolles lost the lower half of his body and an arm in the blast, but he remained conscious long enough to identify Adamson as the person who had set him up. Don Bolles died eleven days later.

That night Adamson and his wife were flown by private plane to Lake Havasu City. The executive suite at the Rodeway Inn had been reserved for them in the name of "Jim Johnson." Dinner reservations had already been made under the same name. Neal Roberts — the Phoenix attorney Tony Serra had identified as an associate of both Ned Warren and Sam Steiger — had phoned in the reservations the day before.[7]

Neal Roberts had become a familiar name to anyone in Phoenix who had read Don Bolles's articles about organized crime. In January 1976, Roberts and Adamson's partner, James Robison, had conspired to blow up a government-leased building in Phoenix.[8] Roberts owned a financial interest in the building and hoped to collect insurance. On that occasion, however, the explosives had been discovered and disarmed by police.

Robison, Adamson, and yet another associate of Neal Roberts, land developer Max Dunlap, were convicted for the Bolles murder.[*] In 1978, Roberts was sentenced to five years in prison for the attempted bombing of the building. He was not, however, indicted in the Bolles case.[9]

When Don Bolles was killed, Tony Serra knew that his life was also in danger. And when the story he had told to Baggot and Frost appeared in the newspaper two months later, there was no doubt in his mind that he was a marked man. He had repeatedly petitioned prison officials for a transfer out of the main prison, where he was most vulnerable to attack. His transfer requests were ignored. In December 1976, Serra was attacked by an unidentified person as he sat on the toilet. Serra, described as a "tough cookie" who could take care of himself if he had to, was beaten about the head and shoulders with a steel pipe before he managed to escape. Hoping to avoid future reprisals, he claimed that he was unable to identify his attacker. But he knew that it wouldn't matter in the long run. There were too many others willing to pick up a contract if the money was right. And he knew it was.

After being treated at the prison infirmary, Serra requested a meeting with the associate warden, Dwight Burd. Burd was in charge of prison security, and Serra believed he was a reasonable man. Serra told him about the attack and what was behind it, and said there had been a "flood of threats on my life." Serra thought Burd seemed sympathetic. He promised to bring the matter to Cardwell's attention and assured Serra that Cardwell would get back to him.

---

[*] Max Dunlap and James Robison were sentenced to death in January 1978. In February 1980, the Supreme Court overturned their convictions, ruling that defense lawyers had not been allowed sufficient opportunity to cross-examine the chief witness for the prosecution, John Harvey Adamson. The charges against Dunlap and Robison were subsequently dismissed.

Cardwell got back to him all right, but not in the way Serra had hoped. In a desperate letter to the interviewer who had broken his word, attorney Atmore Baggot, Serra claimed that not only had his repeated requests for transfer been either denied or ignored, but that when Cardwell finally did see him, it was only to warn him to keep his mouth shut. Even more unsettling was the fact that Cardwell did not come alone: with him was Director of Corrections John Moran. After the first story linking Ned Warren and Sam Steiger appeared on August 13, Moran and Cardwell both came to his cell, Serra said, and warned him about talking to the press.

In his letter to Baggot, Serra wrote:

> On my noon release I returned to my cell to find the warden, Mr. Cardwell, and his boss, Mr. John Morand [*sic*] waiting. This is highly unusual. They would normally send for me, but in this case they were so upset they came to get me. First they were in question as to how I arranged to get you people [Baggot and Frost] in. When I could be of no help along those lines, an order was given to a Major to investigate and report all names [on Serra's approved visitors list] to the warden. Next they started on 'I had better watch out' who I was talking about and what I was saying. I quickly advised them to change their political alliances to Mr. Conlin [*sic*]. Then the threats started. 'Your time here can be very rough.' 'You got a parole coming up,' etc., etc.

Serra closed his letter with a plea:

> Mr. Baggot, many people here die since all of this hell started. I am not afraid for my life but I would be a fool not to be concerned about it. Please be careful about the way you use my name. The newspaper has already referred to me as an informer. In here I already have had to explain. That could get me hurt.[10]

The bitter race for the Republican senatorial nomination so divided the party that, though Steiger won the primary, he lost the November general election to Democrat Dennis DeConcini. Cardwell, who needed Steiger's support, was disappointed and angry, and he blamed Tony Serra. After the general election, Serra's life was rough at best.

On December 30, 1976, four days before he was brutally murdered, Serra wrote a last letter to Baggot:

"The warden was in the yard today," he wrote, "so I know he's here but its become evident he's not intended [*sic*] to see me."[11]

Tony Serra didn't go quietly. He punched and kicked, and it finally took four men to kill him. They stabbed him fifteen times and battered his head with lengths of pipe. One of his ears hung loose, almost torn from his head. The medical examiner later found in Serra's fists large tufts of hair he had ripped from at least one attacker's head. His killers finally had managed to hold him down long enough to smash his skull with a heavy electric drill. Then they used the drill bit to punch a hole in his forehead.

After Serra's murder, both Cardwell and Moran were vague about their earlier meeting with the slain inmate. They admitted speaking with Serra, but denied visiting his cell and making any threats. Moran angrily dismissed Serra's story as "an absolute lie." Claiming that he couldn't recall exactly what they discussed, Moran said that it was "just chitchat." Cardwell was quick to agree. "Moran and I were in a cell block where Serra was about the time he talks about," Cardwell said, "but we saw him only on the run as we were walking through . . . I don't even know where his cell was at that time."[12]

When asked why Serra hadn't been transferred to protective custody after the first attempt on his life, Cardwell claimed ignorance.[13]

Gary Tison was a prime suspect in the Serra slaying, though he was never indicted. Sometime in the autumn of 1976, Joe Tyson visited his brother at the prison. Gary told Joe that he had been contacted about making "a hit on a dude in the land fraud." Gary told his brother the inmate's name was Serra and that he had been offered $50,000 "to take care of it."[14]

Shortly after Serra was killed, an ex-convict, Glenn Scott Thornton, placed a large sum of cash in a safe deposit box at a Scottsdale bank.[15] At one time, Thornton had shared a cell with Gary Tison. Now he was one of Tison's contacts on the outside. Thornton met regularly with Dorothy to deliver money and exchange information.[16] Sometimes he would come to her office at the Collins & Haggard Insurance Agency in Phoenix. More frequently they would meet at a Sambo's Restaurant on East McDowell Road. At one of these meetings, in November 1977, Thornton gave Dorothy ten thousand dollars in cash. That same month, Thornton also retained a Scottsdale attorney, W. Lloyd Benner, who was given power of attorney to manage a trust account that had been established for Dorothy in yet another Scottsdale bank.[17]

By this time Gary had been in the medium-security Annex two

months. Tison's good fortune — his transfer and the money he was paid for the Serra murder — was reflected in the optimism he expressed in the Christmas letter he wrote to his sister Kay. Gary was not only anticipating an escape, he also had visions of sitting down over rum and Cokes in some Central American country to negotiate a movie contract for the script he intended to write about it.

On January 11, 1978, one year after Tony Serra was killed, inmate George Warnock was given a grant of immunity to testify about organized crime within the prison before the Arizona legislature's House Task Force on Organized Crime. Warnock knew Gary Tison well. He had accompanied Gary in his unsuccessful escape attempt of 1972; he had also helped kill Tony Serra for Tison. When Warnock was questioned about the Serra slaying, he told less than he knew. Warnock said land swindler Ned Warren and attorney Neal Roberts, a central figure in the Don Bolles murder investigation, had paid to have Serra killed. The contract had gone out to prevent Serra's scheduled testimony in Warren's trial on land fraud charges. Warnock did not reveal, however (or if he did, it was not reported), that Gary Tison was the person who had picked up that contract. But he did make a point of saying that he had never been paid for his part in the murder; it sounded a little as though Warnock was still expecting to be paid.[18]

On January 13, 1978, the day after Warnock's testimony was reported in the *Republic*, Randy Greenawalt was interviewed by the members of the inter-institutional Transfer Committee, composed of Warden Cardwell and deputy wardens Alfred Grijalva, Andrew Jimenez, and Joseph Martinez. Greenawalt had been petitioning for a transfer out of maximum security almost from the day four years earlier when he began his life sentence. Randy was invariably polite to the point of obsequiousness around authority figures. He exuded sincerity during the questioning, just as he had in letters to prison officials praising Cardwell. Cardwell and his deputies looked approvingly on the deferential Greenawalt.

Still, the fact remained that Randy Greenawalt was in maximum security because he had committed some very ugly crimes. Serial killers are generally regarded as much more dangerous than the typical murderer. Greenawalt had become verbally abusive in a half-dozen or so incidents with guards since his confinement in 1974. The committee decided to give only conditional approval for the transfer, pending the results of a psychiatric examination.[19]

Two weeks later, Greenawalt was examined by Dr. Willard S. Gold, a consulting psychiatrist for the Department of Corrections. Dr. Gold's report, dated January 25, 1978, stated that despite "a fairly large well-spring of unresolved earlier frustration," Greenawalt's "affective display is well-modulated and he controls provocation and surface hostility to good effect." Noting also that Randy's "institutional adjustment has been excellent," Dr. Gold offered this diagnosis:

"The diagnostic assessment is of a passive-aggressive personality disorder. Specifically, I can find no psychiatric evidence to oppose his placement in medium security status in the Trusty Annex."[20]

In fact, the record on Randy Greenawalt was a graphic case history of flowering psychopathology. The only thing that ever kept his aggression in check was tight institutional restrictions on his behavior. Nonetheless, on Gold's recommendation the committee approved Greenawalt's transfer. Gary Tison, Randy Greenawalt, and Bobby Tuzon were now gathered together for Gary's purposes.

After Randy Greenawalt's transfer was approved, Tison gave Dorothy the word to begin preparations for the escape. Shortly after the New Year, 1978, Joe Tyson called his nephew Ray from Casa Grande to tell him that he had the escape car. He told Ray to meet him at Denny's Restaurant at 1343 West Broadway in Tempe, an eastside Phoenix suburb. When Ray arrived at the restaurant with Ricky, Joe was there waiting in his own car. A few minutes later, Ed Meadows, an associate of Joe's, drove up in a cream-colored Lincoln Continental and the exchange was made. Ray followed Ricky in his mother's Galaxie as Ricky drove the Lincoln to Bob Adams's place on the east side of Phoenix. The Lincoln was parked in a storage lot behind Adams's mobile home, to remain there, as it turned out, until July.

A few days later, four tough-looking men were talking over beers at a saloon in Show Low, Arizona. Show Low lies on the high plains of east central Arizona. Located on Route 60, the main street of Show Low, Bill's Bar is an authentic cowboy saloon, with the best country-western jukebox west of Socorro and live music on the weekends. It draws its disparate clientele from all over the area — most of them, as the lyrics of a popular Tom T. Hall song at the time suggested, with a keen interest in faster horses, younger women, older whiskey, and, like the four men sitting at the table in the corner, more money.

Dick Hudson, Jim Crouch, Bill Dutton, and Dick Bilby had all done time, mainly for burglary convictions. They looked like hippies, but they were always ready to earn a little easy money if the chance came along. Dick Hudson told the others that Joe Tyson wanted to trade high-grade marijuana for weapons — pistols, shotguns, it didn't matter, as many as they could steal in the next week or so. Rifles and shotguns adorned the rear-window racks of most of the pickups parked outside every bar. And it was easy to pick a truck-door lock. The demand for marijuana during the ski season in Pinetop and Show Low would be good. It looked like a real profitable venture.[21]

Near the end of January, Joe met Hudson and Crouch at a restaurant in Globe, about eighty miles northeast of Casa Grande.[22] In exchange for two shotguns they had promised earlier — .16- and .20-gauge pumps — Joe gave them a kilo of marijuana. Earlier that same week, Tyson had gone to Nogales, where he picked up another shotgun and a pistol from a drug contact in Santa Ana, a man known only as "Jesus."[23] He obtained additional weapons from other unknown sources.

A few weeks later, Tyson met Crouch, Hudson, and Dutton in the bar of the Doubletree Hotel in Tucson. Tyson paid them $110 as part of their agreement for the guns.[24] The men had four women with them, and Joe bought everyone drinks all evening, paying for each round with $100 bills and leaving big tips. They all got roaring drunk. Joe boasted that the guns he had bought would be used to break his brother out of prison. Everybody laughed.[25] The days of shooting your way out of prison had passed a long time ago.

During the first week of February, Joe met twice again with his nephews and gave them the weapons he had obtained for the escape. Ricky and Ray took the weapons to Bob Adams's place and hid them in the trunk of the Lincoln.[26] That left only the airplane for Joe to worry about.

"About the first or second week of February," Terry Tarr said, "Joe wired me two hundred dollars for air fare, and I flew to Phoenix. Then he rented a private plane and I flew it to an airstrip near Joe's place in Casa Grande. Joe wouldn't let me pay for anything. He always had a roll of hundred dollar bills in his pocket." They spent the next day or two flying around central and southern Arizona, checking out possible landing strips for flying in marijuana. There were three that seemed like good bets: Ryan Field, an old World War II strip about twenty miles beyond the mountains west of Tucson; another just north of Florence, near Florence Junction; and a third in a remote area between Wickenburg and Congress. They also made note of the numerous cropduster strips scattered throughout the rural cotton-growing areas that stretch west from Phoenix along the Gila River to Yuma.[27]

In 1978 it was very easy to steal a small airplane. Manufacturers were not concerned about theft: it hadn't been a big problem. The chances were about one in three that the key to one plane would fit another and airport security was usually lax. Joe said it was almost as easy as stealing a car. He had a pocketful of extra keys that they could try. They needed a plane big enough, he said, to transport the "forty tons" of marijuana that was waiting to be picked up near Santa Ana. Joe introduced Terry to his partners from Pinetop, Bill Dutton and Jim Crouch, who were going to help out. Together the four men spent a day driving around the Phoenix area looking for a plane to steal. They finally found a red-and-white Cessna 180 parked at the edge of the Deer Valley Airport, west of Phoenix, but the plane turned out to be one of the few equipped with a mechanical locking device. They would have to look elsewhere for another plane.[28]

Tarr said Joe regaled him, during the visit, with stories about how easy it was to make money in Arizona. "Why, hell, you could even make your own airstrip if need be," Joe told him, laughing. "One time we stole this Caterpillar bulldozer right outside of Casa Grande, ran it up on a flatbed truck we'd rented, and hauled it away. We scrapped a strip real easy, then hauled the damn thing over to Wickenburg and rented it to some rich doctor from Anchorage, Alaska, who owns a ranch there. I told them I would rent it to them for a couple of months at a thousand a month. He gave me two thousand up front. I don't know what he thought when he never saw me again, but I bet he didn't try too hard to find me, either."

It was always easier to "rent" heavy equipment than sell it, he explained. Something like boats, you could sell. In Tucson, Joe had spotted a twenty-eight-foot cabin cruiser sitting on a trailer in a driveway, and he'd just backed a truck up to the hitch and hauled it away. It was sold within forty-eight hours. "I lost track of all the cars and trucks we picked up," Joe said with a laugh. "But I only did those things when I wasn't doing any weed . . . You know, something would just come to my attention. Maybe it wasn't big money, you know, like weed, but hell, it was so easy."[29]

The load they were going to pick up in Santa Ana was big money. It was all fairly simple, he said. First they'd steal a plane, and Tarr would fly it to Mexico, where he would meet Joe's Mexican contacts and load the plane. The shrewd part of the deal, Joe said, was the financing. He said he had "cut a deal" with the Mexicans. He would make a cash payment when he made the pickup. After Terry got the marijuana safely across the border, he would fly the plane back to Mexico, where Joe's contacts would return a portion of his cash in exchange for the plane. He said Terry could then just catch a bus up Route 15 to Nogales, and the Border Patrol wouldn't give him a second look as he crossed into Arizona. He said the Mexicans liked to deal that way because an airplane was worth more there. And, he said, he didn't need any "hot airplanes sitting around" for the narcs to find.[30] No mention at all was made of a plane's being flown back to Arizona for his brother to use in a prison escape.

By the first week of February, the situation at the prison Annex had become tense. Gary's escape plans continued to revolve around Bobby Tuzon's willingness to fly the airplane. Bobby felt boxed in and was having trouble sleeping. He decided that he had to tell his wife about it. He had to talk with someone.

When he told Irma about his dilemma, she became very upset. At first she begged him not to get involved for fear that he would be killed. But her desire to have him back with her and the children was powerful. All she could think about was the next twenty years without Bobby, and their children growing up without a father. She finally agreed to cooperate, if that's what they had to do to be together again. But she was afraid, and there was no one she could talk to about this — not even her priest.

On Sunday, February 5, Gary told Bobby that everything was set. They were going to break out the following Sunday, February 12. Gary explained that he had made arrangements for Dorothy to contact Bobby's wife. He said Dorothy would give Irma a portion of Bobby's twenty-five thousand dollars in advance, for her and the three children to live on until they could join him after he was settled in Mexico or Costa Rica.

The reality of what was about to happen finally hit Bobby. When he seriously weighed the grave risks involved, he panicked. He immediately wrote to his wife and told her not to come for her customary Sunday visit on the twelfth. He also advised her that Dorothy would be dropping off some money. On February 9, he received a letter from Irma stating that no one had brought her any money; she wanted to know what was going on. Was it a double cross? She was confused and afraid. Should she tell prison authorities or keep her mouth shut? Either way her husband's life would be in great jeopardy.

On Saturday, the day before the scheduled breakout, Bobby's father came to the prison to see him. Irma was upset, he said, and crying a lot. He wanted to know what was going on. Bobby was afraid that if he told his father he would immediately go to the authorities. If that happened, Gary would know he had "snitched," and Bobby's life would be worthless. "It's too late to do anything. I can't talk about it," he told his father. "You'll be reading about it in the papers."

Bobby made up his mind that, short of getting himself murdered, he wasn't going to go along with Tison. Dorothy's failure to give Irma the promised money seemed to provide the argument he needed to back out of the agreement. Gary told him not to worry and promised that the money would arrive. When Tuzon protested, saying he didn't want any part of the escape, Gary shoved him backward onto his bunk. "You're going," he said evenly, "and we're leaving in the morning." Bobby was stuck.

But the next morning nothing happened. Breakfast ended, church services were announced, and inmates lined up to go. Then visitors started arriving, but not the visitors Gary was expecting. By noon Tison was livid. He immediately suspected that Tuzon had told someone about the breakout. When he and LaBarre confronted Tuzon with the accusation, Bobby honestly denied it. Gary seemed to believe him and, at that point, shifted his anger to his brother. Joe suddenly became the prime suspect in the collapse of the plans. Joe was supposed to have arranged the outside part of the breakout and something obviously had gone wrong. Gary wanted to know what.

The arrangements that Joe had to complete outside the prison included providing a get-away car, which he had done; providing guns and ammunition, which he was in the process of doing; and, finally, finding an airplane, which he had not yet done. Joe was also supposed to recruit a dozen or so members of the Mexican Mafia in case they were needed to assist in the escape. Gary planned to have the Mexicans positioned to pin down the tower guards with gunfire should Gary and his group be spotted as they walked to the car waiting outside the Annex. It was perhaps the most bizarre feature of the plan. Gary should have known that the likelihood of finding a dozen men willing to do such a thing was very remote. Joe thought it was just plain crazy and didn't even try.

But there were other reasons no escape took place that Sunday in February. Joe's commitment to his bargain with Gary began to slip. The witness Gary was supposed to eliminate, Mario Castillo, was kept out of reach in the Pinal County Jail instead of being transferred into the state prison as Joe expected, preventing Gary from following through on his end of the bargain. Joe, in turn, had purchased a Lincoln Continental for $1,250 instead of buying a more costly camper van, and the weapons he'd gotten were ordinary handguns and shotguns instead of the automatic weapons Gary wanted. Most important, however, instead of handing over to Dorothy $5,000 that was left from the cash Gary had given him, Joe simply pocketed the money.[31]

Gary said he could accept the compromises Joe had made on the car and weapons, but he wanted to know what Joe had done with the five thousand dollars. "If Joe doesn't come up with that money," he said to Tuzon and Dave LaBarre, "I'll kill him if it's the last thing I ever do." Then, tapping a thick index finger on Bobby's chest, he said, "And if you ever snitch on us, I'll kill you, too."

Gary made sure that Bobby got the message. On February 14, Tuzon was called into the guards' office. Lieutenant Willard Gotcher was holding one of Bobby's white cook's shirts. His name and number had been blotted over with shoe polish and what appeared to be blood. Gotcher asked what was going on, and if Bobby had any idea who did it. Tuzon replied only that he was under a lot of pressure from Gary Tison, but he didn't want to explain why. Gotcher said that he was aware of that, but offered no help other than advising Tuzon to be careful. "Gary Tison can be bad news," he said, as if Bobby needed to be told.

Tison and LaBarre were waiting when Tuzon returned to his cell. Gary immediately asked what he had told Gotcher. Tuzon replied that Gotcher had wanted to know about the blood on his shirt, but he swore truthfully that he had told the lieutenant nothing about the escape plans. Tison fixed Bobby with an unblinking stare before saying to LaBarre that he believed Bobby was telling the truth. Gary then told them about a change in the plans that would exclude any dependence on his brother, Joe. "Joe is out of it from now on," he said. "You never could depend on that motherfucking liar." The new plan on the outside would involve only Dorothy, his three sons, and Gary's old pal, Bob Adams. They were the only ones he could trust.

Tison went on to fantasize about various schemes they could pursue to raise money. There was a bank in Kingman, Arizona, where the Mafia kept large sums raised from its Las Vegas gambling operations. After the breakout, he said, they could fly to Kingman, rob the bank, and, with that money, head for South America and a lucrative future in drug smuggling. He also told Tuzon that he and Dorothy had a large sum of money in a Swiss bank account, a payment for a job that Gary had taken care of in the prison, but he didn't elaborate.

Tuzon thought the plan, and Tison, were crazy. One minute Gary was assuming they would have a plane; the next minute he would be talking about camper vans and survival equipment and a plan to hole up in the mountains somewhere. Bobby also noticed a big change in Tison's outlook. Up until that time, Gary had talked primarily about being reunited with his family in South America. Rejoining his family had seemed to be uppermost in his mind. Now, Tuzon said, "all he talked about was killing people . . . especially his brother Joe."

By the third week of February, Irma Tuzon was veering close to a nervous collapse. She had received phone calls from both Bob Adams and Dorothy Tison, who had gently, but firmly, warned her that her cooperation and confidence were expected. Dorothy was intimidating over the phone. Irma was now too frightened to visit the prison. She was convinced that violence would erupt at any moment. Moreover, she was now afraid to leave her children at home, even with her mother, for fear that they might be kidnapped or harmed.

When Dorothy called, she always asked about the children. She also questioned Irma about her absences from the prison. Irma's excuse was always that she or the children were sick. Dorothy didn't believe her and said so. "Your husband needs you as much as your children do," she said, "and you owe it to him." Dorothy made her feel guilty. "She would tell me a little bit about how long her husband had been there, and how many, you know, the things they had to go through for each other, all the things she did for him. She was very persistent."[32]

On February 25, Irma called Bobby to tell him that she wouldn't be able to visit again that weekend because she was ill. Bobby knew she wasn't. He was sitting on his bunk, upset and depressed, when Gary walked over and handed Bobby a Polaroid snapshot. It was a photograph of Irma getting into her car in the parking lot next to her beauty shop. It was obvious that it had been taken without her knowledge.[33] Bobby flushed, and indignation and anxiety tightened his cheek muscles. Then Gary smiled. "Don't worry, we're keeping an eye on her for you," he said, and winked, squeezing Bobby's shoulder. Bobby flared and warned Tison that no one had better harm his wife or children. "Now, Bobby," Tison replied soothingly, "there's no need for anything like that. We was just hoping that we can keep counting on you both," he said, patting Bobby gently on the back.

On March 1, Gary came to Bobby in a fury. Joe had told Dorothy that he wanted the Lincoln back, claiming the deal he made with Gary was off because Gary hadn't been able to deliver on the Castillo hit, and Joe was going to give the car to his younger sister, Linda. Dorothy had said, untruthfully, that she didn't know where the boys were keeping the car. Then she shot back, asking what Joe had done with the rest of the money Gary had given him. That's when Joe got mad. Whether he actually slapped Dorothy, as she reported to Gary, is debatable.

If there had been any doubt about Joe's fate before, the slapping story erased it. Gary told Bobby that Joe was going to die just like Jim Stiner. Gary's sons were going to take care of Joe, but they couldn't do it until they got hold of a gun that couldn't be traced back to them. He needed Bobby's help. Bobby said that he knew of an old rifle that could not be traced, and that he could have Irma get it for him. With the photograph of his wife still vivid in his mind, Bobby was scared and wanted to do something to placate Tison. "I felt that by giving him the gun," he said later, "it would relieve the pressure on me and my family."[34] Gary was pleased. He said that he would have Dorothy call Irma about picking it up.

A few days later, Gary told Bobby that he had rescheduled the escape for Wednesday, March 12. Was Gary expecting to have a plane for him to fly? Had the Tison brothers settled the argument about the car? Was Gary going to have Joe killed before or after the escape? Plans seemed to change day by day.

They were going to stage a practice run on March 8, Gary said, to make sure everyone had their assignments straight. How, Tuzon asked, were they going to stage a practice run without the guards finding out? "Don't worry about the guards," Tison replied.

The erratic emotions that characterized Gary and Joe's relationship — bitter hatreds quelled by temporary truces, soon violated by shameless betrayals — were typical of relationships in this peculiar family. One night during a bourbon-soaked session at the bar of the Tucson Doubletree Inn, Joe told Terry Tarr that he wanted his sister Carol's husband, John Ericcson, killed, or as he put it, "dusted." But you just visited them, and he painted your car for you, Tarr responded incredulously. Yeah, Joe replied, but you can't trust John. John knew too much about Joe's narcotics operations. That was dangerous, Joe said, because he and John didn't get along.[35] What Joe didn't say was that he had cheated his brother-in-law out of $5,000 in an oil company scam, and John Ericcson wanted his money back.[36]

In the course of another drunken evening with Tarr at a favorite Tucson hangout, the Royal Sun Cocktail Lounge, Joe told Tarr for the first time that he had a brother in the state prison who was planning an escape.[37]

But by the first week of March, after the quarrel over the car, Joe no longer felt that he had a commitment to do any more for Gary. On March 4, Joe and Terry left for Tulsa, where they met Terry's cousin Ed Willingham at the Tradewinds West Motel.[38] Tyson registered along with a girlfriend, under the name of Francis R. Kirklam. They did some partying — but the purpose of the get-together, as usual, was business. Willingham had found an airplane he thought they could steal for their drug-smuggling plan. It was parked at a private airstrip near Hereford, Texas, a small farm and ranch community located between Amarillo and Clovis, New Mexico. The four men drove to Texas. On March 9, they stole the gold-and-brown Cessna 210, with Terry Tarr at the controls.

The following week, Tarr flew across the Mexican border, heading for a primitive airstrip on a ranch between the towns of Santa Ana and Magdalena in northern Sonora, where Joe Tyson's "forty tons" of marijuana was waiting to be picked up.* Joe wanted to get it into

---

*The exact dates of Terry Tarr's Mexican trip are not known other than that it was during the second week of March. According to Dave Harrington of the Pinal County Sheriff's Department, specific records no longer exist in Deaf Smith County, Texas, where Tarr was arrested.

the country quickly, he said, "before the homegrown crop becomes too plentiful, and the market for Mexican weed slows down." He told Tarr that everything was arranged, and the contacts there would be expecting him.[39]

It was dark when Tarr circled over the rugged terrain and began his approach toward a narrow airstrip. The strip was lighted only by bonfires, and Tarr couldn't see that the surface was rough. The landing was hard, then the plane hit something and bounced crazily into the air, and then landed hard again, breaking the wheel strut and pitching the plane forward on its nose. Tarr was knocked unconscious, and he suffered a concussion and broke some ribs. He felt lucky to be alive when he came to.

Tarr made it back across the border a few days later but subsequently was arrested and taken back to Texas to face charges for stealing the airplane in Hereford. There he told the sheriff of Deaf Smith County, Travis McPherson, about the narcotics operation and incidentally mentioned the planned prison escape. McPherson immediately notified Arizona authorities.

Only Joe Tyson and Terry Tarr know whether Tarr was supposed to fly that plane back to Arizona, and whether Joe intended to let Gary use it on March 12. But whatever Joe intended, the plane was too badly damaged to be repaired. The Mexicans involved in the deal dumped gasoline on the plane and set it on fire, presumably to destroy the evidence. As it burned and collapsed in a twisted mass of metal and ashes, so may have Gary's plan for an airborne escape.

Joe Tyson was arrested by agents of the Central Arizona Regional Narcotics Unit the second week of March. At first, Joe denied any knowledge of the prison escape, but, in view of the seriousness of the federal drug charges against him, he was persuaded without much difficulty to talk as part of a plea agreement. Joe wanted Gary to remain right where he was, behind bars. After the "slapping" incident he had received a letter from Gary. He knew what it was going to say, and he didn't want to read it, but his wife, Judy, did. Gary was raging mad and closed the letter with, "I'm going to be out soon and you'll get yours."[40]

Joe had provided guns and a car and that was going to be the extent of his involvement in his brother's plan. Once more, he warned his nephews about getting too involved. He told them it was okay to help their dad set it up, but after that, he said, they should stay out of it. The advice didn't mean much. He didn't know that, at that very moment, Gary was conspiring to have the boys kill him.

The practice run at the prison on March 8 had gone well. According to Bobby Tuzon, everyone walked through their assignments on cue, while the guards went about their business, occasionally looking on with what seemed to be all the interest of cows watching a passing freight train. Tuzon said he recognized Bob Adams as he drove by in a Lincoln Continental, on schedule, outside the fence.

No one said much about the airplane. It was a sensitive point. With or without a plane, Gary said, they were going to break out. His prime objective now was just getting beyond the gate to the car. Then they could work out a way to get across the border, maybe by plane, he said, but if not he would figure out another way. Everything appeared to be set for the escape on Sunday the twelfth, and Gary was chewing gum and smoking more than usual.

On the evening of March 11, it started to rain. It kept Gary awake as it pounded down on the dormitory roof, and it was still pouring when the sun rose the next morning. It was a hard, persistent rain, which made driving on dirt roads through the desert impossible — not to mention a takeoff from a dirt landing strip. The cotton and sorghum fields surrounding the prison were gullied with water, and Gary knew the main washes would be running and impassable. Bobby Tuzon feigned disappointment. It must have been Irma's prayers, he thought. It doesn't usually rain at all in March, let alone pour like this.

Gary was slamming things around and seething with frustration. The weather report said that the rain was supposed to continue for at least another day. Gary had to do something, so he abruptly announced that they were going to have another practice run. Three days later, on March 15, they walked through their routines and, once again, it went well.

About the third week of March, noticeable changes took place at the Annex. The once-indifferent guards suddenly became very attentive and watchful. Their numbers at the Annex and in the surrounding towers were increased. And everyone noticed that the tower guards were now carrying automatic weapons in addition to the usual shotguns. Word spread that the conspirators in the escape had been "snitched off" by one of their own members. Dave LaBarre was convinced that it was Bobby Tuzon and told him so. LaBarre had never liked Tuzon and didn't trust him. With Gary looking on, Tuzon denied that he had been the snitch. LaBarre wasn't satisfied. Gary didn't express an opinion; he just listened and fixed Tuzon with that cold stare.

On March 22, amid a swirl of rumors about a planned escape, Tuzon and Tison were taken for separate interviews with prison officials. The question was whether both inmates should be transferred out of the Annex for security reasons.

Tuzon seized the opportunity to tell his interviewers, Deputy Warden Andrew Jimenez and captains Floyd Turner and Martin Argel, about the escape plan. He pleaded with them to approve his transfer away from Tison and his collaborators, describing how his life and his family had been threatened unless he agreed to cooperate in the escape. To Tuzon's surprise, the committee told him they had already heard about the plan. He was told that his transfer request would be taken under consideration.

On March 24, Gary Tison was moved back into the maximum-security compound of the main prison and placed in "investigative lockup," pending further investigation of the conspiracy-to-escape rumors. As soon as Tison was moved out, Tuzon was approached by inmates Dave LaBarre and Eric Mageary. They told him he was going to die for "snitching off" Gary.[41] Everyone knew now that he was the snitch, and he knew that he couldn't last long. Surely, he thought, the authorities will approve a transfer.

Tuzon was stunned when they didn't. Could the Transfer Committee have wanted him dead? Their decision didn't make any sense otherwise. Believing that he didn't have long to live, Bobby began to put on paper all the things he wanted to say to his wife and children before it happened. But fate intervened.

Within hours of Gary's transfer, Dorothy received a phone call informing her that her husband had been moved to investigative lockup. She was worried. On March 26, she came to the prison to see him. She knew she had to calm him down to avert another disaster like the one in 1967 when he had killed the guard.

What she told Gary probably saved Bobby Tuzon's life. It was true that someone had told prison officials about the escape attempt, she said, but it wasn't Bobby Tuzon. The source, Dorothy said, was not Bobby Tuzon, but Gary's brother Joe.

Dorothy didn't have all the details, but she was right. Joe's questioners in the narcotics investigation had confronted him with the story Terry Tarr had told in Texas about the planned breakout. Joe had thought a minute and then said that he would agree to talk if a plea agreement could be worked out with his attorney on the drug charges. It was, and he did.

7

Setting the Stage:
March–July 1978

The day after Gary learned about his brother's double-cross, on March 27, 1978, Randy Greenawalt was moved at last into the Trusty Annex, where he expected to rejoin his old friend Gary Tison. He had first met Tison when they were doing time in Cell Block 3 at the main prison. They were both loners, both smarter than most inmates, and they developed a friendship. Greenawalt also knew inmate Eric Mageary. They had met four years before in the Coconino County Jail when Randy was standing trial for murder and McGeary was in an adjacent cell awaiting trial for armed robbery. Eric liked Randy, and had introduced him to his mother, Kathy Ehrmentraut.

In March 1978 both Greenawalt and Mageary were aware of the escape plan. Randy had talked with Gary about it months before in the main prison, before Tison's transfer to the Annex was approved. Randy's own involvement had depended upon his successful transfer to the Annex. Now, because of a surprising turn of events, Greenawalt arrived at the Annex only to learn that Gary had just been moved back to the main prison, to investigative lockup. Mageary explained to Randy what had happened.

Two days later, in the main prison, Gary Tison was given a polygraph test. The validity of polygraphs is very doubtful when the subject is a sociopathic personality. Gary had always been able to lie with dry palms and a steady heartbeat, without a twinge of conscience. He welcomed the test.[1]

Tison was serious but relaxed as William Banks of the Department of Public Safety wired him up. Gary answered each of the questions, and the graph lines that traced his physiological reactions moved monotonously within the normal range on all his answers. Only once, when he was asked about his brother Joe, was there any reaction of note, but even this was considered insignificant. Gary's hatred for his brother, now that he knew that it was Joe who had tipped off the authorities, was one emotion he couldn't quite control.

After the test, when Banks casually mentioned to Cardwell the minor reaction, the warden decided to ask Tison personally about his brother. When he did so, Tison denied any escape conspiracy involving his family. He made a point of telling Cardwell that Joe was a liar. "Joe's mixed up in narcotics," he said, "and there's bad blood between us because of that." Piously, he said he had three teenage sons, and it was people like Joe who ruined young people's lives. Cardwell was impressed with Gary's sincerity. In the course of the interview, Tison also reminded the warden of his outspoken support for him a year earlier, during the inmate strike. He said he didn't think his chances would be too good if Cardwell sent him back behind the walls. Cardwell nodded that he understood.

It appeared that Tison was telling the truth, but Cardwell wanted to talk with Randy Greenawalt. He knew Tison and Greenawalt were friends. Randy responded to Cardwell's questions with the same denials, and used many of the same arguments against moving Gary back to the main prison. The escape rumors, he insisted, were nothing but "bullshit." The whole thing, he said, was started by people out to get him and Gary. Randy also reminded Cardwell that he had been one of his few defenders during the strike. He mentioned the letter he had written to the director of corrections. If you send us back behind the walls now, he warned Cardwell, you know what could happen.

Cardwell spoke once again with William Banks, who had given Gary the lie detector test. He told Banks that Tison's slight reaction to the question about his brother was more than likely the result of their "bad blood" than any sensitivity about an escape plan. To be doubly sure, Cardwell requested a second polygraph. Tison was given the test later that same day, and again he passed. The next day, March 30, Cardwell approved Tison's return to the Annex. Amazingly, he had Gary reassigned to share quarters with Bobby Tuzon. Bobby was stunned. Although he had not yet spoken with Cardwell personally, he was sure that the officials he had related his story to eight days before — Jimenez, Turner, and Argel — must have reported to the warden. Bobby saw the move as Cardwell's way of showing his contempt for him.

Randy welcomed his old friend Gary with a slap on the back, while Bobby Tuzon looked on and pretended also to be pleased. To a group that included Tuzon, LaBarre, Mageary, and Greenawalt, Tison joked about Banks's naïveté and described how he had outsmarted the polygraph.[2] "I beat them at their own game," Gary said, laughing. "Hell, if you're cool, them goddamn things don't work at all." He just winked when they asked him about his interview with Cardwell and the Transfer Committee. "That Gary is one cool motherfucker," Greenawalt said afterward, shaking his head. Even Tuzon was impressed.

The storm had passed, it seemed, for Gary. Both he and Randy Greenawalt were now residents of the least secure installation at the state prison. Moreover, he was rooming with a licensed pilot. The stage appeared to be set.

In approving the transfers of Tison and Greenawalt to medium security, Cardwell chose to ignore indisputable evidence that both men were high security risks and very dangerous. But, even more astonishingly, Cardwell ignored two independent and detailed reports of Tison's plan to escape. Cardwell could point to Tison's polygraph results; he could claim that Bobby Tuzon was untrustworthy; but why wouldn't he believe the sheriff of Deaf Smith County, Texas, and the Central Arizona Narcotics Unit?

The timing of the warden's decisions raised even more serious questions. A court-ordered review of the inmate reclassification process was scheduled to begin at the prison on April 1, 1978. From that date forward, a newly appointed Reclassification Committee would pass on such decisions instead of the committee composed of Cardwell and his deputies. The new committee would be made up of mental health professionals drawn from outside the prison system and approved by the state legislature.

There was no chance that the new committee — which would take over only two days later — would have recommended a medium-security reclassification for either Tison or Greenawalt. Harold Cardwell must have known that. Both his judgment and the timing seemed highly suspect.

Harold Cardwell was an arrogant and authoritarian man. He played favorites, and he was easily charmed. He expected deference from his subordinates. It was common knowledge among the inmate population that he was especially susceptible to flattery. Like many arrogant people, he rarely questioned the motives behind the compliments.

Robert Benjamin Smith, an inmate serving a life sentence for murder, described how Cardwell was once duped into a transfer by inmate Charles Schmid. Schmid, who had received national attention in 1964 as "the Pied Piper of Tucson," was serving a life term for killing three teenage girls in Tucson.

Schmid was intent on escape and was constantly scheming to accomplish that objective. Also, like Tison, he had quickly developed a sense of Cardwell's egocentric personality. With that in mind, the articulate Schmid wrote an essay about prison life in which he praised the new warden. It appeared on the front page of the *Arizona Republic,* on January 13, 1974. Schmid told Robert Benjamin Smith that he had written the story for the sole purpose of "getting into Cardwell's good graces so that he would be placed in a minimum custody area." It worked. Cardwell could not conceal his delight with the story. Despite Schmid's criminal record as a multiple murderer and two previous escape attempts, Cardwell approved his transfer request.

"Minimum custody for a lifer was unheard of at the time," Smith said. "It was incredible. Charlie just used Cardwell. It was kind of pathetic."[3] The lesson was not lost on Gary Tison.[*]

The day after Tison was moved back to the Annex, Bobby Tuzon went to the on-duty supervisor, Captain Joseph Barrows, to ask if there had been some mistake in the room assignments. He begged Barrows to recommend that he be transferred *anywhere* as long as it was away from Tison. Barrows said that he couldn't do it, but suggested that Tuzon talk directly with Cardwell.

On April 1, Tuzon was taken to Cardwell's office. It was his first formal interview with the warden about the escape. Bobby repeated what he had discussed with Jimenez, Turner, and Argel on March 22: the detailed plans for the escape, Tison's coercion, and Tuzon's fears for his own safety, which, he said, were even greater

---

[*] Less than a year after his transfer, on March 20, 1975, Charles Schmid was stabbed to death in the minimum-security compound.

now that Tison would be rooming with him. He pleaded for a transfer.

Cardwell wasn't moved. He thought Tuzon was arrogant, that he was demanding, rather than requesting, a change. It made him angry and he showed it. He repeatedly interrupted as Tuzon spoke. Finally Cardwell leaped to his feet, his face reddening, and angrily asked Tuzon who he thought he was talking to. Cardwell ranted about Tison's polygraph results, adding that, in his opinion, Tuzon was the one who was lying. There was one way to find out, Tuzon shot back; but Cardwell refused to give him a test, warning Tuzon that he was sick of his "games."

When Tuzon was returned to the Annex, he was convinced that Cardwell was either incredibly stupid or else had some ulterior motive for his actions.

Gary Tison knew that he had survived a close call. Only someone with ice water in his veins could have faked two polygraph tests. But Gary remained convinced that his brother Joe was the only source of the leak. He still knew nothing about Bobby Tuzon's appeals to prison officials. Maybe Tuzon was right when he had told him that the whole thing was too complicated to work. "Crazy," he had called it.

Gary didn't say anything to anyone, except to Dorothy, but he began to reconsider his situation and his options. Maybe there was another way to get out of prison, or at least to get his sentence reduced. Jimmy Carter seemed like a compassionate president. Dorothy had once suggested that if Gary could do something noteworthy, maybe the president would pardon him. After all, he had recently pardoned those Puerto Rican Nationalists who had tried to assassinate President Truman and members of Congress years before.

Gary got a new idea. Governors were more accessible than presidents. He decided to write a letter to an old friend, Dan Deck, a printing and journalism instructor at the prison. Deck had worked closely with Gary when he served as editor of the prison newspaper, and was very impressed with him. A friendship had developed.[4]

Tison wrote his letter to Dan Deck. The typewritten letter, dated April 3, 1978, read as follows:

Hello Dan:

First of all I trust this letter finds you and your loved ones in the very best of health and good-well [*sic*]. As for myself, I'm alive

NAME RAYMOND CURTIS TISON
AGE 19 YRS. (12-7-58)
HAIR BROWN
EYES HAZEL
HEIGHT 6 FT. 0 IN.
WEIGHT 170
COMPLEXION LIGHT
BUILD MED.

NAME RICKY WAYNE TISON
AGE 18 YRS. (10-31-59)
HAIR BROWN
EYES HAZEL
HEIGHT 6 FT. 0 IN.
WEIGHT 170
COMPLEXION FAIR
BUILD MED.

Raymond Curtis Tison
(birthdate should be 10/31/59)
Right: Ricky Wayne Tison
(birthdate should be 12/7/58)

NAME DONALD JOE TISON
AGE 20 YRS. (1-1-58)
HAIR BROWN
EYES HAZEL
HEIGHT 5 FT. 8 1/4 IN.
WEIGHT 190
COMPLEXION NOT AVAILABLE
BUILD MED.

Dorothy Tison c. 1980

(Dorothy Tison photo printed
with permission of *The Arizona
Republic.* Permission does not
imply endorsement by the
newspaper.)

Donald Joe Tison

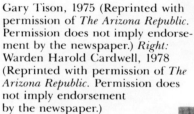

Gary Tison, 1975 (Reprinted with
permission of *The Arizona Republic*.
Permission does not imply endorsement by the newspaper.) *Right:*
Warden Harold Cardwell, 1978
(Reprinted with permission of *The
Arizona Republic*. Permission does
not imply endorsement
by the newspaper.)

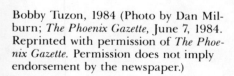

Bobby Tuzon, 1984 (Photo by Dan Mil-
burn; *The Phoenix Gazette,* June 7, 1984.
Reprinted with permission of *The Phoenix Gazette*. Permission does not imply
endorsement by the newspaper.)

Left: John Lyons, New Year's 1978 (Courtesy of Paul Chadwick)
Right: Donnelda Lyons, New Year's 1978 (Courtesy of Paul Chadwick)
Below: Christopher Lyons, 1978 (Courtesy of Paul Chadwick)

Theresa Tyson, 1978
(Courtesy of Mr. and Mrs.
Harry Tyson)

Margene and James Judge leaving for their
honeymoon, August 5, 1978 (Courtesy of
Mr. and Mrs. F. H. Davis)

Randy Greenawalt in custody, August 1978 (Reprinted with permission of *The Arizona Republic*. Permission does not imply endorsement by the newspaper.)

From right to left: Randy Greenawalt, Ricky Tison, Ray Tison; August 11, 1978 (Reprinted with permission of *The Arizona Republic*. Permission does not imply endorsement by the newspaper.)

and still working towards my release date, or at least trying to work for a release date. That's one of the purposes of this letter to you.

Dan, I have given a lot of thought to one of this state's oversized problems . . . Narcotics . . . Especially in the high schools and even grade schools. And the results of this problem is being sent to places like ASP [Arizona State Prison]. It does trouble me to see so many young men come into this damn prison because I know damn well after serving two or three years here, they'll be back and usually with a more serious crime than their first sentence. Of course this isn't news to you.

Dan before I get down to what I really want to ask, there is one question I have on my mind. . . . Would you have any objections if I were to put your name on my visitation list? My reason for such a question is the areas I'd like to discuss with you. I don't think it would be wise in a letter, especially if you were to get the *governor* to go along.

Dan, what I have in mind is to put the narcotic bankers out of business. Just putting the pushers in prison isn't the answer to anyone's problems. Not where narcotics are concerned. But I do have a way that I know will work. Plus, give me something I want badly . . . my freedom. If you know what I mean and I am sure you do.

Dan, if there is any interest on your part to what I am saying, I'd like very much to talk to you about it. . . . As soon as possible. In the mean time I send you and your lady my very best wishes for a good life.

Tison added this closing with a ballpoint pen:

As I remain always Your friend, Gary.[5]

What Tison had in mind, Deck learned, was a plan to provide the new governor, Bruce Babbitt, with information about criminal activities within the prison — as well as their links on the outside — in exchange for Gary's release. Tison could focus on narcotics, but his information extended well beyond into other organized crime activities. As an avid newspaper reader, Tison was aware that there was a great deal of interest in organized crime within the state, especially since the murder of reporter Don Bolles. He was also aware that his old buddy George Warnock had been granted immunity to testify before a legislative committee about it and had been quoted in January on the front page of the *Republic*.[6] Since January, hardly a day went by without a story appearing in the *Republic* about the corruption and violence within the prison. Seven inmates had been killed and twenty-three others had been stabbed in 1977; within the first three months of 1978, there had already been thirteen stabbings and one murder. On March 19, two inmates had been quoted in a front-page story as stating that 15 to 20 percent of the guards were "on the take" in smuggling and extortion operations.[7] Gary had much more to tell; he hoped the governor would be interested.

Bruce Babbitt had become the third Arizona governor in as many years when his predecessor, Wesley Bolin, died on March 4. As state attorney general, Babbitt had been a tough prosecutor of organized crime. The word was out that, unlike some other prominent state politicians, he could not be bought — in fact, his name reportedly had appeared on the same "hit list" that had included Don Bolles. It was also known that Babbitt, like so many others in state government, had strong suspicions about Cardwell's management of the prison.

Tison wanted Dan Deck to negotiate a deal with the new governor. There was no question, Deck said, that Tison had facts and could name names. The deal was an interesting idea, but it was simply too dangerous; the stakes were too high. Deck testified later: "I explained to him that I was honestly concerned that the powers that be — that were involved in this — were much more powerful than I, and I was afraid of getting killed, and that I didn't want to risk my life . . . There were some very powerful figures in the state who may have been involved."

According to Deck, Tison's letter reflected a significant change in his attitude: "It was a statement by Gary Tison basically saying that he had given up any hope of ever earning his release and that, you know, that he was willing to negotiate with the authorities for the first time in his life . . . He had become that desperate."[8]

Gary knew no one else with Deck's talents and respectability, and he apparently decided that it was useless to contact the governor directly. That meant that he had to turn back to his original strategy — escape.

One evening early in April, Irma Tuzon called Dorothy Tison. She hated to make the call but she had to tell Dorothy that she had located the rifle Bobby had promised to get for Gary. Irma said later that she felt she had no choice in the matter. Bobby had told her that if they got the rifle for Gary it might "get him off my back." She was so frightened for Bobby's safety that she agreed to do it.

Dorothy called Ricky to the phone to work out the details with Irma. Ricky suggested that they meet somewhere in central Phoenix. "How about the Denny's Restaurant on Thirty-second Street and Ventura, or maybe the Sambo's on Indian School Road?" he asked. Ricky told her that he would be driving a two-tone green Ford Galaxie.

Irma was nervous as she pulled her station wagon into the Sambo's lot at ten o'clock on Wednesday, April 5, and parked next to the Galaxie Ricky had described. A nice-looking young man got out and walked over to her car. Ricky greeted her with a broad grin and a simple hello. The grin was disarming, and Irma remembered seeing him a few weeks earlier at the prison. They walked around to the rear of the station wagon. Irma looked around to see if anyone was watching before she opened the rear door. Ricky reached in and picked up the antique rifle. He looked at it briefly, then walked over and put it in the back seat of the Galaxie.

"I'm supposed to tell you the firing pin is broken," she called over the traffic noise on Indian School Road.

"Oh, that's okay." Ricky smiled. "I can get it fixed myself. Would you like to have a cup of coffee?"[9]

They went into the restaurant. Irma was more nervous than she thought. She certainly didn't want to talk about the only two things they had in common: the plans for the escape and the rifle she had just given him, which she hoped never to see again. Had she known that it was to be used as part of a scheme to kill Ricky's uncle, she doubtlessly would not have agreed to have coffee with him. Ricky was very courteous and pleasant, and didn't bring up either topic. He also didn't mention the money his mother was supposed to give her. It was as though Ricky had a one-track mind.

"He just started talking about his father," Irma recalled. "You know, how long he had been in prison, how great he was, and that he was a very smart man. He talked like he was very proud of his father."

"How much more time does your father have to do?" she asked.

"Five years," he lied, for whatever reason.

Then, thinking about her own small children, she asked, "How do you feel about him being in prison? What do your friends think about it?"

Ricky's smile faded, then returned quickly. "I don't have very many friends," he said, "and I guess I don't have any *close* friends, except my brothers."[10]

The following Sunday, April 9, Irma visited Bobby at the prison. She told him about her meeting with Ricky and added that she still hadn't received any money from Dorothy Tison. She was also upset about the rifle. She thought they were probably going to use it to kill someone during the escape.

Bobby changed the subject. He told her that Dorothy was going to contact her again about getting passport photographs for the Tuzon children. Irma looked surprised and then began to cry. "I don't want any part of this," she said.

On the following Sunday, April 16, Irma was still too depressed to go to the prison. Bobby called her at home wondering why she hadn't come to see him. He asked her please to bring their children for a visit the next weekend. His situation was becoming desperate. His repeated requests for transfer were being ignored and, under the circumstances, he wasn't sure how much longer he could survive. He wanted to see his children.[11]

It was probably on Monday, April 17, that Irma decided to put a stop to this madness before it was too late. She went to the phone and dialed the state prison and asked to speak to Warden Harold Cardwell. There was only a short delay before Cardwell was on the line. Irma later described the conversation:

> When he answered, I gave him Bobby's name, Robert Tuzon, and his serial number. I told him that I knew there was going to be an escape and I knew several people, or at least some of the guards, were going to be killed during the escape. I told him I was afraid because I knew my husband was a Trusty there.
>
> He sounded like he didn't believe me, so I told him a guy named Gary — I didn't know his number — was behind it, and Gary was taken in behind the walls about a month ago [for investigative lockup] and he was given a polygraph test about an escape.

She said Cardwell just listened, and then he said, "Well, how do you know this? Are you close to this man? How do I know that you're not trying to get even with them for something?"

"Then he asked me who I was," Irma said, "and I told him I couldn't say because I was frightened of these other people that was on the outside who were supposed to help in the escape." She hung up without identifying herself.[12]

Cardwell knew exactly who had made the call. He sent for Bobby Tuzon. The warden cursed Tuzon and berated him as a liar and a troublemaker. He warned Tuzon, as he had warned Tony Serra a year before, that he had better keep his mouth shut.

A day or so later Dorothy Tison called Irma. "She told me that Bobby wanted me to come to see him . . . That it was very important to come and see him . . . That the warden had taken him into the walls [into the main prison], telling him that a woman had made a phone call saying that he was going to escape. Well, she said that Cardwell had given him a hard time, and Bobby was very upset."

Dorothy didn't directly accuse Irma of making the call — she was afraid of what Irma might do next — but her message was clear: don't do it again.

When Irma didn't visit the prison the following weekend, Dorothy called again, and she was irate: "I've been going down there [the prison] for fifteen years," Dorothy said in a voice trembling with emotion. "Every Saturday and Sunday for fifteen years — and my sons have too, just for the moral support of their father. At least you're better off than I am," she continued. "Your husband has a top number [a set term]. Mine has no number at all but his life."

Irma broke down. "Mind your own business," she screamed as she slammed down the receiver.[13]

On April 19, the day after his difficult encounter with the warden over Irma's phone call, Bobby Tuzon went to Major Hernandez and told him that he thought a prison guard who supervised Gary's work in the galley might be involved in the escape plot. That was a fairly serious accusation, Hernandez warned him. Bobby said he knew it. Two days later, on Friday, April 21, Bobby was summoned for the third time that month to the warden's office. Cardwell was waiting with Deputy Warden Burd, Hernandez, and Captain Groves. The officials wanted him to explain about the prison guard he had accused. Tuzon once again went over his story of the escape plan, adding that the guard did favors for Tison. Most notably, Tuzon said, he cooperated with Tison in smuggling narcotics into the prison. A common vehicle for the drugs, he claimed, was the sacks of flour and sugar that were regularly sent to the galley. The sacks were never searched, he said, and he went on to describe how he had personally discovered plastic bags of "white stuff" in one of them. The guard knew the drugs were coming in, Bobby said, but Tison was paying him off. Money from Tison, he said, had enabled the guard to open a restaurant in Florence, near the prison.[14]

Cardwell didn't say a word. He just sat there glaring at Tuzon. When Tuzon finished, the warden rolled his eyes toward the ceiling and asked if anyone had any questions. When there weren't any, Cardwell told Tuzon that he could leave. Tuzon had the feeling that, of the four men, only Dwight Burd believed him.

The prison rumors about this particular guard's collusion with Tison were not new. Tison's former cellmate, Glenn Scott Thornton, later claimed that in 1977, a week before the strike, the guard had given Tison a snubnosed .38 revolver to use for his own protection against the striking prisoners.[15] He was very solicitous of Dorothy when she visited. On one occasion, Karen Hacker, a friend of Kathy Erhmentraut's, accompanied Kathy on one of her visits to her son and Randy Greenawalt. During the course of their day-long visit, Karen was shocked to see Dorothy perform fellatio on Gary — several times. She asked Greenawalt why the guards didn't stop them, especially when there were children around. Randy nodded toward the guard Tuzon had identified and explained that Gary was a "snitch" for one of the guards.[16]

That weekend, the weekend of April 21–23, Gary showed Bobby Tuzon another photograph — this time of a little girl. Bobby couldn't be sure, but it looked like his own little girl, walking a puppy on a leash. Consumed with rage and on the verge of tears, he warned Tison that he would kill him if anyone hurt his children. Tison, uncharacteristically, ignored the threat and remained very calm. Obviously Bobby had gotten the message.

The photograph had been taken at a distance, and Bobby suspected that Tison was trying to bluff him — that maybe it wasn't his daughter after all. His family didn't have a dog. He asked for permission to call his wife. He had to find out for sure.

Without alarming her, he casually suggested that maybe it would be nice if she bought the children a puppy. It could be a present from me, he said. There was a pause on the other end. When Irma spoke he could tell that she was smiling. She said that it was strange that he should suggest that. She had forgotten to tell him, but she had just recently bought a puppy for the children. When he asked her what it looked like, Irma described the little dog in the photograph.[17]

. . .

On Monday, April 24, Tuzon went yet again to Major Hernandez and Captain Groves and asked if there was any way they could transfer him to a job outside the Annex. Again he was unsuccessful. Cardwell wanted him to remain right where he was, as Tison's roommate, they said. Tuzon approached at least three other guards or supervisors about his problem. Their replies were all the same: Cardwell wanted him to remain right where he was.[18]

No one seemed to believe Tuzon's stories about Gary. So Bobby suggested to Tison that their get-away car, the Lincoln, be kept at Irma's house. His hope was that if Tison agreed, Irma could call the police.[19] But Tison told Bobby that the car was well concealed where it was and there was no reason to move it. Tison did make one minor concession, however. He knew that Bobby was worried about doing additional time if they were caught, so he told him that when they left the prison, he would make it look as though Bobby was being taken against his will.[20]

Frustrated with the futility of his efforts to convince anyone inside the prison that he was telling the truth, Tuzon went to a prison counselor named Baxter. He explained his situation and told Baxter that he had to talk with someone outside the prison — someone removed from Cardwell's authority, maybe someone from the Department of Public Safety. The counselor told him that all interviews had to be approved by the warden. The same day, Bobby wrote to William Friedl, his attorney in Phoenix, to describe his desperate and deteriorating situation. He told Friedl that he had already seen weapons inside the Annex. There was no doubt, he said, that something was going to happen, and soon.[21]

On Saturday, May 6, after a visit from Dorothy, Tison excitedly told Bobby and the others that things were quickly falling into place for the escape. Dorothy had just told him that his sons and Bob Adams now had everything "ready to go." The car was loaded with everything they needed. The escape could be as early as the following weekend. He said there was even a chance that they might have an airplane for Bobby to fly. His sons, Dorothy had told him, had learned that Joe had a plane he hadn't told them about. (The new optimism about the airplane was the result of garbled information about the plane Joe and his associates had stolen in Texas two months before. The boys obviously didn't know that it had been destroyed when Terry Tarr crashed it.) The plan to kill Joe was still on, Gary said, but the boys were going to try to find out where he was keeping the plane before they killed him.

Gary was jubilant. He described to Tuzon how they would subdue the guards and lock them inside a storage room. They didn't want to kill anyone if they could help it, he said. He didn't want any shots fired because the noise would alert the whole prison.

To Bobby, this looked like the end of the line. "Gary," he said, "I think you're crazy, and your plan is crazy, and I want out. I'm not going." Gary's expression froze into a snarl as he grabbed Bobby's arm above the elbow and squeezed hard. "I'll be goddamned if you're going to fuck this up now, Bobby," he said. "You're going because we need a pilot for that plane if the boys get lucky. And if you don't go, you're a dead man. It's that simple."[22]

Convinced that he had no other alternative now, Tuzon went to the galley and got a pair of cutting pliers he had hidden there. Tucking them inside his shirt, he walked to a relatively secluded section of the wire fence enclosing the Annex, partially concealed from the view of the tower guards. After some effort, he managed to cut a small opening in the fence and crawled through. Hoping that he would be seen, he climbed over a second fence, twisting his way carefully through the razor wire at the top and dropping to the ground and freedom. But it wasn't freedom he was seeking. Security at the Annex was every bit as bad as everyone said. Nobody was watching. He decided to sit down outside the fence and wait to be discovered. It took ten minutes. Smiling with relief, he held out his hands to be handcuffed. He was promptly taken "back inside the walls" of the maximum-security prison, right where he wanted to be: away from Gary Tison.

Tuzon's mother, Florence, was distraught that he had done such a foolish thing. Now his sentence, instead of being reduced, would only be increased. What were you thinking about? she demanded when she visited him, unaware of his difficulties inside the Annex. Bobby told her what had been going on for the past four months and explained that faking an escape was the only option he had left. "Mom, I told Cardwell about it," he said, "and it didn't do any good. No one believed me. I had a choice to escape or die; I decided to escape."[23]

On May 8, two days later, a prison deputy read Bobby Tuzon his Miranda rights and asked him to restate his allegations about the

Tison escape plot. Tuzon demanded that his attorney and members of the Department of Public Safety be present before he discussed the matter any further. A meeting was scheduled for May 16. In the meantime, Tuzon was held in Cell Block 3, maximum security.

At the May 16 meeting, with attorney William Friedl present, Bobby described the escape plot to prison officials and DPS officers Peter Womack and David Arnett. Tuzon hadn't gotten too far into his story when he noticed that the two officers were less interested in the escape plot than in Bobby's knowledge of how weapons and narcotics were being smuggled into the prison.

The next day there was a surprise shakedown at the Annex. A two-shot derringer was found in a refrigerator in the galley. It was the same kind of weapon that Gary Tison frequently carried in his boot. But guards found no other weapons, nor did they find any drugs. It looked to Womack and Arnett as though Bobby Tuzon had exaggerated. In any shakedown prison officials find contraband, so finding a single derringer was not especially noteworthy. The gun was confiscated, but officials took no interest in finding out who it belonged to.[24]

Twelve days later, on Sunday, May 28, Tuzon once again approached Captain Joseph Barrows and brought up the escape plot. Something needed to be done, he insisted. Barrows sighed and told him everyone, from the warden on down to the guards, was aware of his story. The warden didn't believe it, and that was that. On the first of June, Tuzon read a newspaper story announcing that a new director of corrections would take over on June 5. When Ellis C. MacDougall assumed his duties he would be the fourth person in seven months to head the troubled department. Tuzon noted that MacDougall was an outsider. Could that mean he might have an open mind?

At fifty-one, New Yorker Ellis MacDougall was considered "enlightened" by people outside his profession. Governor Babbitt knew that the prison had been run like a nineteenth-century penal institution since it was built in 1912. He wanted a modern professional in the job. MacDougall had spent twenty-six years in correctional work in four states after receiving an M.A. degree in criminology at New York University. Most recently, he had been an associate dean of the College of Criminal Justice at the University of South Carolina.

In addition, MacDougall was familiar with the problems in Arizona, or so he thought. In 1972, as a consultant during an evaluation of the state's prison system, he wrote that the Arizona State Prison had "every correctional problem existing at all other prisons put together," and that he had "never seen a more difficult institution to operate."[25]

Early in June, Warden Cardwell escorted MacDougall on a tour of the Florence facility. As they were walking through the Trusty Annex, Cardwell lowered his voice and nodded back toward one of the inmates who had greeted them courteously as they passed by. That inmate, Cardwell told MacDougall with obvious satisfaction, was an example of a "bad character" who had been rehabilitated during his administration. It was Gary Tison.[26]

Tison's name came to MacDougall's attention a second time when he received a letter from Bobby Tuzon, describing the escape plan. It was a bizarre story, but the writer seemed intelligent and serious. MacDougall decided that the matter deserved his attention, but his schedule was already filled with appointments. He sent word back to Tuzon that he would talk with him, but he couldn't do it until July 7.

MacDougall decided not to mention the forthcoming Tuzon interview to Cardwell. It sounded as though considerable animosity existed between Tuzon and the warden, and MacDougall didn't want Cardwell to feel that he was indulging a troublesome inmate. It was also conceivable that Cardwell's personal hostility toward Tuzon might be clouding the warden's judgment. MacDougall would discuss it with Cardwell later, if he found the details of Tuzon's story convincing.

MacDougall's interest in Bobby Tuzon's story would have been piqued on Sunday, June 25, if he'd happened to have read a sensational front-page story in that day's *Arizona Republic*. The story by Greg O'Brien, based on an exclusive interview with inmate George Warnock, described in detail how Phoenix attorney Neal Roberts — a central figure in the Don Bolles murder investigation — had put out the contract on Tony Serra.[27] What was news was the identity of the person who had picked up the contract: Gary Tison. It was a story no prison official could have missed; MacDougall must have read it.

Warnock, now safely incarcerated under an assumed name in another state prison, and apparently unhappy that Tison had never paid him for his part in the slaying, had decided to finger his old prison buddy. And he didn't spare the details.

"Tison told me he received a message from a Phoenix attorney named Neal Roberts," Warnock explained. "The message was clear. Ned Warren wanted Serra dead and was willing to pay $25,000. I'd heard of Roberts before. His name popped up quite a bit during conversations about lawyers who were willing to smuggle things into prison on behalf of their clients."

Roberts, Warnock continued, "set the Serra murder in motion" in the fall of 1976, after Steiger won the Republican primary. But when John Harvey Adamson and James Robison were indicted for the Bolles murder, Roberts became worried about his own future. "He [Roberts] said, in a letter smuggled into the prison, that some people connected with the Serra plot, including himself, were concerned that they might be arrested or indicted for the Bolles thing. He told us to keep cool for a while — at least until the heat was off." That's why, Warnock explained, Serra was not killed until the following January. During that whole period, he said, Serra kept hoping Warren's organization "wouldn't be crazy enough to put a contract out on him."

"Well, anyway," Warnock continued, "Tison said he'd split the money with me if I organized the hit. Tison knew a lot about Serra. They worked together in the industrial yard at the prison."[28] Warnock went on to describe how they blackmailed another inmate, Earl Snyder, into taking responsibility for the killing. Snyder was a "snitch" who knew that his own days were numbered. Tison offered him an alternative: Snyder's life would be spared if he took the blame for killing Serra. The way Gary put it, Snyder, already serving life, had nothing to lose if he did take the blame, and everything to lose if he didn't. What Tison and the others kept from Snyder was their plan to kill *him* after he killed Serra. Gary was going to set it up so that it would look as though Snyder and Serra had killed each other.

Part of the plan failed: there was no time to kill Snyder. He confessed to the killing. Warnock was granted immunity as chief witness for the prosecution, and charges against the three other inmates who took part in the killing were dropped. Warnock, as planned, did not implicate Tison in his testimony, but it was no secret among inmates that Gary was involved.[29]

It was quite a story, linking some very familiar names: Don Bolles, John Harvey Adamson, Neal Roberts, Tony Serra, and now Gary Tison. But if Ellis MacDougall (presumably the one person in the state most anxious to inform himself about the troubled prison system) read the story, it apparently did not stir any questions in his mind about how or why Gary Tison had been assigned to a medium-security facility, or, for that matter, whether he might be planning to escape.

MacDougall met with Bobby Tuzon on July 7, twelve days after the O'Brien story appeared. Bobby was impressed by the burly new corrections chief. Except for his wire-rimmed glasses, MacDougall bore a noticeable resemblance to country singer Kenny Rogers, complete with silver mutton-chop sideburns. Nicknamed the "big bear" by inmates elsewhere, MacDougall had the physique of a middle-aged defensive lineman. He talked as though he knew what he was doing.

Tuzon sketched out for MacDougall the broad contours of Tison's escape plan. But when MacDougall asked for details, Tuzon told the new director that he wanted an attorney present so that what he said could be verified later. He was now beginning to consider the possibility of a lawsuit against the state if the escape occurred; and if anything happened to him, he wanted to be sure that his wife and children would be protected.

Tuzon explained to MacDougall that Cardwell had chosen to believe every denial made by Tison, an inmate whose long record of previous escapes raised fundamental questions about his trustworthiness.[30] But wasn't it also true, MacDougall countered, that Tison had passed two polygraph tests in which he was questioned about this alleged plot? Tuzon didn't have an explanation, except to say that polygraphs weren't always reliable. MacDougall agreed. Would Tuzon be willing to submit to one himself? Tuzon said yes, and MacDougall said that he would advise Tuzon's attorney and schedule a test for later that month. That wasn't soon enough, Tuzon protested. The escape was going to happen any day.

It sounded a little hollow to MacDougall. If there was such urgency, why wouldn't Tuzon be more forthcoming with the details?[31] MacDougall wasn't sure who to believe, but he did know that he needed more time to check into this himself. He just didn't know enough about either Bobby Tuzon or Gary Tison; or, for that matter, about Harold Cardwell. In spite of George Warnock's well-publicized statements about Tison, MacDougall was still more inclined to trust his warden than a convicted felon.

But MacDougall did find Cardwell's hostility and indifference to Tuzon odd, under the circumstances. What MacDougall may not have known at this time was that Bobby's story was supported by information the warden had received from two other sources: the March report from Texas authorities after Terry Tarr's arrest, and its confirmation a few days after that by Joe Tyson when he was questioned by narcotics agents in Arizona.

Gary also read Warnock's statements about him in the *Republic*. If he had retained any lingering doubts about his earlier scheme to offer his services to the governor, Warnock's testimony erased them. He was relieved that no follow-up story appeared. (The *Republic* ran no more stories about the prison, as it had almost daily since January.) Gary knew that there was only one way out now, and it had to be soon, before someone like MacDougall asked why one of Tony Serra's killers had been moved to medium security.

On Friday, July 28, Bobby Tuzon, now relatively secure in investigative lockup, sent word to Gary through the prison grapevine that when he went to trial he would testify that his own escape had been a last desperate attempt to avoid involvement in Tison's escape plans. He was going to blow the whistle on Gary. Gary had thought the earlier leaks had come from his brother Joe. Bobby wanted to make sure Tison understood that the supporting information would be filed in open court the following Monday, July 31, before a Pinal County judge and the county district attorney. In the same message, he informed Tison that he had already told his story to the new Arizona director of corrections and was scheduled to take a polygraph test on Monday afternoon when he returned from Court.[32]

Bobby was forcing Tison's hand. It was his way of getting even — not only with Gary Tison, but, more important, with Harold Cardwell. At least one of his two most hated enemies was going to lose — and big. If Tison didn't escape, he would soon be back in maximum security; if he *did* escape, Cardwell would be finished as warden. Bobby was taking control of the final act of the drama he had been living since January. If Tison was going to carry through his escape, he would have to do it *that* weekend. Bobby was betting that the Pinal County judge, unlike Cardwell, would believe his story.

Gary was stunned when he got Bobby's message. It had to be that weekend or never. He immediately asked for permission to call Dorothy.

8

The Weekend:
July 28–30, 1978

On May 20, Dorothy and Ricky Tison had gone to the house of Charles Whittington in Casa Grande, where, a couple of weeks earlier, Ricky had dropped off a .16-gauge semiautomatic shotgun and asked Whittington to saw off the barrel. Chuck Whittington — sometime preacher, sometime gunsmith and gun dealer — was no stranger to the seamier side of life in and about Casa Grande.[1] He could turn down shotgun barrels, attach silencers, and file off serial numbers as well as anyone. While they were at Whittington's house, Dorothy purchased a western-style .45-caliber revolver and thirty rounds of ammunition.[2] It was a real cowboy pistol — just Gary's kind of gun. The Tisons had by this time accumulated a small arsenal of weapons: a .38-caliber revolver with a silencer, a .380 Erma-Werke automatic rifle, and three sawed-off shotguns — two .12 gauges and a .20-gauge Magnum. With the .16 gauge, that would make seven weapons, which, they figured, should be enough.

Now, as the summer desert heat settled in to stay, all the family needed was the go-ahead from Gary.

Gary's sudden call on Friday evening, July 28, caught Dorothy completely off guard. He couldn't be specific over the phone, but Dorothy understood and assured him that she and the boys would be there first thing the next morning when visiting hours began. She reached for her cigarettes and was close to panic when she told the boys.

Up until that time, only she, Ricky, and Ray had been involved in the preparations; and she, like Gary, had hoped none of her sons would have to be involved in the actual escape. Now it was obvious that Ricky and Ray would indeed have to be involved. Joe was out of the picture — and lucky to be alive only because Ricky and Ray could not bring themselves to follow through on Gary's instructions to kill him. Gary's pals Bob Adams, Glenn Thornton, and Bill Anthony had said all along that they would help as much as they could short of participating in the escape itself. That left only Donny, and the escape was one man short.

Donny Tison had been aware of the escape plan from its inception and, according to Bobby Tuzon, might actually have been the driver of the Lincoln Continental in the March 8 rehearsal. Now he wanted no part of it. He had told his mother and his brothers, and even his father, that their constantly changing plans would never work, and somebody would certainly get hurt if they tried. But he knew they were shorthanded, and he realized that they needed him. He had quit his job at the Pizza Hut a few weeks before, explaining to his old friend and supervisor, Mike McBride, that he was having some family problems. He didn't want to talk about it, he said, but he did tell McBride that he needed to have a long talk with his father.[3] Now, on Friday night, July 28, he sat at the kitchen table with his mother and Ray, while Ricky paced.

His mother didn't say much. Ricky did most of the talking. He said that *he* was not going to let *anything* stand in the way of his father's escape. Any slight hint of a reservation about the plan made him angry and more determined than ever to go through with it. He and Ray couldn't do it alone, he explained to Donny; they needed his help. Dorothy sat silently, avoiding Donny's eyes. She smoked one cigarette after another, staring at the ashtray on the table. They owed it to their parents, Ricky said in a voice thick with emotion. Then there was silence.

As Donny listened, he realized that the whole plan now depended on him — the one person who, from the beginning, had opposed it. How could he live with himself if he let his parents and brothers down when they needed him most? Unlike his brothers, up until that point in his life Donny Tison had had his own plans for the future. Suddenly all that changed. Now he was on a one-way ride, and there would never be a way back. He shrugged and sighed and said he would help.

Donny had been worried all along that it was going to come down to this. He hadn't been surprised when, one by one, the others who were involved backed out — his Uncle Joe, Bob Adams, Glenn Thornton, and Bill Anthony; not to mention the constantly changing cast of inmates — Randy Greenawalt, Bobby Tuzon, Dave LaBarre, Gene Vincent, and Eric Mageary. Like Bobby Tuzon he knew that nobody in his right mind would try this.

The night before, Donny had gone to the drive-in movie with his cousin Rhonda Stanford. The two were about the same age and very close. Rhonda was his confidante and he talked with her about things that he couldn't discuss with anyone else. He had been depressed for weeks. The girl he had been dating refused to go out with him anymore because her parents didn't approve of his family. He talked about them, his father and mother and his brothers, and their predicament, and, finally, the crazy escape plan that, by that time, the whole family had been whispering about. Were they going to go through with it? Rhonda asked. He replied that it was crazy, but he guessed that they just might try it.

The two ate snacks and sipped on beer and Cokes and talked, ignoring the movie. They discussed a lot of things, Rhonda said, but mostly the future. Donny was taking criminal justice classes at Central Arizona Community College, and he hoped to get a job eventually with the state police. When the movie ended, he drove Rhonda home, and that was the last conversation they ever had.

After the long planning session with his mother and brothers, Donny wanted to get away. He left Phoenix about nine o'clock and drove down to the El Ranchito Tavern in Casa Grande. Shooting pool at the El Ranchito helped Donny relax, and he also liked one of the waitresses. Linda was pretty and sexy in a friendly, frivolous way, and she liked to kid Donny and watch him blush. But she noticed that he wasn't himself that night. He was too quiet. When she tried to joke with him, he just smiled instead of laughing the way he usually did. He drank beer and shot pool until after midnight. Then he told Linda he had to meet some friends, and left.

Randy Lesser and Sharon Aldridge were already cleaning tables and mopping the floor when Donny arrived at the Pizza Hut on Florence Boulevard. They let him in, and he helped them finish mopping before the three of them sat down at a table in the darkened restaurant with a pitcher of beer. They drank beer and talked the rest of the night.

Just before dawn on Saturday, they were standing in the parking lot about to leave, when another friend, Kevin Sonneman, drove by. Sonneman, who had a job in New Mexico, had just arrived home for the weekend. A chorus of yells turned him around, and the four went back inside for more beer and conversation. Donny wanted to know what it was like living in New Mexico. He said he was in a rut and needed a change of scenery. Kevin, who was working at a large coal mine near Grants, told Donny to come up some weekend. He would take him to some wild bars along the strip in Gallup and they would get drunk with the Navajos.

It was full daylight when the group finally broke up. Donny was fairly drunk and seemed depressed, and he didn't want to leave. As he walked to his car he yelled to Kevin that, if things worked out, he might surprise him some weekend up in Gallup. Then he suggested that they all meet that evening. Donny became serious. "Who knows," he said to Kevin, "how long it'll be before we all get together again?"[4]

When he got back to Phoenix after sunup, his mother and brothers were getting ready to leave for the prison. Get some sleep, they advised him. There was a lot to do in the next twenty-four hours.

Ricky, Ray, and Dorothy were first in line when Saturday visiting hours began at the Annex. Gary was waiting in the visiting area when they entered. Instead of sitting at their usual picnic table, they walked to the far end of the compound and stood as they talked. It was an intense session. Gary did most of the talking. The others nodded or answered his questions.[5] Donny would *have* to help, Gary said. There was no one else. They assured him that Donny had already agreed. They didn't stay as long as they usually did. Dorothy lingered a short while alone with Gary, and then, after a long last embrace, she left to join the boys waiting outside in the car.

They drove to Casa Grande, where the two boys dropped Dorothy off at her parents', and then on to Chuck Whittington's place to buy a box of Federal .16-gauge shotgun shells and a half box of .45s. Whittington sensed something was up from the way they were acting, but he didn't ask any questions. Ray had to go to work at noon, so they drove back to get their mother and left for Phoenix.

Ray had been working for the Gilbert Pump Company in Phoenix since May. He was scheduled to work until six on Saturday evening. Had it not been for a paycheck he wanted to pick up, he wouldn't have gone. He didn't like the job, or the people he worked with. Three weeks earlier he had tried to get a machinist at the company to cut down the barrel of a shotgun he had in his car. Tom Taylor knew sawed-off shotguns were illegal and he refused to do it. Ray became very moody after that and began to miss work. His boss, Bob Schell, wasn't surprised when Ray pulled his time card and punched in at noon, for it was payday. Schell had noticed how surly Ray had become lately. He attributed it to the fact that Ray had been denied a promotion to a night supervisor position. He had a feeling, when he handed Ray his paycheck of $178.31, that he wouldn't see him again on Monday.[6]

Ricky woke Donny that afternoon, and the two boys drove to Bob Adams's place to make last-minute checks on the weapons and other equipment that were packed in the trunk of the Lincoln. They also filled the gas tank and ran the engine some to make sure the battery was charged. It was a good thing they did, because the battery was low and they had to start it with jumper cables. Once that was done, Donny said that he wanted to drive back to Casa Grande for a last visit.

Linda Smith, their aunt and Gary's sister, was surprised to see them when they stopped at her apartment. Gary's oldest sister, Martha, was also there. Linda and Martha, like most of the Tison family except their mother, were aware that an escape was being planned.

Linda said later it was a strange visit. Both boys were extremely nervous. Donny kept talking about how much he loved his father, and how important Gary was to their family. It was usually Ricky or Ray who talked about Gary like that, not Donny. It seemed as though Donny was trying to convince himself that it was true.

Linda mentioned that Joe had promised to give her the Lincoln Continental. That got the boys, especially Ricky, very upset. She shouldn't believe anything Joe said, Ricky told her angrily. The man couldn't be trusted. Linda wasn't prepared to argue that point, but she did offer an explanation. "Gary wouldn't need it," she quoted Joe as saying, because "he couldn't break out of a paper bag." With that remark, Ricky went into a tirade about Joe being a double-crosser. He couldn't tolerate any criticism of his father. Linda interrupted to remind him that Joe wouldn't like to hear him talk that way.

Linda's remark pulled Ricky up short. He was afraid of his uncle; that was obvious from the look on his face. Fortunately, he hadn't mentioned that Gary was planning to have Joe killed, or that he himself had been given the assignment. Finally, as if he was attempting to qualify his attack, Ricky said softly, "Joe's a bad dude, but I have to admit you have to respect him."[7]

Linda didn't want to be put in the position of defending Joe or, for that matter, listening to either of the boys extol Gary's virtues. She knew that Gary was trouble. And Joe was no sweetheart either. Once, in a rage, Joe had threatened to have her beaten and disfigured, and her infant daughter kidnapped, if she testified about his involvement in an attempted robbery and murder. She didn't testify, but as a result she lost her job as a paramedic with the Casa Grande Police Department.[8]

Both women thought their two nephews were behaving oddly. Linda said later that each time she and Martha would change the subject, the boys would steer it back immediately to Gary or Joe.[9] They were glad when Donny finally got up to leave. Still agitated, he said that he was going over to the Stanfords' to see Rhonda. Ricky followed him out.

When Donny arrived at the Stanfords' alone, Rhonda was talking on the telephone. She motioned for him to wait, but he pointed to his watch and shook his head that he couldn't, adding that maybe he would see her later. He didn't. He spent the rest of the afternoon shooting pool and drinking beer at the El Ranchito.[10]

On July 28, the same Friday that Bobby Tuzon set the deadline for Gary Tison, he made an appointment to see prison psychologist Robert Flores.[11] A slight twinge of conscience and some afterthoughts had prompted his request. Bobby knew that revenge was a way of life with Tison, and he really didn't want him on the loose. Tison was dangerous, and Bobby didn't want anyone to get hurt, especially anyone in his own family.

Flores was new to the prison staff, and he was a Mexican-American. For those reasons, Bobby thought that he might have a more open mind than others he had talked to. If he could convince Flores that Tison would attempt to escape from the Annex that weekend, it could produce a confrontation between Tison and Harold Cardwell and would prove the point Bobby had been trying to make for months.

Tuzon was very tense and talked rapidly in his effort to persuade Flores. He told the psychologist that something had to be done immediately if authorities wanted to prevent an escape attempt that was certain to occur within the next forty-eight hours — on either Saturday or Sunday. Bobby explained to Flores that Tison had to make his move or lose the opportunity, since Bobby would be testifying about the escape plot to Pinal County authorities on the following Monday.

Flores listened patiently as Tuzon described the plot, but he mistook Bobby's evident anxiety and intensity for symptoms of emotional instability. He too found Bobby's story incredible. He couldn't believe that Tison would be able to get the news of the Monday deadline to his wife through a prison guard, even though Tuzon insisted that the guard was a "close friend" of Gary's who acted as a go-between for Gary on the outside. Surely no guard is going to risk his job to do that, Flores thought. When Tuzon told him that Tison's wife was a co-conspirator and was going to set in motion the outside component of the plan, Flores couldn't imagine a woman in that role. Tuzon swore that Dorothy had already helped Gary in an earlier escape, just as she was going to do now. In quick, insistent tones, Tuzon described Gary's telling him how he got the pistol he had used to kill the prison guard in 1967. Dorothy had given Gary the pistol as they embraced outside the courtroom after his trial in the Pinal County Courthouse.[12]

Mental health counselors, as a matter of standard practice, rarely disagree outright with their patients. Flores may have raised his eyebrows and pursed his lips thoughtfully, and nodded sympathetically as Bobby talked, but he found the whole story preposterous. Guns inside the prison? Paying off guards for their cooperation? Get-away cars and airplanes, and hideouts in Mexico?

Bobby Tuzon, Flores decided, was paranoid and delusional. "I really still did not believe this was actually going to happen," Flores explained later, "because, as you know, there are always rumors, rumors on top of rumors, going on in the prison. I did not think, at that particular time, that there was any merit to this story, where I should take it to [the] people above me . . . At that particular time, my full diagnosis, if you want to call it a diagnosis, was that he was suffering from a *persecution complex* and *delusions* . . . you know — the warden [and] everybody was after him . . . [It's] pretty hard to believe that everybody in the world is after a guy, or after anybody, unless they're completely negative people. . . . When he mentioned these things, I really didn't believe that there was anything in reality to it . . . this was just made up. . . . It was reality on his part, but not really reality to me."[13]

Less than forty-eight hours later, Bobby Tuzon was sitting on the bunk in his cell in Cell Block 3 when the prison sirens began to wail. It was Sunday morning. He wished that he could see the expression on Harold Cardwell's face. As he lay back on the bunk, hands clasped behind his head, he had to smile.

Was Cardwell involved, he wondered, or was he really that stupid? "I tried to tell that bastard [Cardwell] what was going on," he had told his mother after his bogus escape in May, "and he didn't want to hear it. He had the guards rough me up."[14] Then his thoughts turned to Ellis MacDougall. He wondered whether MacDougall would still want him to take a polygraph test the next day.

Harold Cardwell was only two holes away from completing what had been a pretty decent early round of golf. He was in a great mood until the panting messenger arrived and he heard the sirens in the distance. Cardwell, Assistant Warden Dwight Carey, and Major Don Herndon sped back toward the prison, listening to the Pinal County Sheriff's Department radio alert that the subjects were headed east in a pickup truck.[15] They wondered about that. At least they weren't driving a white Lincoln Continental west toward the Indian reservation, as Bobby Tuzon had predicted months before. When Cardwell arrived at the prison control center, he talked briefly with the officers on duty. He listened, red-faced and grim, as they described what had happened. He had heard it all somewhere before. Then he picked up the phone to make a call he dreaded making, to his new boss, Ellis MacDougall.

MacDougall was shocked when he got the news at home in Phoenix. He immediately left for Florence, Bobby Tuzon's warning ringing inside his head. The moment MacDougall arrived, Cardwell began to blame the escape on the laxity of the guards at the Annex. MacDougall inquired about the procedures being followed to pursue the escapees, then said that he wanted to go to the Annex to look things over. He told Cardwell that he wanted him to show him, step by step, exactly what had happened.

Cardwell could not contain his anger when they met the officers who had been on duty. His shaken subordinates stood quietly as the warden cursed and ranted, blaming the guards for not following prison procedures or, more important, his orders: "My orders [were] not followed with regard to security," he insisted to MacDougall.[16]

MacDougall was skeptical. As Cardwell, who by this time was pale and perspiring heavily, was beginning to wind down, MacDougall interrupted, asking to use a phone in the warden's office to make a confidential phone call. As the two men hurried back to the Administration Building, MacDougall told Cardwell — for the first time — that he had talked with inmate Bobby Tuzon and his attorney earlier that month. Cardwell blanched. MacDougall went on to say that Tuzon had told him that he had tried repeatedly to warn Cardwell that this was going to occur. Now he was going to call Tuzon's attorney to get permission to question his client about where the escapees might be headed. When the attorney could not be reached, MacDougall ordered Cardwell to have Bobby Tuzon brought in anyway. Tuzon, he said pointedly to Cardwell, obviously appeared to have valuable information, and there was no time to waste.

Tuzon wasn't surprised when a guard came to his cell and told him he was wanted in the warden's office. MacDougall immediately asked if he was willing to help with any information he might have about the escapees' destination. He said he would recommend that the escape charges against Bobby be dropped if he cooperated. It was a perfect opportunity to get back at Harold Cardwell. Tuzon said that this time he was willing to talk without an attorney. He asked for a map. MacDougall turned to Cardwell. "Get one," he said. Bobby loved it.

When Cardwell returned, Tuzon proceeded to recount the same story he had told Cardwell before, using the map to point out escape routes and the locations of several airstrips that had been discussed. Cardwell sat silently for the first time since leaving the golf course, staring at the floor, avoiding Tuzon's mocking eyes.

When Tuzon finished, MacDougall told Cardwell that he wanted the information dispatched immediately to all law enforcement agencies. Thus it was that the information that had been discounted by prison officials for months was quickly transmitted across the state. The official bulletin announced: "Prison escapee plan. Armed and extremely dangerous. Will not be taken alive." And, in an ironic twist, "It appears that this escape is well-planned . . ."

Whatever working relationship existed between MacDougall and Cardwell rapidly deteriorated after this. MacDougall knew Cardwell had made, at best, some very serious mistakes; at worst, the warden might have lied. Cardwell, it seemed, had suddenly developed memory problems. After quickly thumbing through the criminal and prison records of Tison and Greenawalt, MacDougall realized just how serious the predicament was. It was obvious to him that neither of the two killers should have been confined anywhere but maximum security — especially Tison, with three previous escape attempts and a dead prison guard on his record. But as Cardwell put it later, MacDougall also knew that there was an immediate need to "cover our ass" by minimizing the problem. Later, with that concern in mind, he met with reporters and made the statement he would forever regret: "The public," MacDougall declared, "has nothing to fear" from Tison and Greenawalt.

Those sirens on Sunday morning had blown away Bobby Tuzon's credibility problem. He couldn't repress a sneer when he was told the next day that the polygraph test had been canceled. As he was being led down a corridor to another of the interviews that had suddenly become so available, he spotted Robert Flores coming down the corridor toward him. It was too late for Flores to turn around.

"See, I told you," Bobby said as they got closer.

"Yes, I guess you hit it on the nut," the psychologist replied, avoiding Tuzon's glare and hurrying on, as if he were late for an appointment.[17]

Tuzon was confined in a "protective custody" area, supposedly for his own safety. Even so, a few days after the escape, he was assaulted by several inmates as he sat in his locked cell. Prison guard Herb Padilla was on the scene but did nothing to stop the attack. He merely looked on as the inmates cursed Tuzon as a snitch and drenched him with feces and urine they had carried to his cell. When they left, Tuzon asked Padilla for permission to take a shower. Permission was denied. Padilla later explained that it was near the end of his shift and he was ready to go home.[18]

"Tuzon was lucky that's all that happened," Tom Brawley observed later. "A whole lot of people in that prison wanted him dead — didn't want him talking to lawyers and investigators like me — and I don't think all of them were inmates. Bobby and his family were well aware of that and wanted him moved out of state; MacDougall finally had to move him to avoid having another prison murder on his hands."[19]

III

The Manhunt

9

Betrayed Again:
August 4–9, 1978

On Friday, August 4, the day after the fugitives narrowly escaped capture outside of Flagstaff, Dorothy Tison was flown there on a plane chartered by television station KTSP, Channel 10 News in Phoenix. Gary's sister Kay Wolfe, who had come from Tulsa to be with Dorothy after the breakout, accompanied her on the flight. The close call in Flagstaff was the big story in Arizona that day. Channel 10 wanted to explore the human-interest angle. How were Dorothy and the rest of the family responding to the unfolding saga of Gary Tison and his sons?

The flood of media attention following the escape was exciting for everyone, especially Dorothy and Kay. After all the years of loneliness, Dorothy was suddenly sought after, pursued by respectable people — the very people she watched on the Phoenix evening news after work. She was nervous about it, of course, but it was flattering in a way, and she and Kay were pleasant and coy with television anchorwoman Mary Jo West as they boarded the chartered plane for Flagstaff. This was the most exciting thing that had happened to Dorothy since Gary's brief parole twelve years before. Someone in California had even called about movie rights. Dear God, she thought, please don't let anything go wrong.

When they landed in Flagstaff, Gary's brother Joe was already waiting at the airport. He had left Casa Grande Friday morning after hearing the news that police had narrowly missed Gary the night before. A massive manhunt was under way. Flagstaff, at the height of its tourist season, was humming with news of the "Tison gang."

Joe was nervous. He liked to talk and enjoyed attention — but on his own terms. He knew Gary was dangerous, and crazy enough to do something stupid, and he didn't like being associated with his older brother's escapades. Not that he was a law-abiding citizen himself, but Joe would have been relieved if his brother and nephews had been captured earlier that morning in Flagstaff. Trailed by reporters full of questions he didn't want to answer, he drove to his brother Larry's house in Williams. His sister Martha was waiting there with Larry and his wife when they arrived.

It was like a family reunion. Everyone was talking about the relatives who didn't show up, but they had to be careful about what they said, with the press there. Dorothy and Kay continued to enjoy it all. Mary Jo West was a sympathetic interviewer, and it was kind of fun, actually. Kay and Dorothy exchanged knowing glances, at times smiling and whispering between themselves, as they dodged important questions.

What was Gary really like? He was a wonderful father, they said. What about the three boys? His sons adored him. Is it true that a boat picked them up in San Diego and took them to Mexico? They had no idea. The Tisons were polite, and Dorothy, especially, seemed refined and very well spoken — not at all what some expected — but it was clear that no hints would get dropped about where Gary and the boys might be headed.

For Joe, the press attention was no fun at all. He had a lot to hide. Gary's Thursday-afternoon call from the phone booth outside the Mountain View Market had been to Bob Adams. Gary had told Adams to tell Dorothy that they were in the Flagstaff area, and that she should have Joe meet them there with a plane. In the meantime, however, unsure if his instructions were followed and having no confidence in Joe, Gary had decided to leave Thursday night. And he didn't call to tell anyone that he had changed his plans.

Joe was upset and still trying to decide what to do when he heard the news that police had just missed Gary in Flagstaff. Now, with a massive manhunt under way and reporters and police swarming over the area and monitoring the family's every move, it was impossible to do anything. And Dorothy knew it; she knew, too, that it wasn't his fault that things had turned out this way. He wanted her to make sure Gary understood that.

Joe was also nervous because he knew that his brother was a killer. He was afraid of Gary and wanted him back behind bars, though he didn't tell his sisters or Dorothy or the press that. Now that Gary was free, Joe was afraid not to help him, for fear that Gary would kill him. It seemed to him that he had only two options: either help Gary get out of the country, or help the police capture him. He decided to let circumstances dictate his choice.

Later that day at Larry's, the family listened carefully to the calls that came over a police radio scanner Larry kept in his house. For everyone except Joe, no news was good news.

About eight o'clock that evening, after all the reporters had left, Dorothy, Kay, and Martha decided to drive back to Flagstaff so that Dorothy could call her contact in Phoenix to see if there had been any word from Gary. An undercover deputy followed them as they drove through the billboard clutter of the business strip and pulled into the parking lot of the Ponderosa Inn. Kay and Martha waited in the car while Dorothy made a call to Phoenix from an outdoor pay phone. Have you heard anything more from Gary? Dorothy asked when Bob Adams answered. Nothing yet today, Adams replied. Well, stay close to the phone, he'll probably be calling soon to let us know what's going on, Dorothy said, adding that she would check back with him later that evening. After the call, the three women returned to Williams.

Police had suspected all along that Dorothy was using at least one intermediary to communicate with her husband. At that point, however, they weren't sure who it was, and they had placed virtually the entire family under surveillance. In every previous escape, Gary had contacted some relative almost immediately. Police knew that Dorothy was worried about the safety of her husband and sons, though not sufficiently to make a convincing appeal to them to turn themselves in; nor was anyone, except maybe Mary Jo West, deceived by Dorothy's feigned perplexity at what had happened. She was deeply involved.

Late that night, Joe, Dorothy, Kay, and Martha returned again to Flagstaff and checked in at the Americana Motel.[1] Dorothy, very worried, called Adams a second time from a pay phone. Still no word, he said.

The next day, Saturday, August 5, Joe, along with his two sisters

and Dorothy, drove back to Williams. They spent the morning monitoring the scanner as police fanned out in an intensive search of the
area surrounding Flagstaff. After lunch, they drove back home to
Phoenix. Joe dropped Dorothy and Kay at Dorothy's place before
continuing on to Casa Grande with Martha.

Later that Saturday night, the phone rang again at Bob Adams's
place. This time it was Gary, calling from a state park near Roswell,
New Mexico. He asked if it was safe to talk. Adams said that it was.
He could tell that Gary was particularly tense as he insisted that he
had to talk with his brother Joe. They had to get a plane somehow,
he said, and Joe was probably the only person who could do it. Things
were getting too hot. He had heard on the radio how close they
had come to being captured the night before in Flagstaff. He said
to tell Joe that he would be giving him a call the next morning. He
was giving Joe a little time to think about the arrangements. Adams
was to tell Joe that if there were any more fuck-ups, he would be
sorry. Then he asked, "How's Dorothy doing?"

"She's okay," Adams replied. "She's back in Phoenix with your sister
Kay. Kay flew out from Tulsa the other day."

"Well, tell her the four are safe and tucked far, far away," Gary
said, and he hung up.[2]

When Dorothy called later from a pay phone, Adams gave her
Gary's message.

It was just about dusk earlier that same Saturday evening in Silver
City, New Mexico, when the five fugitives stopped at a Safeway store
to stock up on supplies. They briefly considered making a run for
the border some fifty miles south at Palomas, but Gary decided that
it would be too risky to attempt crossing in the truck, especially since
he was not familiar with the roads along that part of the border.
Instead, they headed back north and after dark drove into the Bottom-
less Lake State Park fifteen miles southeast of Roswell. Gary made
the call to Bob Adams from a pay phone at the park entrance at
about ten o'clock. They selected a campsite in the Devil's Inkwell
Campground and spread out their sleeping bags and blankets on
the ground. They had had to dump a lot of their equipment earlier
for lack of room in the Mazda; now they had only two sleeping bags.
It was warm even at night, so they didn't need the bags for warmth,
but they had provided a little padding to sleep on. Now they had to

make do with extra clothing and blankets, but no one could get comfortable. Each man, as usual, took a turn standing a two-hour watch.

Patches of mist hugged the ground at dawn Sunday morning, and the air smelled cool and fresh. Gary hadn't slept much that night and was nearly through a fresh pack of Camels before sunrise. He was wondering whether Bob Adams had been able to get hold of Joe. At first light, he decided it was time to call Joe — real early, when he would have the best chance of finding Joe home. He knew it was risky, because Joe's phones might be wired, but he had to take the chance. While the others slept, he walked out to the pay phone at the entrance and dialed Joe's number in Casa Grande.

Joe's young son Jay answered the phone. A strange voice asked for his father. Joe was asleep, so Jay asked his mother, who was already awake, for instructions. "Someone wants to talk to Dad," he whispered, holding his hand over the phone. "What should I do?" Judy Tyson had a funny feeling about who it might be at that hour and she was afraid. She knew that Gary blamed Joe for telling the police about the escape plan earlier that year, and she had read the note Gary sent vowing to get even. She took an extension phone into the bedroom.[3]

Joe sat on the edge of the bed, took a deep breath, and looked at his wife as he lifted the receiver to his ear. "Yeah?" he said, trying to sound as matter-of-fact as possible as he recognized the long distance hum.

"This is GT," said the familiar voice at the other end.

"Yeah, I know it is," Joe replied. "Where are you?"

"Never mind," was the answer. "Is this phone tapped?"

"No, it's okay," Joe lied, as he activated the recording device he had allowed Pinal County detectives to attach to the phone.

Gary got right to the point. "I don't have the time or change for bullshit," he said. In measured tones he said he knew that Joe could get an airplane and that he didn't want to hear any excuses. "I want you to get a plane and meet us in New Mexico. You know the state and the airstrips in these parts," he said. "I want you to meet us with a plane and get us across the border, and I want you to do it *today.*"

Joe's mind was racing as he tried to stall, telling Gary that he couldn't get a plane and a pilot that quickly. "I need more time," he said.

"Today, goddamnit," Gary repeated.

"Okay, okay, I'll see what I can do." Joe said, knowing that there was only one way that he could protect himself and get out of this mess, and that was to go to the police.

"Where can you meet us?" Gary asked with a trace of excitement now instead of hostility.

Joe thought a minute and said that he knew of a small cropduster strip at the edge of town in Clovis, New Mexico, about four miles from the municipal airport. The plane Terry Tarr had crashed in Mexico, a few months before, had been stolen in Hereford, Texas, just up the road from Clovis.[4] Then Joe added a qualifier: "There'll be room for only two of you," he said. "Leave the boys behind. They should give themselves up before they get hurt." Gary agreed.

"It's going to take us a little while to get there from here," Gary said, and then, without revealing specifically where he was, "We're probably about three hours' drive from Clovis." The two brothers agreed to meet there about four o'clock that afternoon.

"I might be a little late," Joe said. "It all depends on how fast I can work this out. If I am, just wait there unless it gets too hot for you."[5]

"It shouldn't, if you get here this afternoon," Gary said. "Nobody knows where we're at." He paused. "Do they, Joe?"

"I guess not," Joe replied. "How would I know?"

"Good. I'm counting on you, brother. Just don't fuck up again."

It was almost 9:00 A.M. on August 6 when park attendant Joe Tomlin came by to collect overnight fees at the campground. He thought to himself that these five guys didn't look like ordinary campers. Their clothes were real dirty, he said later, all smudged with what looked like oil and grease, as if they had been working on their truck, and their equipment was in disarray, as though they had been traveling for a long time and had just dumped everything out on the ground. Too fat to be hippies, though, he thought. Could be bikers, but they're driving a truck. He noticed that they only had two sleeping bags among them. Funny that five guys would go on a camping trip with only two sleeping bags. They seemed a little edgy when he approached, but that wasn't unusual. A lot of people tried to get away without paying the fee — that's why he made his rounds fairly early. He said good morning and asked them to sign a registration form. Gary asked how much it was and then paid the two-dollar fee. He signed the form, "Larry Matthews, Casa Grande, Arizona." It was an alias he had used many times before.[6]

"You're not crazy enough to do that for him, are you?" Judy asked as Joe put down the receiver. He sighed and reached for the cigarettes on the night stand.[7] Lighting his first cigarette of the day, he took a deep drag, then exhaled the thick blue smoke through his nostrils, shaking his head.

In a way the call was a surprise; Adams hadn't reached him to alert him that the call was coming. Yet he had known it was only a matter of time before he would hear from Gary, for Gary had nowhere else to turn. He had been in prison so long that Joe was probably the only person on the outside who could help him. Oh yeah, there were a few paroled ex-cons he knew, but they were just dumb shits, like Bob Adams and most of the people you meet in prison.

"What are going to do?" his wife asked. She hadn't slept a night through since the escape, afraid that every car winding up the gravel drive to their isolated hillside home might have Gary in it. Joe didn't reply. He picked up the receiver and dialed Dave Harrington, a sergeant with the Pinal County Sheriff's Department. After the escape, Joe had called the sheriff and requested police protection for himself and his family. Harrington and two other officers were given the assignment, but there was a condition attached: the sheriff wanted to monitor his phone calls. Without hesitation, Joe agreed. During the two days the officers stayed at the house (they correctly assumed that Gary was out of the area by then), they killed time with pots of coffee and a lot of conversation.

Joe Tyson and Dave Harrington weren't strangers. They both had grown up in Casa Grande. As teenagers, they both cruised Florence Boulevard, hung out at the same drive-in across from the high school, and hustled some of the same girls. One of Dave's best friends had even dated Dorothy Stanford before she got pregnant and married Joe's brother Gary. Joe was more of a cowboy in those days than Dave, with tastes in clothing that ran to boots and Levi's.

Fast cars, airplanes, rock 'n' roll, and, of course, girls were what they had in common. In a town the size of Casa Grande, it was pretty easy for two good-looking boys like Dave Harrington and Joe Tyson to share a good many common experiences.

They went separate ways as adults. Dave graduated from Casa

Grande Union High and joined the local police force; Joe had quit school — didn't see much point in doing anything you didn't get paid for — and spent some time in a detention center for stealing. He had been on probation at the time for helping his father hold up the grocery store. Dave moved on to become a sergeant in the Pinal County Sheriff's Department.

Joe followed in the footsteps of his father and older brother, which led to armed robbery, grand theft, and international smuggling — not only of marijuana, but of cocaine, heavy equipment, and weapons. By 1978, his arrest record showed eight convictions. Sporting an Afro haircut, he dressed and acted like a western dandy — fancy western shirts and designer jeans, held up with monogrammed belts with silver and turquoise buckles, and cut just right above expensive boots. He always carried a wad of hundred-dollar bills — the denomination he found most convenient for business — which he liked to flash for the waitresses in the truckstop at the Sunland Gin Road exit on the Interstate just south of Casa Grande. The waitresses thought Joe Tyson was a pretty cool guy. And he was a big tipper. For his part, Joe enjoyed the attention, so he often met associates there. He liked to be recognized when he walked into a place, and it was as good a spot as any to do business. On his police record he listed his occupation as "pool shooter — self-employed." Joe enjoyed a good joke even when he was being booked.

Despite their divergent paths, Dave and Joe each accepted the other for what he was and let it go at that. They saw each other often because Joe never went more than a year or so without an arrest. They always took it as just business, nothing personal.

"Yeah, I like Joe all right," Harrington said in his western drawl. "You gotta know Joe. He'll only tell you what he wants you to know — and I'd tell Joe that to his face. You know, he's the kind of guy who will tell you a hundred different things, and you know only one or two of them is true. If you understand that, you can get along with him — but never, never trust him."[8]

Dave Harrington was just getting dressed when the phone rang that Sunday morning. He could tell immediately by the tone of Joe's voice that he was nervous, though he was trying to sound calm.

"Dave, Gary just called," he sputtered, "and I agreed to meet him at an airstrip in Clovis, New Mexico. It's all on the tape," he added, as if he didn't expect Harrington to believe him. "What do you want to do?"

Harrington told him to "be cool and just sit tight" until he called back. Then he called Pinal County Sheriff Frank Reyes in Florence, who, in turn, called the coordinator of the statewide manhunt, Captain Jack Dunn of the Department of Public Safety in Phoenix. When Dunn heard the news, he immediately notified authorities in New Mexico. Plans were set in motion to prepare a trap for the five fugitives at the airstrip. The DPS then made arrangements with Sawyer Aviation at Sky Harbor Airport in Phoenix to rent an airplane, since there were no DPS planes available.

In the meantime, Joe called Harrington back and told him that he wanted to go to Clovis to help the police out. "No way Gary's going to come around unless he sees me with that plane," Tyson said. A short time later, Reyes dispatched an officer to pick up Tyson in Casa Grande and drive him to the Florence-Coolidge airport, where Captain Dunn's plane would pick up Harrington as well. Judy Tyson, also anxious to help, suggested that all incoming calls to their home be transferred to the office where she worked in town. Gary might call again while Joe was gone. If he did, she could pass along any new information to the sheriff's office. Sheriff Reyes decided it was a reasonable idea. It was just past noon on Sunday, August 6, when the twin-engine Cessna 441 bounced down at Florence-Coolidge field with Jack Dunn and a DPS pilot on board. They didn't cut the engines. Dave Harrington and Joe Tyson, heads tucked against the prop wash, climbed in, and the plane taxied to the end of the runway for takeoff.

They had just bumped through the summer thermals along the Dripping Spring Mountains and were climbing into the hazy glare above the San Carlos Apache Reservation when the radio crackled with a message for Dunn from the DPS: The bodies of three persons — two adults and a child — had been found in the desert near Quartzsite. The report went on to say that Yuma County investigators believed the Lincoln Continental found at the scene was the same car used by the Tisons and Greenawalt in the escape a week earlier.

When the report ended, Harrington turned to Joe. "What do you think? Was it them?" he yelled above the engine roar. Joe had previously admitted to Harrington that his brother and nephews were traveling in a cream-colored Lincoln. He had bought the car himself, he said, in Albuquerque. Now he shook his head as he stared out the side window at San Carlos Lake glistening below, colorless as molten metal in the brilliant sunshine.

"I can't believe Gary would have the boys involved in something like that," Joe said finally. "I know he could do it . . . but I can't believe he got the boys involved in something like that."[9]

It was close to four o'clock when the Cessna 441 began its descent. Joe directed them over the town and pointed out the cropduster strip on its eastern edge. They could see a single plane parked out on the dirt runway below. When the Cessna banked around to make its approach to the Clovis Municipal Airport on the other side of town, what they saw below was astonishing. There were people and vehicles everywhere.

"When we landed," Dave Harrington said, "there was television cameras, trucks, and equipment sitting all over the place. Television crews and news people were running all over. We asked the New Mexico people about it, and they said someone leaked the story to an Albuquerque television station. There were uniformed police and marked patrol cars plainly visible all around, and there was a plane out there parked on the runway with big bold letters spelling out NEW MEXICO STATE POLICE. Dunn and me couldn't believe our eyes. We knew one thing for sure: We had flown to Clovis for nothing. We weren't going to see Gary Tison anywhere near that place."[10]

He was right. SWAT teams watched for hours as Joe Tyson sat in the decoy plane, or paced around it, rubbing his hands and shivering in the evening chill, until after midnight. There was no sign of Gary. The plan had been ruined.

After Jack Dunn had notified authorities in New Mexico of Tison's plan to meet Joe in Clovis, he called Tom Brawley, who was coordinating the Flagstaff manhunt. He told Brawley about Joe Tyson's tip and his hope that the manhunt could end that afternoon in Clovis. When Brawley hung up, Sheriff Joe Richards was standing by. There had been tension and rivalry between the sheriff and his independent lieutenant for some time. Brawley thought he knew more about police work than Richards. The sheriff, he thought, was just another politician, more worried about reelection than anything else. For his part, Richards thought Brawley was brash, at times insubordinate, and always trying to steal his show. Now he wanted to know what Dunn had said. He didn't want Brawley withholding any information from him, especially on this case. It wasn't just a prison escape any longer; now it was also a triple homicide and possible kidnapping. So Brawley told him and warned him to keep it quiet.

Brawley says Richards didn't. Anxious to appear on top of things, Richards quietly told a reporter from KTVK-TV, Channel 3 News in Phoenix, who was covering the Tison story in Flagstaff. Shortly afterward, the reporter approached Brawley for more details, and he denied the story. The reporter challenged Brawley's denial and identified Richards as his source.[11]

Channel 3 News had immediately called KOB-TV, their ABC affiliate in Albuquerque. News of the Quartzsite discovery had ignited interest in the fugitives, and as word spread of a possible capture that same day, the Department of Public Safety in Phoenix was inundated with calls. The news staff at KTVK-TV had been competing all week for leads on the Tison story — especially with KOOL-TV, their CBS news counterpart on Channel 10. They had been scooped two days before when Channel 10 reporter Mary Jo West accompanied Dorothy and Kay to Flagstaff, but her fluffy interview was nothing compared to the potential of this revelation. It didn't take long for reporters to discover that a plane had been rented at Sky Harbor and a flight plan filed for Clovis, New Mexico. News teams from Phoenix were immediately dispatched to Clovis to join those already on their way from Albuquerque.

It's less than a three-hour drive from Roswell to Clovis, and the fugitives had arrived in Clovis well ahead of Joe and the police. They selected a concealed vantage point near the airstrip and kept it under close observation. They watched New Mexico authorities clear the area and position the decoy plane on the runway. At first they weren't sure what was going on, but it soon became apparent as more cars and men began surveying the area. The focal point, very obviously, was the lone Cessna 172 on the runway. The fugitives left immediately. The blue pickup was already well on its way to Colorado before the SWAT teams arrived and Joe was conveyed across town in an unmarked car to take up his position in the decoy plane. Once again the Tisons and Greenawalt had eluded an elaborate trap.

Gary was beside himself with rage as they sped north on secondary roads away from Clovis. No one else spoke except to voice agreement

with whatever he said. He cursed and swore and vowed over and
over again that he was going to kill the brother who had, for the
second time, double-crossed him. His mood was black. Days before,
he had dropped the military jargon he had been using to discuss
strategy and plans. Now he didn't discuss anything. He didn't want
other opinions. He didn't seem to trust anyone. No one was permitted
to be alone. He gave orders and flew into blasphemous rages. Anything
could trigger them — thoughts of his brother, or an annoying fly.
He was convinced that the plan would have worked except for Joe's
alerting the police. His frustration and sense of betrayal were profound.

The group's constant anxiety and fears, compounded by the almost
nauseating fatigue of over a week's hard traveling and inadequate
sleep, were now beginning to slip into paranoia. When Ray stood
watch at night, he confided to his brothers, he would imagine that
he saw people creeping toward him. Gary Tison would never be
taken alive — he had told his sons that often enough, and there was
less reason to doubt it now than ever. A gun battle was inevitable
and somebody was going to die. It was as certain as sunrise the next
morning, Donny said. They were nearing the limits of their endurance.
They couldn't keep running much longer, and that border kept getting
farther and farther away. The law was closing the distance behind.
They were always looking over their shoulders. This was the second
close call in less than four days. The only question left now was not
whether, but *how*, it was all going to come down, and who was going
to die.

To make matters worse, the truck's transmission was starting to
wear out. Eight years and thousands of grinding miles began to show
as the pickup strained its way up the slopes of the Sangre de Cristo
Mountains near Taos. It wouldn't stay in second gear, and second
gear was essential in these mountains. The engine was starting to
overheat, and the brakes were getting spongy. By the time they reached
Alamosa, Colorado, before dawn on Monday morning, it was obvious
the truck wasn't going to run much longer. They turned west on
Route 160 and drove to the outskirts of the sleeping town, where
they turned north on a dusty road that dead-ends at the Gilmore
Ranch. A few miles later, too tired to look for another site, they
stopped in a grove of giant cottonwoods on the banks of the Rio
Grande.

. . .

Kay Wolfe had always had a special fondness for her oldest brother. She wanted to help Gary, and providing support for Dorothy seemed to be the only way she could. She had flown out from Tulsa as soon as she learned of the escape. She had always believed that Gary was a victim of circumstances and had had a string of bad luck — like when that prison guard "died." Throughout all the years of Gary's imprisonment, they had exchanged weekly letters, and she saved all his. Now she remembered vividly a letter he had written during the last Christmas holidays, saying that, if things worked out, it was going to be his last Christmas in prison. Kay was a born-again Christian like her mother, and she believed that Gary's past sins had been forgiven. Gary had served enough time in prison, she said, and he had changed. His family needed him, and he needed them, and now she told Dorothy, as she had promised Gary in her letters, that she wanted to help them to start a new life.

Kay and Dorothy had a cup of coffee and listened to the morning news on that eventful Sunday — nothing new about Gary and the boys — before driving to Martha's place on a big cotton farm west of Casa Grande. After talking with Bob Adams the night before about getting Joe to help with an airplane, Dorothy decided to ask Martha. Martha's husband, Donald Englund, had a pilot's license and access to cropduster planes. Dorothy believed he was much more reliable than Joe. Kay agreed. Unaware of the arrangements Gary had just made with Joe, they decided to raise the subject with the Englunds.

They drove down the old Maricopa road instead of the Interstate to get to Martha's place near the farm community of Maricopa. It was a short visit. Donald Englund didn't mince any words. He wanted no part in any scheme to fly his brother-in-law and nephews *anywhere*.

Disappointed, Dorothy and Kay drove back to Casa Grande, and Dorothy dropped Kay off at her mother's mobile home in a development on the edge of town. But Dorothy was nervous and didn't want to be alone, so she drove to her parents' home on North Trekell Road, where she spent the rest of the day, completely unaware of the situation developing in New Mexico. Later that afternoon, after a dinner she didn't feel like eating, Dorothy picked up Kay at her mother's and returned to Phoenix to make the pay phone call to Bob Adams. It was nearly eight before she reached him.

Yes, Adams said, Gary had called. Dorothy was shocked when he repeated what Gary had said. There had been police all over Clovis when they got there, and that could mean only one thing: Joe had snitched. He had double-crossed them again.

What are they going to do now? Dorothy asked. Adams said that Gary wasn't sure but had said he needed to talk with Kay. Dorothy was to make sure that Kay stayed in Phoenix until he could.

The foiled attempt to capture Gary and the boys in Clovis was the lead story on the ten o'clock news. Both channels 3 and 10 reported the story live. It had to be Joe, Dorothy muttered as she and Kay watched.

The next morning, Monday, radio reports carried the news that the bodies of a young family had been found the day before near Quartzsite in a Lincoln Continental. Dorothy was at work when she heard. She asked for the rest of the day off and went home. Her head was pounding with a migraine.

Kay Wolfe was at her sister Martha's when she heard the news. She was distraught and called Dorothy repeatedly before she finally reached her at home. She wanted Dorothy to tell her that it wasn't true. Dorothy didn't know what to say. With each news report, evidence of the killers' identity seemed more certain. As she listened, the excitement and satisfaction Dorothy had felt in the planning and success of her husband's remarkable escape slowly drained away, leaving her deeply depressed. Kay tried to encourage her when she arrived in Phoenix later that afternoon. Maybe it was someone else who had killed them after Gary and the boys left. But they both knew it wasn't. Dorothy had accepted the possibility that someone might get hurt in the escape — maybe a prison guard or two, or, God forbid, even Gary and the boys. After all, she had supplied some of their weapons herself. But a young couple? A baby? It was a nightmare. The horror — and shame — were overwhelming.

The day after the escape, the FBI had contacted Kay in Tulsa, seeking her cooperation in locating Gary, and she had refused. News of the slayings changed all that. It broke her heart to do it — she had always stood by her brother — but these murders were beyond anything that she could have imagined. She was completely unnerved, and she felt betrayed. She couldn't deal with the guilt of being part of something so horrible, no matter how much she loved Gary. And now Gary had told Bob Adams that he had to talk with her. Kay no longer wanted anything to do with Gary or his escape. She called the FBI to tell them she wanted to help.

On Tuesday, August 8, Dorothy and Kay, still stunned and disbelieving, were interviewed separately by the FBI. Kay told them everything she knew about the escape. She said that she would be willing to help them further in any way that she could. In return, she asked only for confidentiality and protection for her fourteen-year-old son back in Tulsa. She told the FBI that she was worried that Gary might be on his way to Oklahoma. The FBI agreed to both conditions.

On Wednesday she flew home to make arrangements for her son to stay with friends in another state until Gary was captured. About the time her plane was landing in Tulsa, Dorothy Tison, Joe Tyson, Martha Englund, and Bob Adams were all being served with subpoenas to appear before a grand jury in Phoenix.[12]

10

The Honeymoon:
August 6–9, 1978

The graffiti in the men's room at the Arrowhead Lounge in South Fork, Colorado, is mostly aimed at Texans. "If God wanted Texans to ski, He would have made bullshit white," someone scrawled above the urinal; nearby, "Texans are living proof that Utes was fucking buffalos."

Margene Davis Judge knew that Coloradans liked to kid Texans like herself, but she loved the place anyhow. She had been coming there in the summer since she was a little girl, and it was the place she picked for her honeymoon. She and her new husband, James, arrived on Sunday afternoon, August 6, after driving over from Texline, Texas, where they had spent the night after getting married in Amarillo on Saturday evening. They planned to spend the next three or four days camping in their Ford van, and Margene was going to teach her new husband how to catch trout. They intended to drive back home later in the week through Denver, where they had tickets for a preseason game between the Dallas Cowboys and the Denver Broncos.

But when the Broncos kicked off on the following Sunday afternoon, their two seats at Mile High Stadium were empty. Four days before the game, James and Margene Judge vanished. On Sunday, search parties were organized to search the mountains around South Fork. That day their tickets and the rest of their belongings were found strewn along a lonely stream far away on the other side of the state.

South Fork is situated west of Alamosa, near the headwaters of the Rio Grande, where its north and south forks join. Only some three hundred people live in South Fork year round. But every summer about three thousand tourists and seasonal residents crowd into the cabins and trailer parks tucked away in the mountain valleys that radiate out from the tiny town. The drawls and nasal twangs you hear in the stores and cafes, and the hoots and hollers that echo across still mountain lakes, suggest that most of those summer visitors come from Texas and Oklahoma. When it gets hot back home on the plains, these boisterous flatlanders head for Colorado and the "smoky old pool rooms and cool mountain mornings" Willie Nelson sings about. The abundance of rainbow trout in the clear, cold forks of the Rio Grande is also a big draw.

F. H. and Jenelle Davis and their two daughters, Margene and Pat, had been spending a week or two week in South Fork every summer since 1961. They owned a lot not far from the river. The whole family loved to camp in the Golden Falcon travel trailer they would tow up from their home in Borger, Texas. Over the years, F. H. had built a block fireplace and a small pavilion to cover their picnic table, and he had poured the foundation for the cabin he planned to build there before he retired. He was most proud of the outdoor toilet he had built. "I didn't want one of those awful portable kind construction workers use," Jenelle said, "so F. H. built a real nice one — all redwood and very sturdy."[1]

Borger, Texas, where Margene was raised, is about fifty miles northeast of Amarillo on the rolling plains of West Texas. You can get there from Amarillo by taking U.S. Route 60, whose four lanes run divided to Panhandle and then north on State Route 207, but most folks think it's quicker just to take old Route 136 through Fritch. Either way, traffic is no problem.

Amarillo is surrounded by vast flat fields of wheat and sorghum, but as you drive toward Borger, the ground begins to fall away into gullies and washes, and lush, irrigated grain gives way to tough, thirsty grass and the dried plumes of countless yucca plants that rattle in the wind. There are few trees on this dry land. Brown-and-white Hereford cattle gather near water tanks, chewing indifferently with their backs to a wind that never seems to stop. Oil wells are scattered here and there, looking like huge praying mantises, some nodding monotonously up and down, others standing motionless. An occasional cluster of white grain elevators, visible long before you reach them, contributes to the overwhelming sense of space that looms over the Texas Panhandle. "Out on them plains," an old cowboy said, recalling the loneliness of ranching in the Panhandle, "there was nothing between you and a cold north wind but barbed-wire fence."

Just outside Borger is a large Phillips Petroleum refinery and a couple of smaller petrochemical plants, which define the town's economy and command its loyalty. There are fifty-two churches scattered around town. Except for St. John's Roman Catholic, they're all Protestant and, with only a few exceptions, fundamentalist. One measure of their influence is the absence of saloons and liquor stores. A billboard on the edge of town greets visitors and announces the major source of community pride: "WELCOME TO BORGER," it says in big letters, "Home of the Borger High School Bulldogs." Texans like football, and the folks in Borger love their Bulldogs.

The Borger Bulldogs were a focal point for Margene Davis. Margene was a "twirler" in the high school band. In Borger, twirling batons is for girls what football is for boys. It requires a lot of time and effort and talent, and it doesn't hurt to be pretty. Those who make it are assured the cheers and affection of the whole town. Jenelle Davis proudly recalled that her daughter's passion for twirling began in infancy with a pencil and remained with her all her life.

Margene walked to school from the Davises' comfortable little brick house on West Coolidge Street. On this street of low-slung stucco bungalows, with cars parked in front yards where lawns used to grow, the Davises' house stands out. With its red bricks, steep gabled roof, and two big picture windows, it seems to belong in a nice midwestern suburb instead of right downtown, squeezed between the Church of God of Prophecy and the Foreman Chiropractic Offices. The picture windows look out over only about twenty feet of fenced yard to the sidewalk.

Jenelle and F. H. Davis — everybody called him F. H. — had lived in that house a good part of their lives and had raised their two pretty daughters there. When Pat, who was six years older, married, Margene got her own bedroom upstairs, which she redecorated in pastel yellow with frilly white curtains. During her years in junior high and high school, the walls and the hallway leading to it gradually became a gallery of photographs of happy memories — family, friends, pets, marching bands, and twirling awards. It was hard to imagine that pretty, popular Margene Davis ever had a sad moment in Borger.

The Davises' trip to Amarillo that hot Saturday afternoon on August 5, 1978, was tinged with melancholy, especially for Jenelle, because their "baby" was being married that evening in a big ceremony at the Garden Room of the Amarillo Convention Center. It was a quiet ride. The Davises weren't too pleased with the young man Margene had decided to marry. Moreover, they had always assumed that Margene would be married in Borger, at the First Baptist Church they attended.

"That's what we thought," her mother said, sighing. "But James, her fiancé, was raised in the Church of Christ, and, rather than hurting both families, Margene decided to be married in the Garden Room . . . And it was a real pretty place."

Actually, James Judge didn't care where he was married.

"James . . . well, how should I put it?" his older brother John said. "He just wasn't the churchgoing type. But I think Margene sorta kept that from her folks. Now, it's true that our folks were religious, too. And I mean real religious. You know, self-righteous, hard-core, Texas-style-right-wing — you name it — fundamentalists, but it didn't seem to take on either one of us. When I was home I just sort of rolled with it and was real sneaky when I broke the rules. But James, I think he grew his balls a little earlier than me because he just did as he damn well pleased. Yeah, he got himself into some trouble — two or three arrests for marijuana possession, and I think they got him once for drunk driving. He was a real wild-assed kid for a while, but always likable and friendly. You just couldn't stay mad at him. That's what everybody liked about him, including Margene, I think, when they met."[2]

But the Davises never got to see much of that engaging side of James Judge, or for that matter, any other side, according to Margene's mother. "After she finished secretarial school," Jenelle Davis said, "Margene moved into an apartment with three other girls in Amarillo and was working as a secretary for John Judge, who's a lawyer there. That's where she met his brother James. I think John introduced them. But James only came up to see us twice the whole eighteen months they dated, so we didn't get to know him real well, except through what Margene told us about him. But she'd always call us every day, and we could tell she cared for him. He was a carpenter. We were sure surprised when she told us they wanted to get married."

Margene knew her parents felt hurt about James not coming to visit, and not giving them a chance to know him better, but she needed time to change him. Her plan was working. "James started to tone down after he started courting Margene," his brother John said. "She had quite an influence on him. I guess she had a pretty traditional upbringing and all that, but she was no wilting violet either. She was a good-looking gal, and, at twenty-five, he wasn't the first guy she'd dated by a long shot. She liked to party and have a good time, and when she started working for me after she moved away from home, you could tell she was enjoying the bright lights of Amarillo — if you can imagine that. But compared to Borger, you know, it was the big city. She was a sensible gal, though, and she wasn't going to have any of his dope-smoking and that sort of thing around her, and she had a strong positive influence on my brother. By the time they married, he'd really matured. At twenty-six, he'd finally grown up, thanks to Margene. I was real proud of him."

It was a big wedding by Borger standards. About two hundred guests were invited, and Margene's wedding album is replete with photographs of kisses, cake cutting, formal family poses, and smiles — many, many smiles.

"Just before the ceremony was to begin," John recalled, "I leaned over and asked my brother if he was sure he wanted to go through with it. I said, 'You know, you'll end up teaching a Baptist Sunday school class in five years.' James looked down, kinda shaking his head, and smiled like it didn't bother him a bit to be putting the past behind him. He was real happy."

One of the key points Margene had made in her efforts to convince her parents that she wasn't making a mistake had to do with her fiancé's skills as a carpenter. She knew her mother would have preferred an attorney, but James, Margene said, would be able to help them build the little cabin in South Fork they had all dreamed about for so long.

"He's already said he wants to help Daddy build it," she told her mother excitedly before they were married. "And when we're up there on our honeymoon, he's going to look over the foundation so he'll get some ideas about how we should do it. Don't you be worrying now, Mother, everything's going to work out fine."

• • •

Margene called her parents on Sunday shortly after she and James arrived in South Fork. She had always called her parents regularly when she was away, and her honeymoon was no exception. They always talked longer than they agreed to, but no one seemed worried about the cost.

Margene told her mother that she and James had arrived safely that afternoon after spending their wedding night at a motel they all knew in Texline, on the Texas/New Mexico border. She said it was sunny and cool — "They say it's still downright cold at night here" — and that it hadn't started to rain as it usually did on August afternoons. They had already bought their fishing licenses, she said. That evening they were going to sleep in the van at the campsite and cook out on the fireplace. Then F. H. took the phone. "Daddy?" Margene asked as always when he got on the phone. "Hi, Daddy, how are you? Oh, we're fine and, Daddy, I just have to tell you . . ." Just the sound of her voice made F. H. smile as she happily repeated everything she had just told her mother. How he adored that little girl, who was now, all at once, it seemed to him, a woman. After a while, her mother took the phone back for the final goodbyes.

"Margene, please be careful."

"Oh, Mother," she said, sighing with feigned exasperation, "you'd think I was a child instead of twenty-five years old. You know I'm old enough to take care of myself."

"I know you are, but I just want to say *please* be careful."

"Mother, now don't you worry, we're just fine."[3]

She promised to call again on Tuesday.

A single night at the Gilmore Ranch campsite outside of Alamosa was enough for Gary Tison and his companions. They had camped along an irrigation slough close to the river, where the mosquitoes were thick and hungry. It was maddening. Gary, whose prison-pale skin was already sunburned and peeling, was especially miserable, with stinging, itching welts on his face, neck, and hands. Only their exhaustion and a couple of small bottles of insect repellent, quickly drained, enabled them to get any sleep at all. There was a faint breeze from the mountains after sunrise, but squadrons of mosquitoes continued to rise from the slough.

They left abruptly on Monday morning, August 7. Cooking utensils, army surplus clothing, a pair of boots, an ice chest, shaving gear, toothbrushes, deodorant, and assorted containers and wrappings were left strewn about the campsite, as if they had left in panic and confusion. Someone apparently had added the last of the Prestone coolant to the overheating radiator, then flung the empty container into the trees. It was caught in some branches along with an empty box of shotgun shells.

But the mess wasn't all they left behind. A pair of orange-and-black plaid bucket seats, a sideview mirror — its surface frosted on the edges with gray primer — and a car radio they had taken from the Lyonses' Mazda were all hidden in the brush underneath a green tarpaulin and covered with branches.[4] That morning the fugitives had heard the radio news. The Lyonses' bodies had been discovered, and the Lincoln Continental had been identified. Now the police would be looking for the Mazda, and Gary didn't want someone finding all that incriminating evidence in the truck. The police would now be looking too for a dark blue Chevy pickup with a missing grille.

U.S. Route 160 — the Navajo Trail — is fairly level as it follows the Rio Grande west from Alamosa up the San Luis Valley, through the little towns of Monte Vista and Del Norte, to South Fork. It was a good thing for the fugitives because second gear was almost gone and their truck was overheating on every climb. They knew they had to do something fast about the ailing pickup.

South Fork, Colorado, looked like about as good a place as any to find another vehicle. When they drove into the tiny vacation community that Monday morning, a big sign welcomed them to COLORADO's WONDERLAND FOR VACATIONERS. There sure were a lot of them. The parking lots were crowded with recreational vehicles, vans, and truck campers. Just what they needed, Gary said as they drove through. If they had a van or a camper, they could travel easier during the day.

They took a right turn on Route 149 at the fork and followed it a quarter mile, crossing the two-lane bridge over the river before turning right on a dirt road that winds into the hills along the northern edge of the Rio Grande. A few miles farther they spotted what appeared to be a vacant campsite. It looked okay, far enough away from things. There were no trees or standing water nearby, so the mosquitoes wouldn't be too bad. It had a covered picnic table and a fireplace and, most important, an outdoor toilet. On its side the owner had stenciled PROPERTY OF F. H. DAVIS.

Summer neighbors down the road noticed the five strangers. Both the Trujillios and the Fresques had seen the strange pickup parked on the Davis lot and wondered whose it was. Earlier they had recognized Margene and a young man camping there in a van, but these rough-looking men didn't look like the kind of folks the Davises would know, or would want on their property. Young Patsy Trujillio decided to walk down and have a look. In a neighborly kind of way, she asked if they were looking for the Davises. The reply was a blunt no, but Patsy persisted: "Do you know if the Davises are coming up this summer?" she asked brightly.

"We don't know nothing about the Davises, or whether they're coming up," Greenawalt growled, glaring at her.

"He said it in a real hateful tone," Patsy said later. "It scared me, and I left."

When she got back to her parents' trailer, she told them about her encounter.[5] A few minutes later, they noticed the blue pickup drive away, and it never returned. The Trujillios saw James and Margene come back later that afternoon, but the incident didn't seem important enough to mention. Scruffy-looking fishermen often wandered around looking for campsites on that road in the summertime, and they weren't always friendly or polite.

The fugitives spent the rest of Monday afternoon roaming around the area looking for another campsite and an opportunity to steal another vehicle. That evening near dusk, they headed west on U.S. Route 160. They made it as far as a barricade at the base of the mountain that rises to Wolf Creek Pass. The highway was closed until seven the next morning. Blasting, the sign said. They turned the truck around and drove only a short distance before turning south on a gravel Forest Service road that ran back into the mountains. Just about the time James and Margene were sitting down to have dinner at the Stone Quarry Restaurant in South Fork, the Tison party stopped at a vacant camping area above Pass Creek. Too close to the noisy highway construction for other campers, it seemed like a safe place to spend the night.

The Foothills Market is located on the *Y* in South Fork where State Route 149 turns north from U.S. Route 160. It's the busiest store in town, selling everything for the vacationer: groceries, ice, beer, clothing, camping equipment, fishing licenses, and tackle. In 1978 it was the only such store for fifteen or so miles. At about four o'clock

Tuesday afternoon, the blue pickup pulled into the gravel parking lot out front and parked at the far edge. Randy Greenawalt and Ricky Tison got out and walked into the store. Moments later they were followed by either Donny or Ray. The three strangers looked rough and were behaving suspiciously. The manager pressed the innocuous-sounding "help watch" buzzer that alerted all employees to keep an eye out for shoplifters. Linda Mae Carroll was working at the cash register when she heard the signal.

"I turned around and I saw that three men had come into the store," Linda Mae said. "The one standing nearest the cash register was a young, well-groomed-looking man. There was also a heavy-set man in a kind of sloppy white T-shirt. He looked very dirty and dingy and everything else. He had a growth of beard started. I thought it was kind of funny that this young gentleman who looked so well groomed and clean-cut was with the other man that was so completely different. The younger one did have a very noticeable overbite, but he was still nice-looking. There was another person I didn't get a good look at with them, and they seemed to be more or less wandering around, kind of easing away from each other, looking around the store."[6]

"I noticed when they left," Linda Mae explained, "because they hadn't bought anything — which is very, very strange — because that store has something for everybody, and if somebody walks in, they go out with groceries, or a gift, or something of the sort. But not buying anything? Now, that's unusual."[7]

A few hours earlier that same Tuesday afternoon, Linda Mae had noticed a young woman come into the market. While her companion, a young man with hair below his collar, waited outside in a silver-and-blue Ford van, she picked up a bag of Fritos and a can of dip, a couple of Dr. Peppers, and a roll of Polaroid film. Linda Mae couldn't take her eyes off the woman.

"She was extremely beautiful," she said. "She had a glow to her that you could never forget." When the young woman walked over to the cash register, she smiled and they exchanged pleasantries. "She was so pretty," Linda Mae recalled, "and she had this soft Texas accent when she spoke to me."[8]

Margene and James Judge had gone fishing that morning and stopped at the market to get some film and snacks before leaving on a short sight-seeing drive. James had hinted that he was ready for a break from fishing and the outdoor life. He'd enjoyed the trout Margene had fried in butter for lunch the day before, but he would've preferred it if she hadn't insisted on showing him how to clean them first. He didn't want to say anything to spoil the fun she was having, but when she was trying to light the Coleman stove the next morning he asked if she would like to get a motel room that evening, take nice hot showers, and have dinner out afterward. Margene smiled and said she thought it was a great idea.

Around seven o'clock Tuesday evening, about the time the Tisons and Greenawalt were preparing for a second cold night at their camp-site on Pass Creek Road, James Judge pulled their van into the parking lot of the Rainbow Motel and stopped by the phone booth where Margene had been making her calls. Margene got out and called her parents again, as she had promised to do the night before.

Margene was laughing as she described how James had caught three trout that day. The weather was nice, she said, and they were having a great time. She went on to say that they had tried to get a motel room that night, but everything in South Fork was full. So, they would spend the night at the campsite after all. They were going to get up early the next morning and drive up to fish at Millions Reservoir, a lake high in the mountains southwest of South Point. After that, they planned to drive over to try Shaw Lake, near Wolf Creek Pass. James was going to take her to dinner at the Arrowhead, a restaurant about a half mile up the road. When she said goodbye, her mother asked her to call again on Wednesday evening, and she laughed and said she would.

The Arrowhead Restaurant and Lounge was a good place to get eggs and hashbrowns or a big bowl of Texas-style chili. It was popular with truckers. At night the lounge was a fairly rowdy hangout for beer-swilling cowboys and their women. James liked places like that, and, after three days of listening to crickets and staring at stars at night, he may have been ready to do something more lively — maybe listen to a country band and do a little dancing with his bride. When they pulled into the parking lot at the Arrowhead, he would have heard that fiddle and those strumming guitars, and all the laughter coming from inside, and thought that he'd made the right choice.

That summer, the highway that runs past the Arrowhead Lounge and climbs ten thousand feet up over Wolf Creek Pass was being widened on the South Fork side. Bulldozers scraped back and forth all day, and giant earth movers laden with rock and dirt rumbled past. Flagmen at either end took turns waving a slow line of one-way traffic through the construction area. Highway crews were working around the clock to finish before winter. Big snows in the Colorado high country, they knew, could come anytime after Labor Day. A lot of blasting was done at night. As the fugitives had discovered, the highway was closed at seven and not reopened until seven the next morning. Though it created quite a problem for unknowing travelers, it was a boon to the motel operators on both sides of the mountain.

By late Tuesday night, the temperature was dropping down into the thirties. On the side of one of those mountains, Gary, Randy, and the boys huddled shivering around a small fire. The Coleman stove and tarp they had used to keep warm had been left at the Gilmore Ranch the day before.[9] The five men moved restlessly between the cab of the pickup and the small fire, pulling on whatever excess clothing they could find.

Brian Lieske operated a road grader on the day shift at the Wolf Creek construction site. At quitting time on Tuesday evening, he took off his coveralls, as he always did, and left them in the cab of the grader. When Lieske came to work early the next morning, they were gone. Donny Tison had climbed into the grader, found Lieske's coveralls, and pulled them on over his own clothes. The next morning, after it had warmed up, Donny had thrown the coveralls into the back of the pickup in case he needed them again.[10]

Aching with fatigue and cold, the Tisons and Greenawalt stayed at the campsite longer than usual on Wednesday morning, trying to thaw out in the sun's warming rays. It was about ten o'clock before Gary said that they had to get moving. They had been in the area too long, he said. He was afraid someone was going to spot them. But they were unsure where to go. There had been no place in South Fork to get the old truck repaired, and there had always been too many people around when they wanted to steal another. For two days and nights they had prowled the camping areas around South Fork, like hungry predators looking for prey.

Sometime after Margene Judge called her parents on Tuesday evening, she and her husband disappeared. The exact circumstances of their disappearance remain a matter of dispute.[11] Some Colorado investigators believe that the young couple was abducted at the phone booth in the parking lot of the Rainbow Motel on Tuesday evening, moments after Margene spoke with her parents. According to this theory, the fugitives either followed them to the phone booth or were waiting there when they arrived. The abduction occurred, they believe, after Margene completed the call. Others suspect the abduction occurred several hours later, when the Judges left the Arrowhead Lounge. In either case, the supposition is that the couple was forced at gunpoint into the van and taken to the campsite at Pass Creek Road, where they were held hostage overnight. As soon as the road opened the next morning, they were driven over Wolf Creek Pass and taken to an isolated area west of Pagosa Springs, where they were killed. Advocates of both these theories presume that the fugitives stalked the young couple for at least a day before the abduction. The stalking presumption is based on the fact that the fugitives were seen both at the Davises' campsite and later at the Foothills Market.[12]

Although there is no reason to doubt that the fugitives appeared at both places, more than likely it was pure coincidence that they did. James and Margene Judge were seen alive and well on Wednesday morning — the morning *after* the supposed abduction — by two independent and credible witnesses.

Bob Lewis, the owner, by coincidence, of Bob's Western Wear in Borger, Texas, was fishing at Millions Reservoir on Wednesday morning. At about eight-thirty, Lewis said, he noticed a young couple walk down to the lake from the parking area. He didn't pay much attention to them until they started to fish from the shoreline directly across from him. Then he said he noticed that the woman was fly-fishing with "a great deal of skill." That was really something, he thought. He had never seen a woman handle a flyrod so well. Her companion, he noticed, was just "bait-fishing" and seemed a little bored. It wasn't long before the trout became interested in those dry flies the young woman whipped out so gracefully, and she started to catch fish. "You knew when she did, even if you weren't watching," Lewis said. "Every time she had one hooked, she would squeal and holler."

When Lewis left about midmorning, he said, the couple was still fishing, and there was no one else on the lake. Although he had never met Margene and James, he recognized their pictures later when he saw them in the *Borger News-Herald.* "I'm ninety-nine-point-nine percent certain that it was them on the lake that morning," he said.[13]

Consistent with Lewis's recollection was that of Gloria Chisum, who was also at the Millions Reservoir that Wednesday morning. Mrs. Chisum, a resident of Malone, New York, was vacationing with her son. Moreover, by an odd coincidence, she happened to be a distant cousin of Jenelle Davis. Although she had never met Margene, nor had she seen her cousin Jenelle in some years, Margene and James had known she was vacationing in the area. They planned to visit her later that week at the cabin she was renting.

Mrs. Chisum has vivid memories of that morning. As she and her son were driving in on the dirt road to the reservoir, they were forced into a ditch by a dark-colored pickup truck speeding in the opposite direction. She said the driver of the truck was alone and didn't stop. When they arrived, a bit shaken, at the parking area a few minutes later, it was about ten-thirty and a young couple was putting their fishing rods into a silver-and-blue van and preparing to leave. They were laughing and talking together. Mrs. Chisum later positively identified the couple from photographs she was shown.[14]

When she got down to the lake, Gloria Chisum noticed two young men lounging on the other side. She wondered what they were doing there, since they weren't fishing. The two men must have arrived sometime within the fifteen minutes or so between Bob Lewis's departure and Gloria Chisum's arrival. Later that day, about three o'clock, Mrs. Chisum said, the two young men were joined by a heavy-set man who walked down from the parking area. He was dressed in what looked like green work clothes, or army fatigues. The three men squatted on the lake shore and had a brief conversation before all three walked back up to the parking area. When Mrs. Chisum and her son left a few minutes later, the parking lot was empty. Later, after seeing photographs of the fugitives, she said the three men she saw at a distance could have been Gary Tison and two of his sons.

On the basis of the Lewis and Chisum sightings, Margene's parents disagreed with Colorado authorities and were convinced that their daughter and her husband were abducted in the parking area at Millions Reservoir by Gary, Randy, and one of the boys, while the other two boys waited down by the lake. But this theory was also incorrect.

What actually happened was this:

After fishing at Millions Reservoir for a couple of hours on Wednesday morning, James and Margene left only a few minutes after Bob Lewis and walked to their van in the parking lot. They were there, as Gloria Chisum said, when she drove in and saw them. But they were not abducted there. When James and Margene pulled out of the parking area unmolested, the Tisons and Greenawalt were still back at their campsite on Pass Creek Road, some ten miles away. Later that afternoon, when the person who resembled Gary Tison came to get the two young men at the lake, Gary and the boys were actually nearly two hundred miles away, across the state in Cortez.

The Judges were headed for Shaw Lake, about fifteen miles to the west, where they were going to fish, just as Margene had told her parents when she called the evening before. To reach Shaw Lake, they had to get back on Route 160 and follow it west from South Fork all the way to Wolf Creek Mountain. A mile or two past the Pass Creek Road, in the middle of the construction area, another Forest Service road angles off and winds back into the mountains past the Big Meadows Reservoir and on to Shaw Lake, a few miles farther up the valley. Less than half an hour after the couple left Millions Reservoir, James stopped the van in a line of traffic that was stopped in the Wolf Creek construction zone.

A dark blue pickup with a noisy transmission had turned onto the highway from Pass Creek Road just after they had passed by. Gary had decided to try make it over the mountain to Pagosa Springs or Durango, where they hoped to find a Chevrolet garage and get the transmission fixed. The meeting at the roadblock was completely fortuitous. They pulled up behind the Judges' van and stopped. The dirty blue pickup was the last vehicle in the line, and midweek traffic was light.

Gary immediately noticed the van — just what they had been looking for. Someone, either Randy or, most probably, one of the boys, climbed out and walked a short distance up along the line of cars, pretending to be curious about the construction and trying to gauge the duration of the wait.[15] A casual glance revealed only two people inside. Moments later, Gary and Randy, looking ugly and unshaven, startled the young couple by appearing at the open windows on either side of the van. Almost simultaneously they jerked open the doors, Gary on the driver's side, Randy on the other, pointing the pistol he held into Margene's face. Gary pushed John Lyons's vintage .45 hard against James's ribs.

Within seconds Gary had squeezed in behind the steering wheel, while Randy held the stunned young couple at gunpoint in the back. When more cars stopped behind the pickup, everything was quiet and seemed normal. The flagman finally began waving the stopped traffic through, and Donny, Ricky, and Ray in the pickup followed the van in a grim procession up the mountain. As they passed the ski area at the top and started down into the beautiful San Juan Valley on the other side, James and Margene Judge sat helplessly in the back of their van under Randy Greenawalt's indifferent stare.[16] In less than two hours, they were dead.

Looking back on the last time she saw her daughter that warm Saturday evening after the wedding in Amarillo, Jenelle Davis recalled: "When Margene got to the east door and she started out, she turned around and looked back, and gave that funny little wave of hers, like she always did, and I looked at her and I thought to myself, 'I will probably never see my child again.' And why that went through me, I don't know. I have no earthly idea."[17]

The last photograph in the wedding album shows two happy young people, dressed in casual clothes, sitting in the front seat of their Ford van, about to leave for their Colorado honeymoon. Underneath, Margene's mother affixed a poem that Margene had selected for their wedding. It was titled, "Our Life, Our Beginning," and closed with these words,

> This is only a tiny message,
>   but it's written just for you
> who found time in your busy life,
>   to give us a moment or two.
> We hope that you can feel
>   As we, light hearted and gay,
> And share with us the magic,
>   Of this enchanting day.
>
>   James and Margene
>   August 5, 1978

Four days later, her mother gave the photograph to the FBI to use in the missing persons bulletins.

11

Malfeasance

Warden Harold Cardwell's immediate reaction to the prison break was to blame everyone but himself. First, he blamed the American Civil Liberties Union, whose lawsuit in behalf of the strikers caused the court to order a reduction in the number of inmates confined in the main prison. Second, Cardwell blamed the Department of Public Safety and the director of corrections, Ellis MacDougall, who, Cardwell claimed, had withheld important information from him. Third, he blamed his subordinates, who hadn't followed correct procedures. In retaliating, Cardwell started, characteristically, at the bottom.

Two days after the escape, Major John Avenenti and Captain William Groves, the two supervisors who had been on duty at the Annex at the time of the escape, were formally reprimanded and transferred. Two weeks later, they, in turn, passed the buck, in the form of written reprimands, to three officers of lower rank, George Goswick, Marquis Hodo, and Wayne Wrisk, who were under their supervision that day. These reprimands charged that the three were negligent when they permitted Randy Greenawalt into the control area.[1]

Greenawalt should surely not have been permitted into a supposedly secure area, but Marquis Hodo decided that he wasn't going to roll over on that charge. Hodo was still smarting from the humiliating tongue-lashing Cardwell had administered on the day of the escape, and he refused to sign the reprimand. He produced an official memorandum that had been circulated to the guards, containing formal instructions to admit Greenawalt into the control area on Sundays to type the "gang sheets," as the Monday work assignments were called. Hodo handed it to Major Avenenti and watched the expression on Avenenti's face change as his eyes scanned its contents. When he finished, Avenenti looked over at Groves for a long moment, then without a word tore up the three reprimands and walked out.[2] Bill Groves had a lot of tracks to cover. He had served on the committee, with Cardwell, that had recommended both Tison's and Greenawalt's initial transfers to the Annex.

On August 11, Governor Babbitt called for a complete investigation of the escape. There were too many unanswered questions. How had three men been able to carry a box of weapons directly into a prison without being detected? The governor told Ellis MacDougall that he wanted some answers, and that he expected them in short order, "in a matter of days, or weeks, at the most."[3] The state legislature also wanted some answers. Why had Cardwell not acted on the earlier information he had received that an escape was imminent? "Incredibly, prison officials were notified this year by law enforcement officials that Tison was planning a breakout," Representative Peter Dunn fumed, "and officials left him in medium security. Why?" Dunn wanted to know, adding that "whoever is responsible . . . should be fired immediately."[4]

Stung earlier by the deluge of criticism following his assurance that the two escapees were not dangerous to the public, and now under mounting pressure to account for the escape, MacDougall asked a respected criminologist, Arthur B. Huffman, to give him an independent evaluation of the records of both Tison and Greenawalt. In specific terms, MacDougall wanted to know if there was any sound clinical or factual evidence to support the decisions Cardwell and his Transfer Committee had made to move both escapees to the Annex in the first place.

On August 16, Huffman submitted his detailed report. It was a devastating indictment of Cardwell's judgment and his committee's recommendations.

> In conclusion, it develops that in Gary Gene Tison you're concerned with a repetitively violent criminal. Repetitively violent offenders cannot be regarded as those most likely to succeed, either intramurally or extramurally.
>
> Tison represents the prototypical criminal in the public's mind,

especially because he is the kind of criminal [who is] an irrationally violent man who kills [and, therefore,] generates the most pervasive fear. As such, his record mandates that he be maintained in close and safe custody . . . No one can doubt that for years Tison constituted a high security risk and, as such, responsible prison officials were remiss in not having provided a range of physical devices to limit, or preclude, physical contact and visiting.[5]

In a similarly sweeping condemnation of Randy Greenawalt's transfer, Huffman's assessment completely contradicted the earlier positive evaluation submitted by psychiatrist Willard Gold. There could be little disagreement about the long history of patterned violence that characterized the life of this deceptively genial psychopath.

> In brief [Huffman wrote], it is this reviewer's impression that Randy Greenawalt is a chronically antisocial individual who will profit neither from experience nor punishment, and, as such, requires permanent and safe confinement away from society.
> The history of this man reveals 1) an unsatisfactory military career; 2) a history of numerous arrests including arson and crimes of violence; 3) an impersonal, emotionally trivial and poorly integrated response to life; and finally, 4) a psychiatric diagnosis of psychopathy.

Huffman concluded with this blunt statement:

> In conclusion, it is this reviewer's judgment that sufficient evidence existed in the institutional files on Randy Greenawalt to indicate that anything less than maximum and/or close custody clearly was contraindicated and that his placement outside the prison walls, in view of his criminal history, the detainer from Arkansas [Greenawalt still had charges pending against him in that state for the murder of another truck driver], and other precursors of his potential dangerousness and propensity toward aggressive behavior constituted malfeasance.[6]

Malfeasance. MacDougall had no alternative. On August 18, Harold Cardwell was removed as warden and given a "special assignment" in MacDougall's office, pending the conclusion of the investigation. Denying unconvincingly that he was acting under any political pressure, MacDougall cautioned that Cardwell's removal "should not be construed" as punishment for the escape. When asked, however, about reports that the warden might have been involved in the escape, MacDougall swallowed and allowed that "it's possible."[7] He was aware, he said, that an unsigned letter, reportedly from a number of inmates, had been sent after the escape to a Phoenix television station. The letter charged that a deal had been made between Cardwell and the two escapees during the inmate strike. Cardwell, the letter claimed, had promised transfers to Tison, Greenawalt, and also to David La-Barre in return for information on the strikers.[8] On the surface, such a deal sounded plausible. It wasn't the first time anyone had heard that the three inmates were "snitches" for prison officials.

MacDougall was also privately aware that, in his words, "covering our ass"[9] was going to require a Herculean effort. Governor Babbitt's instructions notwithstanding, it was quite apparent that the less the public learned about this, the better. With that in mind, MacDougall did not want to dig a beleaguered Harold Cardwell any deeper into the hole; nor did he want to risk needlessly antagonizing a volatile, thoughtlessly impulsive man whose judgment was notoriously poor. MacDougall subsequently denied that he had said that Cardwell might have been involved in the escape. "Cardwell has made a lot of mistakes," MacDougall told the press, "but I have no evidence that he is other than an honest man."[10] Then he decided to soften the warden's ouster with a pay raise.[11]

MacDougall's desire to keep the lid on things was also reflected in the way he announced his plan to reorganize the prison administration. "It was my feeling we needed new people, new blood down there," MacDougall said at the same press interview, and then proceeded to read off names that sounded very familiar. Dwight Burd, former assistant warden, would replace Cardwell. New organization units within the prison would be headed by four other Cardwell assistants: Joseph Martinez, Andrew Jimenez, Dwight Carey, and John Avenenti.

"New blood? Where?" a reporter asked. Joe Martinez, who had made the initial transfer recommendations on both Tison and Greenawalt, had recommended Tison's transfer, so inmates claimed, as a "payoff."[12] If true, was it a payoff for Tison's support during the strike? Or did it have something to do with the widely publicized contract on Tony Serra? Inmate Raymond Celenza claimed the alleged threats against Tison's life for his support of Cardwell during the strike were fabricated by Martinez to justify a decision that had already been made for other reasons.[13] Moreover, Martinez's recommendation on Tison was subsequently approved by all three of MacDougall's appointees: Burd, Jimenez, and Carey. Only John Avenenti appeared to be unsoiled by what Arthur Huffman had called "malfeasance."

Ellis MacDougall thought that he could have averted the whole disaster if he had had more time. But he didn't. Now he was trying to cut his losses, thinking only about damage control in a badly listing prison administration, nearly sunk by an incompetent, and possibly corrupt, skipper. The less the public learned, the better it would be for the Department of Corrections. Self-interest would ensure that none of MacDougall's new appointees would stir things up.

Harold Cardwell, however, was another matter. The recently removed commander was now a loose cannon. Cardwell was not affected by his boss's leniency or his generosity. Nor did he seem to understand MacDougall's attempt to provide shelter with his new appointments. To Cardwell it must have looked as though he was being set up as the scapegoat. The specter of a criminal indictment could not be ignored. Realizing that his reputation and career were at stake, Cardwell decided that his best defense was a good offense. Having failed earlier to shift blame convincingly to those below him, he now lashed out at those above. On August 31, he volunteered his own explanation for the escape to the governor.

Cardwell emphatically denied any knowledge of an escape plot. He blamed the American Civil Liberties Union and Judge Muecke for the transfers (they wouldn't have been made, he said, except for the court order). He blamed MacDougall and Department of Public Safety investigators for withholding information about the plot from him. The reports he had received from the Central Arizona Narcotics Unit and the Sheriff's Department in Deaf Smith County, Texas? Unreliable, Cardwell said of the Arizona information. It "could not have come from an inmate." Had the report come directly from the Department of Public Safety, Cardwell continued, he would have considered it "more reliable" because "the source would have been one *inside* the prison."[14] His logic was difficult to understand. He seemed to be saying that he did not trust anyone *outside* the prison, or beyond his own supervision — even another law enforcement agency that had, presumably, nothing to gain with false information. He didn't bother to mention the report from Texas.

What about Bobby Tuzon's futile warnings? Initially Cardwell flatly denied ever talking with Tuzon about the escape before the day it happened.[15] Later, he changed his story, admitting that he had interviewed Tuzon once on April 1 in his office.[16] He claimed that this single conversation with Tuzon "concluded with the inmate stating that he would contact me if he had any problems or learned of any escape plot involving any inmates."[17] And, Cardwell implied, Tuzon never did.[18] Cardwell didn't mention the call he had received from Irma Tuzon; nor did he mention the second bitter interrogation it had prompted with her husband.[19] Cardwell even denied that he knew that Tison and Tuzon were cellmates. "I never made cell assignments," he explained.[20]

Cardwell claimed that Tuzon chose to talk to others about the escape, and these other persons kept this information from him. Had he been given this information, Cardwell protested, he could have done something to prevent what happened.[21]

Who kept Cardwell in the dark about the escape plot? Everyone Tuzon talked to, Cardwell claimed: the guards and supervisors at the Annex (who, after the escape, of course, also denied that Tuzon had warned them about it); Department of Public Safety investigators Peter Womack and David Arnett; prison psychologist Robert Flores; and Ellis MacDougall himself.

"Had either Director MacDougall or DPS advised me that they had any information concerning a possible escape plot involving Tison or any inmate," Cardwell insisted, "I would have taken immediate steps to place Tison, or any such inmate, in the maximum-security prison yard investigative lock-up, pending further investigation of the matter."[22]

He reminded the governor that he had followed that procedure when he first received the Central Arizona Narcotic Unit's report in March.[23] Cardwell placed the blame squarely on MacDougall and the Department of Public Safety: "I must state that, to me, it is inconceivable and inexcusable that the information obtained by the Director and the DPS concerning a possible escape plot of a prisoner in the medium-security facility was not reported to me, the Warden, the man on the scene with the primary responsibility for prison security."[24]

Cardwell did not mention that he had also been warned of the escape a second time by Texas authorities in June. Several months had passed since Sheriff Travis McPherson had first warned prison officials about the escape plan described by Terry Tarr. Concerned that Cardwell had not received the earlier report, McPherson sent his chief deputy, Art Burton, in person, to confirm what his department believed to be a serious and imminent threat at the prison. Burton met with members of the Department of Public Safety in Coolidge, a little town ten miles west of Florence. Sergeant David Audsley, in turn, reported the information directly to prison officials.[25]

McPherson received no response from Cardwell. He was surprised and annoyed by the apparent indifference and lack of courtesy, but at that point he decided that he had done all he could.[26] When Cardwell was asked about the second report from Texas, he denied receiving it.

Cardwell did tell the truth about not receiving one report. Prison psychologist Robert Flores had not bothered to mention his interview with Bobby Tuzon to Cardwell because he thought Bobby's story was symptomatic of mental disturbance.[27]

Nowhere in his lengthy report did Cardwell suggest that Tison's and Greenawalt's transfers had been approved because their lives were in danger.[28]

Cardwell's statement was also interesting in view of his response to two related personnel decisions: his denials of the repeated pleas for transfer from Bobby Tuzon and, earlier, Tony Serra — despite spotless prison records and compelling reasons of personal safety. How could he have approved the transfers of both Tison and Greenawalt — both with dismal criminal and prison records — notwithstanding the numerous and repeated warnings about their escape plot? And how could he have missed inmate George Warnock's description of Tison's role in the Serra murder, which appeared on the front page of the *Arizona Republic* only a month before the escape?[29] And why did he rush to approve their transfers to medium security within hours of an outside evaluation?

Cardwell claimed that he had simply followed the recommendations made by the Transfer Committee in making the two controversial transfers. But members of the committee denied ever making the recommendations. In fact, they told MacDougall that they had never met to review the transfer requests of Tison and Greenawalt.[30] Only one committee member, Deputy Warden Joe Martinez, admitted making the recommendation to Cardwell, explaining defensively that he "wouldn't be afraid to do it again." There wasn't much else Martinez could say.[31]

"[The Transfer Committee] just rubber-stamped what Cardwell wanted," MacDougall concluded after his own investigation.[32] Cardwell had independently decided to make the transfers out of some sense of obligation to Tison and Greenawalt. The nature of that obligation wasn't exactly clear. Cardwell had instructed the committee to sign the recommendations.

There were just too many strange coincidences left unexplained.

It wasn't just one thing, it was a pattern of events. And it didn't appear to be random.

That's the way it seemed far away in Nevada and Texas and Nebraska as the grieving families of Gary Tison's and Randy Greenawalt's six victims tried to cope with the tragedies that had befallen them. Their losses were incalculable, and they wanted a more convincing explanation for how these men had escaped so easily from prison than either Harold Cardwell or Ellis MacDougall seemed willing to give. In Amarillo, James Judge's lawyer brother John sensed a cover-up. A friend recommended that he call attorney Frank Lewis in Phoenix to look into the possibility of a lawsuit against the state.

12

Chimney Rock:
August 9, 1978

At the same hour that James and Margene Judge were pulling on sweaters and windbreakers that chilly, bright last Wednesday morning of their lives, before leaving for Millions Reservoir, newspaper readers in Arizona sat over their morning coffee and read, for the second day, about the ghastly massacre of a young family in Quartzsite and the intensified manhunt for their killers. Outrage spilled across the editorial pages of newspapers around the state. The *Arizona Republic* was typical:

"Society Has Had It!" began the editorial. "[It] has reached its limit to endure the criminal justice system's coddling of the Tisons and Greenawalts of the world. . . . The criminal justice system has failed the public. It has stalled and derailed attempts to restore punishment to match crimes.

"The victors in this legal skirmish have been bloodthirsty criminals. The victims have been innocent, law-abiding men, women, and children who have been maimed for life, or lie almost forgotten in their graves."[1]

A few pages later, columnist Paul Dean described the bloody horror of a murder scene that "made tough investigators gag." Not even a Peckinpah film, he wrote, could match the "filthy, primeval insanity" of the heartless slaughter that brought "My Lai to a roadside near Quartzsite." "These men," he continued, "two escaped murderers and

Tison's sons, who are apparently up to their animal armpits in dad's crimes and possibly new revolting killings, may well have decided any public doubts concerning gas chamber justice and soft-touch penal systems."[2]

If Chimney Rock were in New Jersey instead of Colorado, it would probably be a national monument, crawling with camera-festooned sightseers. Out West it hardly gets more than an occasional passing snapshot, although it's hard to miss there, above the Shell Oil sign and the Chimney Rock Café. A column of rock at the top of a steep, brushy hill that would be called a mountain back East, the natural formation faintly resembles a chimney. U.S. Route 160 passes right by. If you're a vacationer traveling east, you've probably just seen the Grand Canyon only a day or two before, and you may have just driven through the spectacular monoliths and colors of Monument Valley or viewed the ruins at Mesa Verde. If you're headed west, you've just crossed over the snowcapped San Juan Mountains at Wolf Creek Pass and looked down deep into the verdant, stream-laced valley east of Pagosa Springs. So unless your bladder was aching for a rest room or you needed a cup of coffee to stay awake, you'd probably pass right by Chimney Rock without giving it a second glance. Now it marks the site of two brutal murders.

Just up the road from the café is an intersection, from which State Route 151 runs south following the Piedra River down a long valley that gradually widens and disappears into the open expanses of the Southern Ute Indian Reservation. Here the colors are burnt shades of brown, like Indian pottery. The land becomes arid quickly, and the tall pines become shorter and more stubbly with each mile, until they give way to the junipers and high desert scrub of the reservation.

About two miles down the road from the intersection, Cabison Canyon cuts back into the foothills. A graded dirt road follows the canyon along tiny Cabison Creek, trickling and gurgling unseen through the thick, dry underbrush of late summer. In August, the canyon gets hot by midday. Hunters know that it's good deer country, but a little too brushy and dry for elk.

Gary spotted the turnoff as he approached Chimney Rock. He snapped on the turn signal to let the boys, following behind, know what he was going to do. A few minutes later, the van turned left again on Cabison Creek Road and stopped near a line of mailboxes.

When the pickup pulled in behind, Gary got out and walked over while Randy remained inside the van with the Judges. "You guys wait right here," he said to his sons. Then, lowering his voice, "I have to take care of that couple."[3]

He climbed back into the van and drove off, following the road east around a curve and out of sight. It was just past noon. The air was still and dry.

The boys could hear the engine as it labored up a slight grade into the canyon. They waited silently in the bright sunlight, sometimes sitting, sometimes leaning up against the truck, knowing what was going to happen. They heard the van's engine stop in the distance. It seemed very quiet.

Less than two miles down the road, Gary had turned the van around so that it was heading back out of the canyon. When he turned off the ignition, it was still except for the melancholy din of cicadas droning in the pines on either side of the road.

He opened the door and eased himself to the ground. He was wearing army fatigues and held the .45 in his hand. First Margene and then James climbed out, blinking in the bright sunlight. They were both frightened but in control, pleading only that their lives be spared. Take the van if you want it, James said, just don't hurt us. Nodding toward the trees and brush on the north side of the road, Gary told Randy to take James there. Then he made Margene walk ahead of him in the opposite direction toward the creek. They walked about fifty yards through the trees and mottled midday sunlight, pushing deeper into the thick brush that grew along the creek. When they reached its banks, Gary told Margene to stop.

Randy forced James to walk a little farther off the other side of the road. The brush wasn't as thick away from the creek, and he didn't want to have to drag James's body out of sight. James walked as if he were in shock. They were about seventy-five yards from the road when Randy told him that was far enough and warned him not to turn around. Randy hesitated a moment, as if he were waiting for Gary to go first. Then he raised his .38 caliber pistol and shot James once in the back of the head. James was standing with his teeth clenched tightly when he died.[4]

Moments after the first shot, a second echoed through the canyon. Gary shot Margene once at the base of her skull. The .45-caliber bullet exploded through her head at the hairline and she toppled face down into a little pond that had formed in the creek behind a log that stretched across its width.[5]

Gary didn't try to move Margene's body far. There was too much blood. He rolled the body over against a tree that had fallen a few feet from the creek, then covered the exposed side with brush and as much grass and dirt as he could kick loose.

Randy scraped out a shallow grave and rolled James's body into it, face up. A little blood never bothered Randy. He was used to rummaging through the pockets of people he had shot. He twisted the gold wedding band from James Judge's finger before he covered the body with about six inches of loose dirt, leaves, and brush.[6] When he finished, he noticed the toes of James's running shoes were visible through the covering. The hell with it, he thought as he left. He was hot and sweaty and the brush made him itchy.

It was another very quiet ride after Chimney Rock. The van and the pickup headed west on the Navajo Trail across the southern edge of Colorado. In nine days, Donny, Ricky, and Ray Tison had watched, and heard, and had not interfered while their father and Randy killed six innocent people. At around one o'clock that afternoon, they stopped in the little town of Bayfield. They were getting low on cigarettes.

Martha Jane Sauer was working in the town's only store, the Shur Value Store, when Randy and two of the boys walked in. Randy was wearing blue jeans and a soiled T-shirt; he was dirty, and he smelled bad. They looked around the store for a few minutes, mumbling to one another occasionally, before picking up three cartons of Pall Malls. Martha Jane recalled that when she rang up the $13.47 for the cigarettes, one of the two younger men handed her a crisp hundred-dollar bill.[7] It was the gift F. H. Davis had pressed into his daughter's hand as he kissed her goodbye four days before.

At about three-thirty that afternoon, Donny Tison drove up to the service entrance of Bob Gabriel Chevrolet in Cortez, a small town in the southwestern corner of Colorado where it meets the borders of Utah, New Mexico, and Arizona. Dale Todeschi, the assistant service manager, walked over, clipboard in hand, and asked what needed to be done.

"I've been using my mother's pickup," Donny replied, "and it got torn up some in the mountains. It keeps jumping out of second gear, it's heating up on long pulls, and there's not much brake pedal left, either."

Bill Lucas, the service manager, who was standing nearby, came over and asked how soon he needed the truck. Donny replied that there was no rush on it.

"I'm going back into the mountains again," he said, "so I won't be needing it for another ten days."

He seemed nervous and anxious to leave as Lucas told him they would work up an estimate.

"Good," he said. "I'll check back with you later." As he was leaving, he hesitated. "Oh yeah," he said, "I can't spend more than fifteen hundred dollars for this." That was the last time they saw him.[8]

Did Donny intend to return to get the truck after it was fixed? Hardly. Once the fugitives had the van, they did not need the truck. The problem was what to do with it. Initially Gary wanted to abandon it as they had the Mazda. It was Donny who suggested that they leave it at a garage. That way, he reasoned, no one will find it and report it to the police as they would an abandoned vehicle. By the time the garage realized that no one was going to pick it up, he said, two or three weeks would have passed and they would be long gone. Gary thought it was a pretty good idea.[9]

While Donny was talking with Todeshi and Lucas, his companions sat in the van across the highway at the Sonic Drive-in, gulping down hamburgers, fries, milkshakes, and Cokes. They had been too busy to eat since leaving Pass Creek that morning, and everyone was famished. When he left the garage, Donny walked over and joined them. The van was a lucky break, Gary mumbled between swallows. They could never risk eating in public like this in the pickup. Right, Randy agreed through a mouthful of food, adding that maybe their luck was changing.

After the meal, they loaded up with bags of extra food for later that evening and drove back through town, turning north on State Route 145. The two-lane road winds up through the narrow Dolores River Valley and over Lizard Head Pass to Telluride. They were looking for a campsite, but there were a lot of campers at this time of year, and a public campground was just too risky. Now that they had the van, Gary needed some time to rethink their plans. They were looking for an isolated spot.

At Milepost 19, they turned right toward the river on a narrow dirt road. A faded NO TRESPASSING warning dangled loosely from what had been a gatepost. The van bounced and scraped over the deep ruts, pushing through the thick underbrush on either side until they broke out into a clearing by the river. There was a small house on the edge of the clearing next to some huge cottonwood trees, but from the broken door and windows, and waist-high weeds around it, they could tell it was empty. It was almost dusk, and they were a secluded three hundred yards from the main road. Gary decided it would be okay for the night.

Earlier in the day they had stopped at a rest area near the Mesa Verde National Monument and transferred all their belongings from the truck to the van. The van was now piled high with their clothing and equipment as well as the Judges'. The first order of business was to make more room. They sorted through the Judges' things, scattering whatever they didn't want in a wide semicircle around the van.

At about the same time the fugitives were pulling up to the abandoned house, a vacationing Arizona couple and their three-year-old son were eating dinner at a Mexican restaurant in Cortez. The restaurant was just down the street from Bob Gabriel Chevrolet. It was almost dark when they finished, and they were the last customers to leave. A waitress locked the door behind them. As they walked to their truck camper parked a short distance away, they noticed that their pickup was the only vehicle of any kind parked on the street, which also happens to be U.S. Route 160. It reminded them of the opening scene in Michael Crichton's novel *The Andromeda Strain,* in which two scientists discover all the inhabitants of a small desert town dead one night. They chuckled about the similarities as they drove down the empty street and turned north on Route 145 to look for a campsite along the Dolores River.

As every outdoorsman knows, you don't wait until dark to look for a campsite. The vacationers spent the next couple of hours on unfamiliar roads, unable to see very far in any direction, before they finally pulled off on a rough dirt road and, in frustration, parked. Thick underbrush pressed against the camper, making it almost impossible to walk around one side. They thought the road continued down to the river, but it was too rough, too dark, and they were too tired to find out. When they got out and walked to the rear of the truck to enter the camper, they could hear the river, but the underbrush was too thick to see water, even with a high-beam flashlight.

Two hours later they were still awake and very nervous. The stillness and blackness of the night seemed strange and, for some reason they didn't understand, dangerous. Periodically they flashed the light out into the darkness and anxiously eyed the fluttering shadows cast by its beam for some clue to their growing apprehension. Both had spent a good deal of time in the outdoors, so this wasn't a new experience, but there was something ominous about that particular night and place. Strange, they thought, that there were no crickets or other night sounds of the sort they expected to hear along a river, only the soft sound of the river itself.

"Do you think there's someone out there?" the woman whispered finally.

"I doubt it," he said. "We didn't see any other cars on the road when we were coming in, and there's been no one since."

"But what about down by the river? What if somebody was down there before we arrived? Do you think there could be someone —"

"I don't think so," he interrupted. "The road's too rough."

But that was precisely what he had been thinking. Without saying so directly, they were both, by that time, convinced that there was someone, or something, else — some malevolent force — out in the darkness near the river. They talked about leaving, but didn't know where to go. Then they admitted that they were both too afraid to get out of the camper and walk around to the cab of the truck. What if someone was right outside the door, maybe even listening as they talked? Finally, at the woman's insistence, the man got up and took a shotgun he hadn't fired in twenty-five years from a storage compartment. It wasn't even assembled. They were afraid to turn on the light, so he put it together in the dark and laid it on the floor beside them. He left it unloaded but placed two shells beneath his pillow.

After a fitful few hours of sleep, they awakened with the morning sunlight streaming through the window. Sleepy eyed, they drank instant coffee at the side of the truck and talked about what a strange night it had been. They left without taking the walk they had promised each other to take down to the river.

The following Sunday, two other campers walked down the same road to the clearing by the river. They were outraged by the mess someone had left: clothing, towels, a Coleman stove, two sleeping bags, camping and fishing equipment, and an expensive-looking set of luggage were scattered about the clearing, along with Sonic food and drink containers, an August 6 receipt from someplace called the Devil's Inkwell Campground in New Mexico, and a pair of coveralls that belonged to someone named Brian Lieske. Amarillo newspapers were blowing everywhere. "Hey, look at this," one of them said, stooping to the ground. "Two tickets to a Broncos-Cowboys game, and it's today." Something's funny here, they agreed. Everybody knows Texans are junking up Colorado with their trash, but unless this guy Brian Lieske represents a new breed of trasher, not even Texans throw this kind of stuff away. They decided to report their find to the sheriff.[10]

On Wednesday evening of the day her daughter was murdered, back in Borger, Texas, Jenelle Davis was waiting for the phone call Margene had promised to make. "By ten o'clock, Margene still hadn't called, and I was worried," she said later. "But I didn't want to make too much of it because F. H. was starting on graveyards [the midnight-to-eight shift at the refinery] the next night, and I didn't want to keep him up with me worrying."

But when she finally went to bed that night, Jenelle couldn't sleep. She kept thinking about her daughter and her own feelings five days earlier at the wedding reception, when Margene looked back smiling, "gave that funny little wave of hers," and was gone.[11]

13

Fate:
August 10–11, 1978

On Thursday morning, the day after he and Randy had killed James and Margene Judge, Gary Tison paced the campsite along the Dolores River, pondering his next move. Ever since Clovis, Gary had been turning an idea over in his head. After they had taken possession of the Judges' van, he announced it: now that they had a good, reliable vehicle, he said, they were going to backtrack into Arizona and head south for the Mexican border on the roads that Gary knew best. Once again that peculiar homing instinct was undermining his judgment. It had been twelve days since the escape, he said. Security had probably eased up along the Arizona border after everyone's attention had shifted to New Mexico. Casa Grande and the area south of there, he reasoned, would be the last place authorities would be looking now. It wasn't a bad guess.

Gary was familiar with the rugged, empty terrain between Casa Grande and the Mexican border, and he was confident that he could still deal with the Papago Indians and the Mexicans they might encounter along the way. He had smuggled guns and farm machinery into Mexico through that country. The *federales* at the border, he sneered, were a joke. If they could make it to the border, they could bribe their way across. Money talks real loud in Mexico, he said. They don't give a damn about American laws. An inmate friend, convicted drug dealer Arden Lee Smith, had a *rancho* near Caborca, only an

hour or so from the border. If we can get across that border, he
said, we can hide out there as long as we want.

The van was their hole card. But before he played it, he wanted
to make one last effort to get an airplane. Even though he was familiar
with the roads along that part of the border, flying over would still
be a hell of a lot quicker, easier, and safer, he said. His double-crossing
brother was out — and he intended to kill him for what he did at
Clovis, he said, if he ever got the chance — but Don Englund, his
sister Martha's husband, had a pilot's license and access to cropduster
planes, and possibly others, on the large cotton farm he managed
about twenty miles northwest of Casa Grande. Gary knew a cropduster
plane could only carry one passenger, at most, and their range was
limited, but there was only one passenger he was much worried about.

Gary didn't know his sister's husband very well. He had been in
prison practically the whole time they had been married, and Englund
had had no great desire to get acquainted with his notorious brother-
in-law. But maybe, Gary thought, Don would be willing to help them
for Martha's sake. At least it was worth a phone call. What Gary
either didn't know, or had decided to ignore, was that Dorothy had
already approached Englund about helping them four days before,
and he had already refused.

The other possible source of help was Bill Anthony, an inmate on
parole who had been one of Tison's contacts outside the prison. Anthony had a pilot's license, Gary said, and maybe he could help them
out.[1] Even if Englund wouldn't fly them all out himself, maybe he
could still get them an airplane. Even a single-seat cropduster would
be big enough for him to squeeze into, and with Anthony at the
controls, *he* — if not the others — could make it to Mexico. Anthony
could set that sonofabitch down right on that dirt strip at Smitty's
ranch.

Before the escape, Gary had considered several isolated landing
strips on the Papago Reservation, south of Casa Grande. From any
one of them, it would be a short, easy hop across the border. If
they couldn't get a plane and someone to fly it, Gary said, then they
would go ahead with the plan to make a nighttime run for the border
in the van. But whatever they did, they had to do it quick, before
someone reported that van missing. The pressure was intense. It
was a desperate gamble.

At about eleven o'clock on Thursday morning, they left their campsite on the Dolores River. They timed their departure to arrive in the Casa Grande area after dark. They drove south on U.S. Route 666 across the northeastern corner of the Navajo Reservation, through Gallup, and out over the windy tableland of the Zuñi Reservation before turning west into the early afternoon sun, and Arizona. They drove cautiously through St. Johns — the second time they had driven through Tom Brawley's hometown — and continued west through Concho to Show Low. At Show Low they took Route 260, which follows the cool, pine-forested curve of the Mogollon Rim west before it winds down a series of switchbacks over the rim's edge and descends now as Route 87 through Payson to the hot desert valley below.

John Chilson, Tom Connally, and Dave Garrels were having a few beers after work that afternoon in a Payson saloon. In fact, they had quite a few, and their mood quickly became festive. It was about five-thirty when they left the saloon and climbed into the battered pickup parked outside. They were driving south through a dusty construction zone on Route 87 when they noticed a van with Texas plates trying to pass them. The three cowboys, in good spirits and not wanting to miss out on a little fun with these dudes from "back East," waited until the van pulled alongside. "Watch this," Chilson said to his buddies as he snapped the ignition key off. When he snapped it back on seconds later there was a muffler-rattling explosion that sounded just like a gunshot as the truck backfired. With tears of laughter flooding their eyes, they watched the driver — the only person visible in the van — jump and duck convulsively from view as the van swerved away from them. "I mean, that poor bastard jumped like he really had been shot," Chilson said. It had been "a hell of a lucky day," they agreed a couple of days later, when they learned that it was a guy named Donald Tison who had ducked.[2]

A short time later that same Thursday evening, Donald Englund was talking with Ron Narcia and Quinnie Hernandez at the cotton farm outside of Casa Grande when the phone rang and Englund answered it. He didn't recognize the rasping voice at first and was stunned when Gary identified himself. He hadn't talked to his brother-in-law in years. As usual, Gary got right to the point. I need an airplane, he said, and I need it tonight. Can you get me one? Englund didn't know how to respond. He started to say that he had already explained to Dorothy that he wanted no part in the whole business, but then he decided not to. Gary sounded too tense, and he didn't want to make matters worse; he was well aware of his brother-in-law's violent reputation. He told Gary that the only planes he could get didn't have the fuel capacity to make it into Mexico and back. Gary continued to press him. Narcia and Hernandez said they could tell by the way Englund was talking that it was a "get-me-an-airplane-tonight-or-else" demand the caller was making, and Englund was taken totally off guard.[3]

While it is virtually certain that Englund would not have voluntarily provided, or flown, a plane for Gary under any circumstances, he managed to collect his wits in time to offer a convenient excuse. He told Gary that the problem was no longer the availability of an airplane, or its range and fuel capacity; the problem was that neither he, nor Martha, nor anyone else in the family could do anything to help him because the police had been watching their every move since the escape. Since last Sunday, he said, without mentioning the discovery of the Lyonses' bodies, the surveillance had increased. Tison cursed and slammed down the receiver. They would be heading for the border in the van, Gary said angrily to Randy and the boys, but on the way they were going to make one last stop in Casa Grande — to take care of some business. Everyone knew that he was talking about Joe. There was only one thing that was more important to Gary Tison than his freedom, and that was revenge.

At about eleven o'clock that night, several hours after Gary had called Donald Englund, Casa Grande police officer J. R. Pike was cruising north on Pinal Avenue when he noticed a silver-and-blue van, with out-of-state plates, traveling too fast in the opposite direction. Pike made a U-turn and followed it, clocking its speed at forty-five miles an hour in a thirty-five-mile-an-hour zone. He was about to snap on his siren when another call crackled over his radio.

Someone had reported a break-in at the Border Patrol Armory in Gila Bend, and an alert was being sent out to police in Maricopa, Yuma, and Pinal counties to be on the lookout for a small foreign car, painted gray or silver, that was reportedly seen leaving the area near the armory. The report went on to say that there was reason to believe that this might be the Tison gang. The Lyonses' repainted Mazda had not yet been found, and police assumed that the fugitives might still be traveling in it. Police also knew that back in 1961 Gary Tison had broken into the armory in Casa Grande and left with a trunkload of weapons he hoped to sell in Mexico. The locale of the break-in also fit with Tison's well-known pattern of returning home. It looked like the first solid lead police had had since the fiasco on the previous Sunday at Clovis. Orders were issued immediately to set up roadblocks on all roads leading south from Gila Bend toward the Mexican border.

Dave Harrington was at home watching television when Captain Minor Stephens, the staff duty officer, called and gave him the report.

"Everybody in law enforcement, in this area, said all along that Gary would be caught somewhere around Casa Grande," Harrington explained later. "Every time he's escaped, he always showed up in Casa Grande, regardless of what he'd done. It wouldn't make sense; seems like he just couldn't help coming home. And every time he did, we'd be waiting on him. Funny, ol' Gary was just like a boomerang — kept repeating the same mistakes. And some people say he was smart."[4]

That night it looked as though Gary Tison was, once again, going to live up to his reputation as a hometown boy. Three roadblocks were set up in the Pinal County area within half an hour. But though the police were correct in guessing that Tison was in the area, their reasons for thinking so were wrong. The Tisons and Greenawalt had been nowhere near the armory in Gila Bend, and the police had no idea whatsoever that, at that very moment, the fugitives were in Casa Grande, right under their noses. A short time after the patrolman noticed the van with Texas plates, a police informant saw it drive up the road to Joe Tyson's house. It didn't remain there long.[5] Fortunately no one was home, or Joe Tyson would surely have been added to the growing list of his brother's victims.

When Dave Harrington arrived at the roadblock at the intersection of Battaglia and Chuichu Roads, a few miles south of Casa Grande, he found six fellow officers already in position. It was close to midnight.

At about two-thirty on Friday morning, J. R. Pike was still cruising the streets of Casa Grande, keeping an eye out for the silver-colored compact, when he again noticed the Ford van with the Texas plates that he had nearly ticketed some three hours before. This time it was driving west on Florence Boulevard, the main road through town. He watched as it turned left on Florence Street and headed south toward the outskirts of town. Strange, he thought, that that van is still cruising around town. Must be some young kids. But with out-

of-state plates? For a moment he thought about stopping it for a
routine check, but then decided not to. For what? he thought. Some
kids out late doing forty-five in a thirty-five zone? It just wasn't worth
the time, especially with everything else that was happening that night.
An hour or so later he heard a report that the occupants of a van
matching that description had tried to shoot their way through two
roadblocks south of town. That's when he realized that his decision
to ignore the van had undoubtedly saved his life.[6] The Tison gang
had spent at least three or four hours cruising in and around Casa
Grande without being spotted.

Chuichu Road is the only paved road that runs south through the
Papago Indian Reservation. It's a straight shot sixty lonely miles down
the desolate Santa Rosa Valley to Covered Wells. Then it gets tricky.
Any number of dirt roads trail off from it. There aren't any signs,
and not all those rutted tracks lead to the border, but Pinal County
authorities knew that Gary Tison knew which ones did. Chuichu Road
seemed like a good place for a roadblock.[7] But a couple of hours
had passed now, and everything was quiet. The sheriff's deputies
manning the roadblock were getting bored and thinking about all
the sleep they were losing while they stopped a few boozy Papagos
on their way back home.

Unknown to the officers of Pinal County, the state alert had been
called off shortly before midnight and all roadblocks ordered lifted.
Investigators at the scene in Gila Bend had concluded the alleged
burglary attempt at the armory was a false report. There might have
been a prowler, they said, but there was no evidence of an attempted
break-in. It was just another of the scores of supposed sightings that
were being called in to police daily since the escape, a good number
of them by cranks.

For some reason, Pinal County didn't get the word, and as a result
their roadblocks remained in place. The decision to set up the roadblocks had been purely fortuitous, based on erroneous information;
they remained in place as long as they did only because of a breakdown
in communications. As someone said later, it was a couple of lucky
damn mistakes.[8]

At about 2:00 A.M. — some two hours after the roadblocks were
to have been lifted — Captain Minor Stephens sent word that he
wanted a second roadblock set up about seven miles south of the

first on Chuichu Road, at the intersection of Cockleburr Road, just south of where the road cuts through a pass in the low, jagged peaks of the Tot Momoli Mountains. Stephens had a hunch that if the fugitives were heading south as everyone assumed, they might come along Cockleburr Road to connect with Chuichu in order to by-pass Casa Grande. Dave Harrington, Perry Holmes, and Tom Scott were given the assignment and left to man the second roadblock, each driving a Sheriff's Department pickup truck. At two-thirty or so, Dave Warren, who had just joined the Sheriff's Department, arrived with sandwiches and hot coffee. It looked like a long night ahead.

Sergeant Armando Valenzuela and deputies Wade Williams, Steve Greb, and Billy Jewel were sitting in two of the three patrol vehicles parked at the first roadblock, sipping the coffee Dave Warren had just dropped off, when they noticed headlights turn onto Chuichu from a dirt road a mile or so to the north. As the headlights drew closer, the four men put down their coffee and routinely took up positions on either side of the road. Five minutes before, a Papago family had been stopped, and Valenzuela had made the routine call to the second roadblock to describe the car that was on its way. They assumed the approaching vehicle was probably more Indians on their way home. When it was about five hundred yards away, they switched on their headlights and flashers and noticed the glow of the van's brake lights as it hesitated momentarily. Then it continued slowly toward them with its high beams on.

Sergeant Valenzuela walked toward the open space at the center of the road between the two patrol cars and a station wagon, as the van, its engine idling, coasted slowly toward him. He was about six feet away and the thought had just started to run through his mind that this one might be different — A van? Papagos drive pickup trucks, not vans. And Texas plates? — when shots exploded from the passenger window. The van suddenly lurched forward, its tires squealing on the asphalt, as it broke through the roadblock. Two of the bullets narrowly missed Valenzuela, tearing holes the size of golf balls in the left front fender of the station wagon about two feet from where he was standing. Lunging for cover, the four officers quickly returned the fire, but the van was already speeding out of range.

Valenzuela leaped backward and dropped to the ground before dashing for the station wagon. "The first thing that went through my mind was to get the hell out of the way," he said. "They took us completely by surprise. . . . We weren't sure what we had because we were looking for a Mazda."[9]

Valenzuela dove into the station wagon, slammed it into gear, and stomped the accelerator to the floor. Nothing happened. Thinking it had stalled, he grabbed the radio and alerted the officers at the second roadblock. As he sat there fuming with frustration, he suddenly noticed that, in the excitement, he hadn't turned on the ignition.

Wade Williams scrambled low to his patrol car and wheeled it around in a shower of gravel and dust as Steve Greb swung in on the other side. Billy Jewel was already in pursuit in another car by the time the squealing wheels of Williams's car caught the pavement and fishtailed after him. Greb was fumbling big double .00 buckshot shells into the .12-gauge semiautomatic shotgun he held between his knees while Williams kept his eyes on the flickering tail lights ahead. A couple of miles down the road, Williams and Greb realized that Jewel was alone and unable to return the gunfire they could see flashing from the rear of the van. His car was also blocking Greb's line of fire. "I'm going to pass him," Williams said as he accelerated and moved to the left side of the narrow road. Jewel slowed enough to let them pass. Greb leaned out the side window, took aim with the shotgun, and opened fire, pointing now more than aiming at the taillights ahead as Williams slowly pulled within range.

"That van must have been hitting ninety-five on the straightaways," Williams said. "I couldn't take my eyes off the road long enough to look at the speedometer, but I could tell the way my car was vibrating and handling that they had to be moving somewhere near that speed. We'd closed to about fifty yards, I guess, when I realized those muzzle flashes up ahead were starting to bother me a little. We're programmed to do certain things, but I hadn't been paying too much attention to the muzzle flashes until then. I mean, I knew what they were and what they *could* mean, but it hadn't sunk in. And then after a while and we're still on their tail and we keep seeing these flashes and then your brain starts thinking and then it started dawning on me that every time I saw a flash out of the back of that van, I'd blink my eyes, waiting for that bullet to come smashing through that windshield. You have training on how to react and all that in those kind of situations, but those flashes really made me start thinking that a bullet comes awful fast, but if I can blink my eyes and open them again

. . . Well, I said to myself, 'Boy, if you can keep doing that, then you got it made.' "[10]

The three men at the second roadblock had finished their sandwiches and were still drinking coffee and talking with Dave Warren when an excited voice from the police radio broke into the conversation. A van had just shot its way through the first roadblock, Armando Valenzuela stammered, and it was speeding south on Chuichu toward them.

Styrofoam coffee cups and cigarettes were tossed into the air. The four officers rushed to move the two vehicles from their position on Cockleburr Road across the intersection to Chuichu. Warren watched as Holmes waved Tom Scott's truck into position diagonally across the southbound lane. "We have to leave room for that car with the Papagoes to get through," Dave Harrington yelled as he parked his Ford pickup in the northbound lane just far enough from the other truck to permit a car to pass through. "Unless they turned off," he said, "we can't have those Indians in the way and getting hurt when that van gets here. We've got to wave them right through, and fast." Both vehicles faced north with headlights on and dome lights flashing.

Conversation ended as each man picked up a rifle: Scott, a .45-caliber semiautomatic; Holmes, a .223 Ruger Mini-14 and a clip of copper-jacketed bullets; and Harrington, a .308 Winchester. A shaken Dave Warren, getting more than he bargained for in delivering coffee and sandwiches, was handed a 30/30 Winchester as they scrambled to take up positions among the rocks and brush on a gentle slope about seventy-five feet from the roadblock, just beyond the glow of the domelights. They had to stay close enough to the road so that someone could race down to wave the car through if it got there before the van. Then they waited.[11]

The situation inside the speeding van was chaotic. The fugitives were all stunned by the unexpected sight of the roadblock. Chuichu Road, pitch dark except for the soft glow of Casa Grande behind them on the horizon, should have been deserted at this hour. Randy was sitting in the front passenger seat and Gary, Ricky, and Ray were in the back resting when Donny, who was driving, said, "There's some cars parked along the road up ahead."

"What? Cropdusters?" Gary asked as he sat up in the rear just as headlights and domelights flashed on, illuminating the road five hundred yards in front of them.

"Oh, Christ," Donny said softly, as he hit the brakes briefly, "it's a roadblock."

"Cops?" Gary asked in disbelief. He and the others in the back struggled to their knees and leaned forward to look. "How the fuck did they know?" he said. "How in the fuck did they know?" It was Gary's nightmare.

"Goddammit to motherfucking hell," he raged over and over again before he got control of himself. "Okay, okay, do what I tell you," he snapped to Donny. "Just slow down like nothing's wrong so they think we're going to stop, until we get real close, then be ready to floor it when I tell you."

"Dad, it's no use," Donny protested. "We can't make it."

"God damn you, do what I say," he spat into Donny's ear as he positioned himself, pistol in hand, behind the driver's seat.

"Randy, be ready on that side," he said to Greenawalt, who was sitting in the front passenger seat, a .357 Magnum at the ready just beneath the side window.

"I'm going to kill that motherfucker, just watch," Greenawalt said. He cranked back the hammer on his .357 as a police officer stepped out from between the cars.

"Dad, look up there," Donny said. As they drew closer, he could see Valenzuela standing by the patrol car, waiting for them to stop as other officers looked on from either side. "Look, will you? It's no use trying to —"

"God damn you, you do what I say," Gary repeated, his voice choking with rage. Then, as they slowed almost to a stop and Valenzuela took a step toward them, Gary said, "Okay, run it!" When Donny hesitated, Gary screamed, "Hit it, God damn you!" just as Randy's pistol exploded out the side window.

"Donny didn't want to do it," Ray explained later, "and Dad yelled, 'Hit it' again, and . . . well . . . he did."[12]

Randy fired three shots at Valenzuela as the van squeezed between the two parked patrol vehicles. As Donny accelerated down the road, Gary yelled for Randy to move to the back with him. He picked up a rifle, smashed the glass out of one of the rear windows, and began firing. There was no return fire until a second patrol car passed the first; a few seconds later, they saw a muzzle flash as a slug from

Steve Greb's .12 gauge shattered the other rear window. Ray crawled out of their way and stretched out on the floor, covering his head as the two killers began firing at the police car moving closer behind them and now returning their fire. Ricky crawled to the front and crouched down in the passenger seat next to Donny as they sped south. Gary's rifle jammed; cursing, he threw it down and pulled the Colt .45 he always carried from his belt and quickly emptied a clip at the headlights behind. Slugs from Greb's shotgun hit the rear of the van three more times. Despite the loud thuds, they were beyond effective range; the marble-sized slugs, devastating at close range, only dented the doors. The noise inside the van was deafening.

Donny had thought all along it was going to end like this, and it was all coming down now. It would have been easy for him to roll out of the van at the first roadblock, but he couldn't. He had said once that he never wanted to end up like his dad; now it must have seemed certain that he would, as he pressed down on the accelerator and tried to concentrate on the road ahead.

The night was an astronomer's dream, clear with no moon, and the stars were spectacular. But Dave Harrington, Tom Scott, Perry Holmes, and Dave Warren weren't aware of the stars as they waited silently at the second roadblock. Their eyes were fixed on White Horse Pass, a slash in the rocky slopes of the Tot Momoli Mountains, backlit by the distant lights of Casa Grande. The pass lay at the end of less than a mile of straight road to the north.

They heard the chase before they saw it: the approaching wail of the sirens over the high-pitched whine of engines straining to capacity, and then the squeal of tires barely adhering to the asphalt surface as they rounded the curves leading up the mountain. Then, just as the rocks on the east side of the pass lit up in the glow of rushing light, they heard the gunfire, seconds before two headlights appeared rounding the curve and now racing toward them. When Wade Williams crossed the pass seconds later, he saw the van accelerating down the long straight slope toward the flashing lights marking the roadblock ahead. He dropped back to avoid the fusillade of bullets about to meet it.

At the roadblock, none of the officers spoke or took their eyes from the rapidly approaching headlights as they raised their rifles. "It's a van all right," someone said. Dave Harrington sighed. "Yep, and it's not going to stop." He spoke the words softly, as if to himself. When the van was about two hundred yards away, he took a deep breath and said, "Okay, open up."[13]

It was rapid fire. They were reloading almost before the first hot clips hit the ground. No one sat or knelt behind cover; they just stood there in the open, firing at the windshield from an upright position, as they would at a carnival shooting gallery, concealed only by the blackness of the night. Except for the muzzle flashes of other weapons, the sights at the end of their barrels would have been impossible to see in the darkness.

Dave Harrington was squeezing off rounds as fast as he could when he suddenly realized there was no recoil. My God, he thought, it's empty already. He fumbled a clip and tried to reload without taking his eyes off the van, but the clip wouldn't go, and he finally slammed it, jamming the rifle. Later he saw that he had managed to force the .303 clip in backward, a virtually impossible feat under ordinary circumstances. He had wedged it in with such force that it took a gunsmith to pry it out.

The others were still firing, and Harrington was struggling frantically to dislodge the clip, when the van slowed slightly as it approached the narrow corridor between the two trucks. Then it swerved as the driver adjusted. The van passed through without scraping either truck, in spite of the bullets Harrington and the others could now hear smacking into the metal and glass. But just as it cleared the roadblock and began to accelerate, it suddenly lost momentum, as if the driver had lifted his foot from the accelerator. Then it began to veer slowly to the right, and went off the road into a broad, gently sloping drainage ditch, in a shower of gravel and dust. The driverless van continued forward a short distance, guided by the sloping sides of the ditch, before the right tire hit a rock outcropping. It twisted around sharply, nearly upsetting, as it slid sideways through the gravel and brush until it struck a palo verde tree and spun completely around, its single headlight now pointing back toward the roadblock. It rocked almost over on its side before slamming back down to an upright position. The headlight flashed and went out in a swirling cloud of dust a quarter mile beyond the roadblock.

Seconds later, Wade Williams steered his car through the roadblock, continuing another three hundred yards before skidding sideways to a quick stop, his headlights directed toward the wrecked van shrouded in dust. Williams and Greb immediately took up positions behind their opened doors. Billy Jewel screeched to a stop beside them, his headlights illuminating the desert behind the van. The deputies strained their eyes and ears for some sign of the van's occupants. Except for the hiss of steam billowing up beneath it, and the shadows fluttering across it from the rotating domelights, the van was still and quiet.[14]

When the van came over the pass and Donny and Ricky saw more lights flashing ahead, Ricky said, they knew it was all over. They yelled back to tell their dad, who was still firing at the headlights behind. "Run it, goddammit," was the shrill reply.

Ricky knelt down on the floor between the passenger seat and the dashboard and covered his head with his hands, trying to stop the roaring in his ears as they sped toward the lights. Then the bullets began coming from the front — or was it the side?

They could hear their father's cursing and heavy breathing, now at their necks, as he crouched behind and between the two front seats, ignoring the cars behind and preparing to fire out the passenger window when they got to the roadblock. At first came the faint but deadly hissing sound of the misses; they heard and felt the impact of the hits. Ricky looked up from the floor at Donny and saw him hunched low over the wheel, as if he was trying to draw his head into his shoulders. Donny couldn't have seen beyond the edges of the road — the lights in front of him were too bright — but he may have guessed the drainage ditches at the sides were too deep, and there were too many big rocks and saguaros beyond to risk trying to go around. All he could do was hold to the broken yellow centerline as it flashed beneath him. He was squinting, trying to gauge the width of the blurred opening between the dazzling lights. A bullet smacked like a loud handclap as it glanced off the curve of the windshield, cracking the glass to his left before whining off into the darkness. He ducked again as another hit at an angle, shattering the glass directly in front of him. Clinging tightly to the steering wheel, he forced himself to lean forward toward the windshield. Straining to see through its lethal glittering surface and the sweat burning his eyes, trying not to flinch or blink and afraid to lift a hand from the wheel, he steered into the deadly gauntlet of fire between the two trucks. Bullets were now hitting like hailstones; it seemed as though the van was being dragged backward by their force. Another bullet tore through the right front door post; another ripped through the bottom of the right front door, miraculously missing Ricky, pressed against the floor, as the van somehow broke clear of the roadblock.[15]

Then there was a loud metallic ring and a frightening whine. A copper-jacketed bullet had hit the top of the vent on the passenger window and ricocheted inside. Donny never heard it. His neck snapped back as the bullet exploded through the right side of his head, tearing a gaping wound from his hairline back behind his ear. Its force lifted him from the seat and slammed him against the door frame. The impact knocked him back upright again, momentarily, before he fell forward. "I looked up," Ricky said later, "and I seen Donny flopping on the steering wheel." Then Donny toppled slowly sideways toward him. Blood and brain tissue splattered the interior and ran down the steering column; large crimson splotches marked every spot his head hit as it bounced loosely from one object to another, while the driverless van slid sideways down the drainage ditch. When the van finally stopped, Donny lay unconscious and dying, his arms draped limply over his younger brother's back as Ricky crouched on the floor. His head looked as though someone had hit him with an ax, then twisted it out.

As soon as the van rocked to a halt, while the air was still too thick with dust for the patrol cars' headlights to penetrate, Gary frantically climbed over Ray, who was lying on the floor in the back, and shoved Randy aside to slide the side door open. "Ev'ry man for hisself," he rasped over his shoulder as he leaped out and fled into the night. No one remembers him even looking at Donny.

Ricky tried to ease himself out from under his brother's bleeding, convulsing body as gently as he could. Then he pushed and rolled him up onto the seat so he was lying on his chest with his head turned sideways. It was hard to do; Donny was heavy and limp. There was a groan. "Don?" Ricky asked as he leaned down close, but all he could hear was labored breathing. "Help me," Ricky said. Ray leaned over and helped straighten his oldest brother's legs. They looked at each other and then at their brother for a split second, before scrambling out the side door behind Randy, who was already running into the desert.

Greenawalt was about twenty-five yards from the van when Williams and Greb saw him emerging from the dust into the clearer air. Greb quickly slid his shotgun across the doorframe, took aim, and fired. Greenawalt dropped and lay motionless on the ground. Greb thought he had a hit.

A few minutes later, with Greb providing cover, Wade Williams cautiously approached the van from its dark side, away from the headlights of the patrol cars. He opened the door on the driver's side and saw a body lying face down on the passenger seat, its legs stretched out beneath the steering wheel. He could tell from the irregular breathing and muscle spasms that the man was unconscious. After hesitating a moment, he leaned in and flashed his light into the back of the van and saw that it was empty except for the debris strewn everywhere. He crawled in, pulled the man's arms behind his back, and handcuffed him before checking his vital signs. There was a moan. The man's pulse was fluttering and his breathing rattled. Then Williams noticed the blood puddling on the floor beneath the man's head. Williams slipped a wallet from the man's hip pocket and turned to go back to the car. He was startled when another car pulled up and stopped beside him. It was a deputy from the Papago Reservation. He had been driving north on a routine patrol when he came upon the commotion at the roadblock.[16]

"Here," Williams said, handing him the wallet, "run this up to the roadblock and give it to the officers there. Tell them we got one shot, laying in the van with a real major headache. The others are gone. Turn your lights off. There's been a lot of shooting and they're still out there somewhere."[17]

Harrington, Jewel, Scott, and Warren had moved from their position on the hillside and were down at the roadblock when the Papago deputy pulled alongside and handed Harrington the wallet. With his hand cupped over a flashlight, Harrington pulled out the driver's license. "I'll be damned," he whispered. "Will you look at this? It's Donald Tison."

Until that moment, the police had no idea who was in the van. Although the roadblock had been set up with the Tisons and Greenawalt in mind, the police were still looking for a gray Mazda with Arizona plates — not a Ford van from Texas. When Harrington radioed the news to the three officers covering the van, they were astonished.[18]

With the knowledge that it was the Tison gang out there in the darkness, Dave Harrington ordered all officers on the scene to hold their positions and turn out all lights until a helicopter arrived with searchlights. Only the headlights trained on the van and the motionless figure lying beyond in the desert were left on. Headlights made easy targets and there was little doubt about how Gary would choose to end this. They knew he was armed, and no one had to remind them that he was extremely dangerous, or that there was little likelihood that he would be taken alive, or that he would try to take as many of them with him as he could.

A steady stream of patrol cars began arriving in response to the calls for assistance that went out following the identification of Donald Tison. A half hour later, a Department of Public Safety helicopter thumped into view and was immediately instructed to direct its powerful searchlight on the motionless body Steve Greb had presumably shot. When it did, two more figures could be seen nearby, lying face down on the ground. Ray and Ricky, like Greenawalt, had dropped to the ground, frightened but unharmed, when Greb fired.[19]

One by one the three fugitives were ordered to stand, leaving their weapons on the ground. They stood there, hands raised, heads bowed against the bright lights, as the helicopter blades thumped overhead, encircling them in swirling clouds of dust. One of its lights beamed directly down on them; the other moved in slow methodical arcs over the terrain beyond, searching for Gary.

The three captives offered no resistance. None of them had been hit; they were just scared. Randy was lying on an army field jacket, its pockets bulging with ammunition for the .264 Winchester rifle and .357 Magnum pistol he had beside him and had chosen not to use. The three were quickly handcuffed, and the helicopter was signaled to turn off its light. Officers were afraid Gary might fire on them if they left it on. In the covering darkness, the captives were hurried back to the relative security of the vehicles at the roadblock while the helicopter banked away to resume its search for Gary. There, surrounded by tense deputies, the three were stripped naked and searched.

In addition to Randy's guns, deputies found a .38-caliber Smith and Wesson in the shoulder holster Ray wore beneath his shirt. Ricky was unarmed; he had lost his .45-caliber pistol in the confusion. Their clothes were marked and placed in plastic bags as evidence.

After they were searched, each of the captives was taken to a separate pickup. They were made to lie on their backs in the metal truckbeds and their wrists and ankles were shackled. Nearly all the police officers who flooded into the area walked over to take a look at the three nude captives lying in the pickups. Somehow the humiliation seemed appropriate. Finally it made someone uncomfortable, and each was covered with a blanket.

In the manner of men familiar with danger, and expecting a fight, the lawmen displayed a good bit of contempt. After Quartzsite, the soft answers and good manners of these three frightened men were irritating. It was hard to imagine, but, in a way, Wade Williams said later, they seemed even more despicable than Gary. He sure as hell wouldn't give up like that — you could count on it. Everyone knew that he was one mean, twisted-up, sadistic sonofabitch; but he was no coward. As far as anyone knew, the only thing Gary Tison had ever been afraid of was getting caught. And now he was out there somewhere in the blackness with a gun, watching them.

14

Ordeals:
August 11, 1978

Jenelle Davis was at work at her beauty shop on Friday morning, August 11, when Jim Judge, James's father, called from Amarillo.

"There were three ladies in the shop and I was just combing out Bertha Eller's hair when he called," Jenelle later remembered. "He was wanting to know where F. H. was. I said he was at home asleep because he had just started graveyards. And then I said, 'Jim, is there something wrong?' And he said, 'Well I'd rather talk to F. H.'" And I said, "No, you tell me right now 'cause something's wrong, isn't there? Where's the kids? Have you heard from them?' And he said, 'Yes, and it's not going to be good news for you, Jenelle.' 'Well,' I said, 'You go ahead and tell me, Jim. I can take it better than anybody.' Then he said, 'They found the kids' van early this morning in Arizona, and they don't know where the kids are."[1]

Jenelle Davis swallowed hard and said she would tell F. H. She felt sick to her stomach.

"It was the same feeling I had when I saw her leave," she said. "It was almost like I knew what Jim was going to say before he told me."

A few minutes later, when F. H. brought her lunch down to the beauty shop, as he always did when he was home, graveyards or not, she told him and closed the shop. They went home and called their pastor at the First Baptist Church and asked him to tell others at the church to please pray for Margene's and James's safety. Then they got down on their knees and prayed. At about three-thirty that afternoon, an FBI agent from Amarillo came to the house and asked for recent photographs and a description of Margene. The wedding photographs had just arrived from the photographer, and they gave him one of Margene alone, formally posed and smiling over her bouquet, and another of her and James in the van, about to leave on their honeymoon.

Thursday, the day before Arizona authorities called his father with the bad news, John Judge left his law offices in Amarillo at noon and, with his girlfriend, headed for Denver and what they hoped would be a long weekend of fun. Late that afternoon they checked into a motel in Trinidad, Colorado, where they whiled away an hour or two before calling the friends they planned to meet there that evening. John, especially, had been looking forward to this trip. He had been working hard and was overdue for some fun and relaxation. On Saturday, John and his friend were to meet his brother and Margene in Denver. The two couples would have dinner at the Brown Palace or some other fancy restaurant, then spend the night on the town John had promised them before they were married. On Sunday they were all going to see the Cowboys play the Broncos at Mile High Stadium. Weeks before, Margene, an avid Dallas fan, had gotten four seats just twenty rows up on the fifty-yard line. When John Judge tumbled into bed after midnight on Thursday, he was a happy man. Those good feelings ended with a phone call early the next morning.

John was fast asleep and a little hung over when the phone rang at seven. Who the hell could be calling me here? he thought as he reached across his sleeping companion, groping for the phone. The drapes were drawn, and it seemed like the middle of the night. "Hello," he mumbled into the receiver.

"John? Is that you?" It was his father, and the old feelings of dread and guilt flooded into his stomach, as vivid as they had been when, as a child, he'd been caught in some transgression. How did he know where to find me? John wondered. Jim Judge was a religious man, and he didn't approve of unmarried couples taking overnight trips together. His two sons' persistence in doing so was a continuing source of distress to him and their mother.

Before his son could say more than "Yes, sir," he said, "John, they found your brother's van last night down in Arizona. It was being operated by some escaped convicts. Nobody knows where your brother or Margene is. Have you heard from them? They were supposed to leave South Fork yesterday."

"Wait, Dad, slow down," John said, trying to clear his head and wanting to make sure he heard what he thought he had heard. "You say some convicts had their van in Arizona?"

"That's what they told us just a little while ago," his father replied, and then repeated what he had just said.

"No, I haven't heard from them," John answered, "but I wasn't expecting to until tonight in Denver. They were supposed to meet us at the motel there."

"Oh," his father said, "then you haven't heard from them at all? That's too bad. I was hoping maybe you had . . . John, your mother and I are worried."

"So am I. What do you think I ought to do?"

"I don't know what to do," his father said. "I just don't know what to do but pray. Well, I better not keep this line tied up in case there's someone trying to reach us."

John put down the phone and walked into the bathroom, ignoring his companion's questions. "James has gotten himself into another mess," was all he said. What is it with that guy? he thought angrily as he stood over the commode. Seems like all my life he's been getting himself into one kind of trouble or another. And then his eyes started to burn.

"It was the beginning of the worst weekend of my life," John said. "After sitting around in that damned depressing motel room and stewing for a couple of hours, trying to figure out what to do, we decided to forget Denver and drive over to South Fork to help look for them. It was awful. I felt so helpless. The police were doing all they could, but there were few clues as to where they might be. The police figured that they had probably been abducted on Tuesday night at the phone booth there by the motel, and that meant they could be anywhere between South Fork and southern Arizona where they found the van. Unless their abductors decided to talk, it looked pretty hopeless to me.

"The longer we stayed, the more frustrated and angry I became. I knew they were dead and I was just hoping they'd be able to find their bodies. Oh, there was some talk — you know, my folks and the Davises, and other well-meaning folks trying to make you feel better — that maybe they escaped and they'll find them walking down out of the mountains. Well, I didn't say anything, but, hell, I heard who was in that van when it wrecked — I mean, their van was being driven some five hundred miles off course by convicted murderers. Once I knew that, it just seemed logical to me that my brother and Margene were dead. So I spent that awful weekend there, and a long time after that, just trying not to think about how they might've died, and hoping they'd be able to find the bodies."[2]

The morning sun was bright and well above majestic Picacho Peak before an ambulance and paramedics were permitted into the tightly secured area of desert surrounding the second roadblock. The decision to keep them out, when there was a wounded man who desperately needed medical attention, created some controversy. Pinal County Sheriff Frank Reyes explained that all "civilians," including the paramedics, were kept out until daylight because the area surrounding the roadblock was considered too dangerous. Gary Tison was out there — a cold-blooded killer, very frustrated, very angry, and presumably well armed; the risk was simply too great, Reyes said. While the paramedics waited a half mile away, Donald Tison died. "He wouldn't have lived anyway," one lawman said. "Did you take a look at his head?" When the paramedics arrived, they agreed; there was little anyone could have done for Donald Tison. A reporter asked later if they would have done the same thing if a deputy had been wounded. There was no reply.

After Donald Tison was officially pronounced dead, his body was photographed from various angles as it lay in the van. When the passenger door was opened to photograph his position inside the van from that side, grisly crimson strands of brain tissue and congealed blood dangled over the splash rail. Officers lifted him out and stretched him on his back on the pavement for several frontal photographs to establish his identity. It reminded you of the way they used to prop up and photograph the dead bodies of outlaws you see in books about the Old West. Photographers from the Department of Public Safety and the Pinal County Sheriff's Department must have taken two or three rolls of particularly vivid color prints that morning. When they were done, they lifted the body onto a stretcher and rolled it into an ambulance. That's when someone noticed that Donny Tison was wearing a wedding band. It had belonged to James Judge.[3]

The wrecked van had stopped just short of a cluster of six small white crosses that had been staked into the ground. The Papago Indians, like the Mexicans, have a custom of using crosses to mark the places loved ones have died in traffic accidents. They're often adorned with plastic flowers. The crosses weren't noticed until the sun came up, and then they seemed an omen of what everyone feared: that Terri Jo Tyson and James and Margene Judge would not be found alive, and the toll of innocent victims would rise to six.

Ricky and Raymond Tison never saw their brother again after they left the van. At first, authorities thought Ricky had been shot. He had a lot of blood on the back of his neck and smeared across the upper portion of his body and arms; the back of his T-shirt and the legs of his jeans were also heavily stained. When he was being stripped, they asked if he was injured.

"I'm okay," he said quietly. "That's my brother's blood. He needs help."[4]

After sunrise the temperature began to climb and the three captives were moved from the pickups, still naked, and taken to separate patrol cars. Greenawalt was walked to a car, where Warden Harold Cardwell and Associate Warden Dwight Burd were waiting. Authorities had thought that Terri Jo Tyson might have been in the van with them. When it was discovered that she wasn't, the two immediate concerns were to determine her whereabouts, as well as that of the Judges, who had been identified through their Texas license plate number.

Harold Cardwell thought he knew Randy Greenawalt as well as anyone in law enforcement did. When he learned that Randy wasn't being very cooperative — he was upset about being stripped — Cardwell suggested that Randy might be willing to talk with him. He thought he might be able to get more information from him than the Pinal County detectives could. But Randy barely grunted "Hello, Warden" when he saw him. Greenawalt remained sullen, squeezed into the back seat of the patrol car, looking out the window, while he was read his Miranda rights. Before Cardwell and Burd got into the car — Cardwell in back, Burd up front — Cardwell asked for a blanket so Randy could be covered. Someone reached in and stretched a blanket across his lap, covering the thick folds of perspiring flesh that draped down over his genitals. He seemed relieved, and Cardwell thought that maybe he would loosen up.

After some small talk, the two prison officials began to ask questions about Terri Jo Tyson and the Judges. Burd said that Greenawalt was "polite and alert" when they first greeted him, but he refused to talk without an attorney.[5] They persisted anyway, with more small talk interspersed with questions, but it didn't work.

"Randy, where's the girl you took with you at Quartzsite?" Cardwell asked. "It would be a big help to us if you could tell us where she is."

"I told you, Warden, I can't talk about that."

"Well, what about the people who owned the van, Randy. Will you tell us where they are?"

"I'm not going to talk about anything until I see an attorney."

The questioning continued until about 7:00 A.M., when the two prison officials gave up.[6]

While Cardwell and Burd were questioning Greenawalt, Raymond Tison was being questioned nearby by two Pinal County detectives, Tom Solis and Ed Harville, and by Dan Martinez, a criminal investigator from the Papago Reservation. No familiarity existed to smooth the interrogation, and the three questioners made no attempt to establish some rapport as Cardwell and Burd had tried to do with Greenawalt; the questioning was direct and aggressive. Eighteen-year-old Raymond was scared and too unsophisticated in the ways of the law to demand an attorney. He responded to the questions with stammering and disconnected answers, denying any knowledge of either Terri Jo or the Judges. As with Greenawalt, the humiliation in the back of the truck had stirred some indignation.

"Okay, where's the girl at?" one detective asked.

"Don't know where the girl is."

"At one time, did you have the girl with you?"

"I don't know what you're talking about, man."

"Where did you get the van you were driving? Who does it belong to?"

"My old man drove the van over to the boonies where we were at . . . We been with the old man since a week ago last Sunday."

Then Ray interrupted the next question with one of his own. "Do you know how my brother Donny is?"

"Do you want to see him? He's not going nowhere, I can tell you that," Martinez sneered. "We can take you over to that van and you can have a real good look. Would you like that?"

Raymond looked right at Martinez for a split second and then dropped his eyes. He didn't reply.[7]

Solis and Harville gave Martinez a look and then resumed the questioning:

"How long have you had the van you were driving?"

"I don't know how long we had . . . Is today Thursday? No today is Friday already . . . We had the van since last Friday or Saturday . . . I know we were near Flagstaff, up in the woods."

"How many people were in the van?"

"I don't know how many people were in the van . . . Left Flagstaff about three days ago . . . Not sure, man . . . I can't tell you too much about the van . . . I don't know what town we've been to last . . ."

"Where are the people who own the van?"

"Don't know where the people of the van are, or the girl," he mumbled.[8]

Twenty minutes later, the same team interrogated Ricky. The questioning got rougher. Like his brother, Ricky chose to talk without an attorney, and the answers were the same. But when the suggestion was made that Terri Jo had been raped, Ricky got angry.

"The hell we did. We never raped no one. I ain't no sex maniac. We never did have any sixteen-year-old girl with us . . . I don't know anything about that girl you're telling me about. We were never in Quartzsite . . ."

After that, most of Ricky's remarks were less answers to questions than a rambling and disjointed account of the previous week.

"Where did you get that van you were using?"

"The old man got the van up north a couple days ago. He was by himself out in the pines. I don't know how he got it, but I guess he had it waiting for him. The old man was gone a few hours, and he just came back with the van."

"When did you leave Flagstaff?"

"In Flagstaff, we went into a store and got some supplies. From Flagstaff we came south to try to cross the border. We covered the truck in the trees — the green Ford in some trees — orchards, I guess."

"What about the white Lincoln Continental with New Mexico plates?"

"We did have a white car with New Mexico plates. No idea what happened to it. The whole idea of breaking the old man out of jail was ours — just pulling a spree. The old man was doing the shooting, then Greenawalt got in the back. Don got shot . . . fell over on me . . . The old man had the rifle at that time. I was on the floor with Ray . . ."[9]

Ricky wasn't making much sense, and his questioners weren't sure whether he was lying, confused, or both. It was clear to them, however, that he wasn't going to give them the information they wanted most about the Tyson girl and the couple from Texas. They ended the questioning after about thirty minutes. Then the three captives were loaded into separate cars for the trip to the Pinal County Jail in Florence.

The two brothers had not been specifically told that Donny was dead. They probably assumed that he was, but it wasn't until the three cars queued up behind the ambulance that was to lead the procession north on Chuichu Road that they knew for sure. It wouldn't have been waiting there if he wasn't. There was a lot to think about as they looked ahead at that ambulance and retraced the route back to the first roadblock and on toward Casa Grande. What if Donny had refused to run it, like he wanted to? What would Dad have done? Well, it probably wouldn't have mattered anyhow. Either way, somebody was going to die, that's for sure, because there was no way Dad would've just handed his gun over to a cop. Too bad it had to be Donny. He never did think it was a good idea, and now he's dead.

News of the capture and Gary Tison's escape spread quickly across the state and made the television network news that Friday morning. In Casa Grande, many people were arming themselves, afraid that Tison might appear anywhere. Sheriff Frank Reyes decided that it would be best for the three-car caravan carrying the two brothers and Greenawalt to by-pass town. It was a prudent decision. Animosity toward the Tisons was running high, and Reyes was worried that someone might follow through on one of numerous threats. After the prison break, some of the locals had kind of laughed about it, not because they liked the Tisons, but because they thought it was funny the way they duped those prison guards without firing a shot. Prison guards didn't enjoy great public esteem. But that jocular mood had changed after Quartzsite. So just outside Casa Grande, the caravan turned east on the by-pass and headed toward Florence, while the ambulance followed the interstate to the Coroner's Office in Phoenix.

Since there's only one funeral home in Casa Grande, it wasn't hard to guess where Donny Tison's body would be taken after the autopsy. The phone at the Cole and Maud Mortuary started to ring as soon as his death was reported on the news, the calls mostly profanity and threats.

"It was disturbing," a spokesman for the mortuary said. "A lot of people were calling and asking us how we could even think of burying the boy. They wanted us just to leave him rot."[10]

While the Tisons and Greenawalt were being questioned as to the whereabouts of Terri Jo Tyson, her parents, Jo Ann and Harry, were sitting in the Westside Chapel on Seventy-second Street in Omaha waiting for the funeral service to begin for Jo Ann's brother and his family. They had driven straight through to Omaha from Las Vegas and had arrived the day before. Word about the capture at the road-block had reached them just before they had left for the church, and Jo Ann wept when they learned that Terri Jo wasn't with the fugitives. Now they were praying for a miracle, but it seemed hopeless. Neither of them believed any longer that their daughter would be found alive. Jo Ann's grief that day was like a terrible physical presence that dried her throat and knotted her insides.

The chapel was packed and too warm. People crowded the pews and lined the vestibule and spilled outside into the hazy Nebraska sunshine. The service was delayed as people kept coming. Despair settled over the chapel and deepened with each somber note from the organ, until Jo Ann thought that she would scream.

Once it started, the service was dignified and mercifully brief. The pastor realized that there wasn't much he could say to lessen the grief felt for a family that had died so young and so unjustly; and somehow even the comforting words about the hope of eternal life seemed hollow. The caskets were carried out by marine pallbearers. There were only two caskets. Paul Chadwick, Donna's brother, didn't want his infant nephew to be buried alone. "I just couldn't stand the thought of them being apart . . . so I asked that he be buried in Donna's arms."[11]

It was a big funeral. The procession of cars from the chapel to the cemetery was over two miles long. At the gravesite, it took an hour before the crowd could assemble and the pastor begin. Once again, he was brief and simple. The families, overwhelmed by it all, sat numbly staring at the two coffins, one covered with flowers, the other with an American flag.

"That military ceremony really brought it home to me," Donna's brother said, taking a deep breath. "You know, the marines know how to bury their dead, and when that marine honor guard snapped to attention and fired a twenty-one-gun salute, it really got me. Then a bugler started to play taps, and then the tears welled up and I couldn't see . . . I guess that happened to a lot of people that day."[12]

Tom Brawley was in Phoenix, working with the Department of Public Safety in coordinating the manhunt, when he got word of the capture. Rather than go to the capture site, he left about nine-thirty the morning of August 11 for the Pinal County Jail in Florence, where the Tisons and Greenawalt had been taken. Brawley had been told that Terri Jo Tyson was not in the van, and he especially wanted to find out what they had done with her, to say nothing of James and Margene Judge. Greenawalt had refused to answer questions, he had been told, and the Tison boys denied any knowledge of the missing persons. Brawley thought that just maybe his old friend Randy would be willing to talk with him. He always had before.

"Tom Brawley. I'm working with DPS," he said, showing his identification to a deputy outside the jail. "I'm here to question the Tisons and Greenawalt." Brawley was taken first to the main compound, where Ricky and Ray were being held in separate cells at opposite ends of the jail. They were still naked.

Ray Tison was polite but uncooperative. He continued to deny any knowledge of what happened at Quartzsite, and even of being there. Brawley knew he was lying. He didn't have time to spare. It was important to find the three missing persons as quickly as possible.

Ricky's questioning started out the same way. He simply denied knowledge of anything. But Brawley tried a different approach and it got to him.

"You took that little girl with you and raped her, didn't you," Brawley suggested.

"The hell we did," Ricky blurted out.

"Come on, Ricky." Brawley sighed. "You're not going to deny that, are you?"

"No one was raped," he insisted angrily. "Hey, man, I ain't no sex maniac. I didn't rape no one."

"That's the only thing I was able to get out of Ricky," Brawley told a group of investigators after he completed the interview. "That's all he would say. But he got so upset when I suggested that to him, it's possible that maybe they didn't take her with them like we thought when she wasn't found. But where the hell is she?"

Then he asked where Greenawalt was being held.

"He says he's not going to talk with anyone without an attorney," the jailer said as he motioned toward a holding cell down the hallway from the main cell block.

"Hell, we don't have that much time," Brawley said. "It'll be another three or four hours before they're arraigned and they appoint an attorney for him. Has he said anything at all about the Tyson girl yet?"

"Nothing. Not a word. They thought Cardwell might get something out of him, but he didn't."

"Well, let me talk to that sonofabitch," Brawley said. "Ol' Randy loves to shoot the breeze with me."

Greenawalt had lost his thick glasses in the confusion after the van wrecked, and without them he couldn't see well across an ordinary room. He was sitting on a bench in the small holding cell when the jailer let Brawley in. Like Ray and Ricky, he was still naked.

"How you doing, Randy," Brawley said in a folksy way as he walked in.

Randy recognized the voice and leaned forward, squinting. "Is that you, Tom? Tom Brawley?"

"Sure as hell is," Brawley said as he swung a chair around backward and sat down. "What's going on? Looks like you got yourself in trouble again."

Randy just shrugged and smiled his shy little smile as he looked down at his handcuffed hands clasped over his genitals.

"How about a smoke?" Brawley asked, shaking out a cigarette in Randy's direction. "You ain't quit smoking, have you?"

"Thanks, Tom," Greenawalt said, smiling again and leaning forward for the cigarette. You could tell he was glad Brawley had come. Brawley held out a lighter and lit the cigarette. Randy inhaled deeply and sat back, the shackles rattling as he crossed his legs at the knee to cover himself.

Brawley had learned from his many earlier conversations with Randy, when he was standing trial for murder in Flagstaff, that Randy liked to talk about what he had done — if there was nothing to lose; which is to say, if Randy knew the authorities already had the goods on him. And at first it looked as though this interview would go that way too. Greenawalt was obviously glad to see him, but when Brawley interrupted their small talk to read him his Miranda rights again, Randy hesitated and then refused to sign the waiver. At that moment his mood and expression changed. He sucked his lower lip into a pout and slipped back into the sullen mood he had been in before Brawley arrived. It was as if he was hurt that an old friend had made such an unseemly request.

Brawley had seen him act this way before. On the one hand, Greenawalt didn't want to jeopardize his case by saying too much; on the other, he didn't want his friend, Tom Brawley, to leave right away. Brawley played him just right.

"Now, come on, Randy, you're not going to give me a hard time over this, are you?"

Greenawalt didn't reply. He just sat there staring at the cigarette he was holding while Brawley waited.

"Okay, if that's the way you're going to be, I guess I'm just wasting my time," Brawley said as he rose to his feet and scraped the chair back around. "I thought you wanted to talk, and you know we can't do that unless you sign this paper. That's not my rule, Randy, that's the law."

"Wait a minute, Tom," Greenawalt blurted out. "Don't leave yet. Just let me think a minute."

Brawley hesitated but didn't sit down.

"Okay, okay," Greenawalt said, "I'll talk about a few things, but not everything."

"Great. I was hoping you'd — " Brawley was saying as he sat back down. Greenawalt interrupted.

"The first thing I want to clear up, Tom, is that we did not kidnap the girl. She has got to be near the car. We left her right there in the car."

"Well, did you shoot her like the others?" Brawley asked.

Randy looked right at him before answering. "You're goddamed right she was shot," Greenawalt said, with that smirk that Brawley was waiting for, the one Randy always had on his face when he bragged. It was impossible for that sadistic sonofabitch to conceal his pride.

"Well, was she hurt bad?" Brawley asked matter-of-factly. He didn't look up, because the revulsion he felt for the man across from him was so deep that he wasn't sure he could conceal it.

"Well, she may have walked away," Randy said, raising his eyebrows and cocking his head to a jaunty angle. "But she couldn't be far because she sure as hell was shot."

Randy tried hard, but he wasn't quite able to stop his grin.

"What about the people in the van?" Brawley asked. "Will you tell me where they are?"

Greenawalt hesitated, gazing thoughtfully up at the ceiling. Then he sighed, exhaling a stream of smoke. "No, Tom, I'm sorry, but I can't talk about that."

"Well, are they hurt?"

"Sorry, Tom." Greenawalt smiled benignly.

"You know that if they're hurt and you tell me where they are, and we can get there in time to help them, it'll help your case," Brawley countered.

Greenawalt looked up at the ceiling again and took a deep breath. "It's too late for that, Tom." He sighed again. "You don't have to worry none about those two."

He almost chuckled after he said it. Then, sensing what he thought was disappointment in Brawley, he added, "But remember, Tom, I told you about the girl. It's just that on this other deal . . . Well, I want to do the same thing I did in Flagstaff, Tom. I want to see what my attorney is like. I want to see if there are any loopholes where I can beat you guys, and if there is not, I'll tell you the whole story, just like I did in Flagstaff."[13]

As soon as Brawley left the interview, he called Cecil Crowe at the Yuma County Sheriff's Office.

"Greenawalt says they left the Tyson girl at the car with the others," he said, "and I think he's telling the truth. Better get your people back out there right away and go over that whole area real good another time. She's got to be out there somewhere."

Then Brawley called Assistant Attorney General William Schafer, who would direct the prosecution for the state. He told Schafer that they had some very messy cases to prosecute on this one and, given the multiple jurisdictions involved — at least three counties and the state of Colorado — he suggested that it might be a good idea to set up a team to coordinate the investigation. Schafer agreed and told him to call the governor. Governor Babbitt also agreed and, after asking for Brawley's suggestions, appointed a seven-member team of investigators, selected from the various jurisdictions involved, to coordinate the preparation of the state's case. He asked Brawley to head up the new group, which he labeled the Arizona Cooperative Investigative Team. This was one case no one wanted to botch with a sloppy investigation. There was enough controversy already. The governor said he would make an announcement the next day.[14]

While this was going on, across the state near Palm Canyon, Ken Lewis of the Yuma County Search and Rescue Team and Game Warden Larry Young had once again scoured the desert, looking for some sign of Terri Jo Tyson. They were two of the scores of men sent out early that afternoon to search the area after Brawley's phone call. They hadn't been there more than a half hour when they spotted her body in a shallow wash. She had dragged herself about a thousand feet west of the car, trying to get to the highway, when she collapsed. She knew she was going to die, and had stopped to make it easier. She was lying on her side with her knees drawn up slightly, as if she had gone to sleep. The Lyonses' little Chihuahua had died there with her, pressed close against her stomach. She had removed its identification collar and had fastened it around her ankle. She wanted someone to know who she was when they found her.[15]

It was late afternoon in Omaha by the time Terri Jo's identity was officially confirmed. Jo Ann Tyson's Uncle Fran had taken both the Lyons and Chadwick families to a restaurant after the funeral. It was a simple little place in a shopping mall. The people gathered around the long table were quiet. There was no release from the sadness, as there sometimes is when a loved one has died when it is time to die. It was quiet except for the occasional sound of coffee cups scraping on saucers. There was simply nothing to say about a tragedy so profound. Neither Jo Ann nor Harry Tyson could eat. Exhausted from worry and sleeplessness and their long trip from Las Vegas, they struggled against the awful sense of dread that ached deep inside.

They were sitting there staring at their plates when a voice broke into the Muzak. "Harry or Jo Ann Tyson," it said, "please go to the information booth . . . You have a phone call." For Harry and Jo Ann, it was like the voice of doom. Jo Ann felt dizzy, then ill, and thought she was going to faint. Her husband reached over and squeezed her hand.

All eyes turned toward them as the voice repeated the message in

its indifferent monotone, as if it was saying that someone's car was
blocking a driveway, or that a lost child had been found in the toy
department. Suddenly Jo Ann leaped up and bolted from the table,
upsetting her water glass and spilling silverware as her husband tried
to restrain her. She walked, then started to run, toward the door,
trying to get away from that voice and what she knew it meant. Out
in the crowded mall, she pushed and elbowed her way through startled
shoppers, stumbling as she ran down a long walkway, throwing herself
against the doors and out into the parking area. A car swerved and
blew its horn as she ran across its path, by this time screaming, "No,
no, no . . ."[16]

15

Judgment:
August 22, 1978

A large green fly buzzed angrily against the inside of the screen door at the office of the Papago Chemical Company. Flies come with livestock and the summer rains, but there seemed to be more flies than usual the past few days. Ray Thomas scraped his chair back from a worn wooden desk and walked outside, squinting against the bright morning sun that reflected off the white block walls of the plant's other building across the three-acre fenced enclosure. The plant, which manufactures agricultural fertilizers and employs a handful of workers, is owned by the Papago Indian Tribe and located on the reservation. About six miles south of Casa Grande on Chuichu Road near White Horse Pass, it sits off to the west on a one-lane gravel road up against a spiny ridge of cactus and rock. A mile south of the ridge is where the van had been wrecked.

It was one of those scorching, breezeless August mornings in Arizona that, except for the angle of the sunlight, could be the middle of a hot afternoon anywhere else in the country. It was never really busy at the plant, but summers were especially slow because of the heat. Every day the thermometer outside the door of the tiny cement-block building Ray Thomas shared with the plant bookkeeper climbed well past 100 degrees and never dropped much below 85 at night. Official high temperatures had averaged 106 degrees for the past two weeks. The most you could hope for was a seasonal monsoon — those intense thunderstorms that blow up from the Yucatan on August afternoons — to cool things off for an hour or two.

The screen door slammed behind Ray Thomas and the buzzing stopped as he bent over the water cooler outside the door, letting the hot water run out before he took a drink. It was quiet except for the swamp cooler vibrating on its shelf at the side of the building and the distant drone of a small airplane. He watched the plane flying in slow circles over a ridge a few miles away. Still looking for that guy, he thought. No one could survive out there this long in the heat. It had only rained briefly a couple of times in the last week, and not enough to matter. Most days, the clouds would billow up in the afternoon and the wind would start to kick up, and you would swear it was going to rain. And it would. The problem was, the rain never reached the ground. It would trail down from the clouds in tantalizing gray sheets and ribbons that evaporated long before they reached the hot desert valleys below. Dry showers like that were real pretty to look at, especially with the sun setting behind, but they were not much good for anything else, especially to a man dying of thirst. It was Tuesday, August 22. Eleven days since the chase and shoot-out a mile down the road, and they still hadn't found Gary Tison.

Since Saturday, Thomas had smelled a foul odor at the plant. He first noticed it as he drove in and out of the plant road. At first he thought it was just the decaying flesh of a dead animal and would pass in a day or so. But it kept getting worse, and this morning, in the still air, the nauseating stench seemed to have settled over the whole area. Something needed to be buried or covered with lye, he thought. He decided to take a look around.

Gary Tison hadn't died easily. When Ray Thomas found him, he was lying on his back, his face twisted in an ugly grimace, and you could see that he had kicked a deep furrow into the ground. Tison's face was blackened by decomposition and was unsettling to look at. His mouth was opened wide and turned downward at the corners, exposing his discolored lower teeth, as if he had died screaming a final curse. His right arm was bent awkwardly behind his back; a cocked .45 that had slipped from his right hand had been ground into the sand by his writhing. His large, thick body had swelled, and in places the flesh had split open in the heat like an overcooked sausage.

He had hidden in a cocoonlike tunnel he had made in thick brush next to an ironwood tree, vainly seeking the feathery shade that quickly faded away in the merciless summer sun. The heels on his cowboy boots, the symbol of his status in prison, were badly scraped and torn loose, the result either of convulsions or a futile attempt to dig for water. The furrow at his feet, about eighteen inches deep, was only three hundred feet from Ray Thomas's office, from the water cooler, and from a spigot with a hose trailing away from it.

Tison wore an olive-green army fatigue shirt. It was hard to tell about his trousers. They were discolored with dark stains, and they might have been jeans. His writhing had twisted his clothes tightly around his bloated body. Flesh so badly swollen that it cracked open had almost enveloped the wide leather watch band on his left wrist. He had taken off one of his socks and used it to carry cactus fruit he had found and sucked for the little moisture and nutrition they offered. A black flashlight lay near his head. In his pockets he had a pair of glasses in a brown case, a penknife, a Zippo lighter, a Chap Stick, and a half-empty pack of Camels in a silver cigarette case with the monogram "D.T." on it. A girlfriend had given the case to Donny for his twentieth birthday.

Thomas walked back to his office and called the sheriff's office. He told them that he thought it was probably Gary Tison. By 9:00 A.M., there were half a dozen patrol cars and an ambulance parked on the road to Papago Chemical. Thomas's guess was confirmed when the body was positively identified by representatives of the Department of Public Safety and the Pinal County Sheriff's Department. The discovery ended the largest manhunt in Arizona history.

For eleven days, hundreds of police and volunteers had combed a ten-square-mile area on foot, on horseback, and in jeeps, looking for Gary Tison. Tear-gas grenades were used by SWAT teams who repeatedly searched the numerous caves and abandoned mine shafts that honeycomb the nearby Sawtooth Mountains. Searchers with bloodhounds had roamed back and forth through the gullies and washes that lace the area. Helicopters and planes had looked for some sign of Gary from the air, some at night with infrared equipment. The best technology was employed in the search, but no one ever found Tison's hiding place, a stone's throw from the Papago Chemical Plant road, only about a thousand feet from Chuichu Road, and no more than a mile from where he had escaped from the van.

While he was on the loose, the town of Casa Grande became an armed camp. On some days as many as five hundred armed volunteers participated in the search. Those who stayed at home or went to work kept their doors locked and weapons handy. Children were chauffeured back and forth to school by anxious parents. Deputy Dave Warren recalled that the whole community was nervous, but none more so than the men who were out in the desert looking for Gary Tison.

"Knowing Tison was out there," Warren said, "and that he'd kill you as soon as look at you, kind of made the hair crawl up on your back, especially [if you were] on horseback where you're sitting up there high so you can see, but it's always in your mind that he can see you easier too, like coming down into a wash where there's ample cover for someone to hide."[1]

But at least one of the searchers claimed that he wasn't nervous. "Afraid of Tison? Underneath, Gary Tison is a cowardly sonofabitch," retired prison warden Frank Eyman scoffed from the back of the palomino he rode during the search. "Sonofabitch never did kill anyone in a fair fight. But now he's got nothing to lose so he's dangerous. But afraid of him? Hell, no."

The eighty-one-year-old Eyman had known a lot of hardened criminals over a long career in law enforcement. An album he kept in his den at home is filled with the photographs of men he brought to justice, two of them prison escapees strapped lifeless over the backs of mules after they were found and shot dead in the desert. Eyman was one of the lawmen who stormed a Tucson house in 1934 and captured desperado John Dillinger and his gang. He took particular pride in his tough reputation for swift and certain justice and the fact that, as warden, he had personally presided over "twelve or thirteen" executions during his seventeen-year tenure at the state prison. The last three photographs in his album are eight-by-ten glossies of the new gas chamber. But of all the evil people he had known over the years, Eyman said, he hated none more than Gary Tison. Tison had killed one of his best friends in a previous escape in 1967.

Eyman rode his own horse during the search, armed with a .45 revolver with a barrel that reached halfway to his knee. Even as an old man, he still had the stride and lean, sinewy look of a nineteenth-century gunfighter. Horses and guns. Times had changed, but Frank Eyman hadn't. Law enforcement remained a very personal matter with him. And so was Gary Tison.

"I knew we'd get him, whether it was a few days, or a few weeks," Eyman said when Tison's body was found. "I wanted a body and we got one. Who knows what some goddamn liberal judge would have done, if he'd gone to trial," he continued, his hard gray eyes squinting beneath the brim of his Stetson. "Probably would've said he was criminally insane and put him in a hospital and served him chicken every Sunday. To me, criminal insanity is just a nice word for sonofabitch. I just wish I'd killed that heartless bastard years before when I had the chance. If I had, those six young people he killed would be alive today, and his three sons might've grown up to be decent boys. Now look at them."[2]

Then the wiry old man turned his contempt on federal judge Carl Muecke, who had declared Arizona's death penalty unconstitutional a few years before.

"They should've taken Muecke to Quartzsite and made him look at that little baby with his face blown off. When I heard about that, I wanted to kill that bastard so bad."[3]

"Who? Muecke or Tison?" someone asked.

Eyman didn't reply.

After photographs were taken, men wearing surgical masks and rubber gloves gingerly dragged Tison's corpse out of the brush to a plastic sheet spread out between some creosote bushes in an open area by the wash. More photographs were taken before the sheet was folded over the body. A deputy held his breath and leaned over with a 35-mm. camera for a close-up of Gary's face. Then six men lifted the body into a black plastic body bag and onto a stretcher, which they carried to an ambulance parked on the plant road. The body was taken first to the Cole and Maud Mortuary in Casa Grande, the same place that had buried Donny Tison nine days before, and then on to Phoenix for an autopsy.

What amazed almost everyone was Tison's decision — not to mention the determination required — to die such an agonizing death rather than surrender for a drink of cool water. He surely knew that there was water just a short distance away at the chemical plant; yet he remained where he was until he died.

Dave Harrington said that he believed Tison made it to that spot within a few hours after he escaped and never left.

"That night after they hit our roadblock," Harrington explained, "while we was waiting for the chopper to arrive with lights, Perry Holmes said he thought he saw a flashlight back up the road that way toward the pass — and now we know he had a flashlight with him. We didn't pay much attention to it then because we were concentrating on the three people we could see lying in the desert. But we now think Gary crossed over to the opposite side of the road after they wrecked, figuring we would be concentrating on the west side — which we were — so he just made it back up to the other side of the pass — probably sticking fairly close to the road because he was way overweight and that's a rugged climb otherwise — before daylight. Then he crossed back to the west side of the road again on the other side of the pass. The trees and brush are thick along that wash where we found him, and I don't think he ever moved from that spot. He might've figured he had a chance for some water running through that little drainage when it rained — and we did have a couple of thunderstorms — but there wasn't enough runoff to make any difference to him."[4]

"We must've walked by him at least four different times in that area," Sheriff Frank Reyes said, shaking his head. "It's hard to spot something in the desert that's not moving, and Gary knew that. I think that's why he stayed right there."[5]

One of Gary's biggest mistakes, Dave Harrington decided, was wasting those precious hours in Casa Grande earlier that night, trying to find his brother Joe.

"If they had headed straight for the border," Harrington said, "they probably would've made it across without any problem. The roadblocks weren't up yet, and the additional manpower and surveillance we had down there right after the escape had been pulled off. Getting across would've been easy for someone like Gary. But he spent all that time looking for Joe. He wanted to even the score."[6]

"Pretty amazing," someone said quietly as the body was rolled into the ambulance. "He was one mean sonofabitch. Aren't too many men who could do that — go without water like that, I mean. I'm glad he's dead . . . and he sure as hell suffered."

"Yeah, but I wanted to see Tison bleed," a sheriff's deputy replied. "He should've been subjected to the same torture his victims suffered. I hope his soul rots in hell."[7]

"Torture?" countered the first. "Did you see those ruts he kicked in the ground? You think dying slow like that wasn't torture? Hell, I'll tell you that bastard suffered."

"Yeah, but nobody caught him," said Bernie Lawrence, a well-known tracker brought in with his dogs from Mohave County to help in the search. "He said he wouldn't be taken alive, and, by God, he wasn't. You've got to give the guy credit . . . even if he was a rat."[8]

That was the kindest thing anyone had to say about Gary Tison, and the closest he ever got to a eulogy.

There was a grisly continuity to the work performed by Maricopa County Medical Examiner Thomas B. Jarvis that day. He had done autopsies on five of Tison's victims, beginning in 1967 with the prison guard, followed recently by the four Quartzsite victims. Eleven days before, he had done the autopsy on Donny Tison, and now Gary himself. Even if you were used to it, it made you think.

Tom Brawley looked on as Jarvis and an assistant went to work on Tison. Brawley and Jarvis were cousins from St. Johns. Folks back there still called them both Tommy. Now they only saw each other across dead bodies.

"Funny," Brawley said, "when Tommy went on to medical school and I went into police work, I never thought we'd see as much of each other as we have, but I couldn't begin to remember all the autopsies I've had to watch him do over the years. But I'll tell you, this was one of the messiest."[9]

In death Tison was still a tough person to understand. As nearly as Jarvis could tell, Gary had died slowly of thirst and exposure in the intense heat. There was a possibility that he had had a heart attack brought on by the stress, but the corpse was too badly decomposed to be certain. Despite its bloated appearance, Tison's body weighed only 138 pounds at the autopsy — a hundred pounds less than he weighed in life. Gaseous decay accounted for most of the lost bulk.

On August 24, members of the Tison clan gathered at the far end of the Mountain View Cemetery for a graveside service. The cemetery, at the western base of Casa Grande Mountain, about halfway between the house where Gary and his young bride had set up housekeeping in 1957 and the spot where he died twenty-one years later, isn't much to look at. Behind the arched entrance it's just a flat piece of desert scraped clean and replanted with some thirsty-looking pine trees that struggle for life along the driveways. Here and there, patches of coarse Bermuda grass grow near the water spigots. It's drab and colorless except for the plastic flowers and a few tiny American flags that mark scattered graves; everything else is some shade of brown or gray and more desolate than the desert cleared to make it.

A heavy police escort accompanied the funeral procession to the cemetery. Authorities were concerned about an attempt to disrupt the funeral. Dave Warren, who was following directly behind the hearse in one of the patrol cars, was more worried about having to pull out of the procession to vomit.

"Maybe it was the hot day," Warren said, "or me just remembering what it smelled like when we found his body, because the windows were up and the air conditioner was on, but I swear that awful smell was still there, like it was seeping out of that casket, and it was making me sick to my stomach."[10]

A group of reporters and television camera crews were already waiting at the cemetery when the procession arrived around nine-thirty. Fifteen minutes later, Gary's brother Joe drove up in a late-model Cadillac, scattering reporters in an intimidating swirl of dust and gravel as he parked between them and the gravesite. He was the last to arrive. A snarling Doberman leaped from the back seat when he got out, dressed as always in western shirt, flared slacks, boots, and dark glasses. No one can remember Joe ever wearing a coat and tie, brother's funeral or not. You could tell he was in a bad mood.

"Get back and no pictures," he said to the reporters as they began to reposition themselves across the driveway from the grave. "This dog ain't been fed today," he said, "and he seems pretty hungry."[11]

Joe snapped his fingers and the panting Doberman jumped to the hood of the Cadillac. The big dog remained there, panting and whining as it pranced on the hot metal, its eyes fixed on the group of strangers as Joe flipped his cigarette and walked over to join the rest of his family.

About forty relatives and friends were there. No one spoke as Joe walked to the edge of the gathering, away from the coffin. He nodded to his brother Larry. Dorothy sat beside the coffin on a folding chair. Dorothy's mother, Valle Mae Stanford, and Gary's mother, both wearing light summer dresses and dark glasses, as Dorothy did, sat on either side. Dorothy looked bad. The strain of the past three weeks showed. Or was it the past twenty-one years? Gaunt and very pale, she appeared as old as the two women sitting on either side of her.

There were only three folding chairs. Everyone else stood behind them, all the women dressed for the occasion, the men tieless and in shirtsleeves, like Joe. Only the preacher wore a suit and tie.

Some reporters thought that Ricky and Raymond, who were denied permission to attend their brother's funeral, might have been permitted to attend their father's.

"Are you kidding?" Sheriff Frank Reyes asked. "Too dangerous. Too many people around here that think a trial's just a waste of money after what's happened. And it's my job to see they don't get the chance to do anything about it."

Dorothy's father, Robert Stanford — looking weary and stooped, with a thin, leathery face lined like those of the men and women Dorothea Lange photographed in California forty years before — stood behind Dorothy, a peaked cap with an auto-parts label on his head, his left hand resting gently on his daughter's shoulder. Gary's sister Kay stood beside him, weeping softly. Two weeks before, when the same group assembled to bury Donny, there were also younger people — Donny's friends and cousins — in attendance. Today there were none.

A helicopter carrying a television crew from KTAR-TV in Phoenix thumped noisily to a dusty landing nearby, blowing flowers from the bouquets. "Vultures," whispered a tight-lipped woman in dark glasses, standing at the edge of the gathering.

The service began about ten o'clock, and it was brief. There was no sermon or eulogy. Reverend Jerry Totty, Mary Tison's pastor at the Glad Tidings Pentecostal Church, stood at the head of the casket and, in a soft drawl that sounded like Oklahoma, read some Scripture about turning to God in the time of trouble. As far as anyone can remember, he mentioned Gary Tison's name only once, when he said, "The life of Gary Tison rests in the hands of a just God." The preacher concluded with a short prayer for the living — about being prepared to meet the Lord when your time comes — then he stooped and picked a red carnation from the casket and handed it to Gary's mother. Mary Tison lifted a white handkerchief to her face and began to weep.

It was all over in ten minutes. Other members of the family hugged each other briefly and walked silently back to their cars. Joe Tyson stood back as a few people went over to speak to Dorothy and his mother by the casket. Then Joe moved closer. As he bent down to whisper something to his mother, Dorothy turned her back to him. Mary Tison slowly got to her feet and held her son's arm as he walked her to one of the processional cars. After helping her inside, he turned and said to no one in particular that he had room in his car if anyone needed a ride. No one did.

After the family left, a reporter asked Reverend Totty about Gary's mother.

"She's a very religious person," he replied. "The only thing that's seen her through all this is relying on God and the prayers of Christian people."[12]

Reverend Elzia J. Elliott, an old family friend, attended the funeral with his wife, Shirley. "I felt a special sorrow for sister Tison [Gary's mother]," Reverend Elliott said. "She's a fine Christian woman, but that made it even harder to find words to say to her. I've had a lot of funerals where folks have died without God; about all you can do is say that this person is in the hands of a just God . . . and, well, that's about it. It's very hard. There's just not much comfort to give in those situations, except maybe saying that something might've happened that no one knows about, and maybe they repented their sins before they died; other than that . . . well, you know . . . the Bible just flat-out says they're lost and in hell. But most folks try to believe that something did happen, and that's the way she was. She said that she was just praying and trusting the Lord that Gary'd repented his sins and asked God for forgiveness out there in the desert before he died."

But Elliott had some doubts. About twenty years before, he had tried to talk with Gary about making some changes in his life.

"He was young — late teens or early twenties — nice-looking young fella," Elliott recalled. "I tried to speak with him about his soul — about getting right with God. It was just about the time he was starting to get into serious trouble. I was having special meetings there at the Casa Grande church and it seemed like he was under conviction during the altar call one Sunday night. I put my hand on his shoulder and asked if things were right between him and the Lord.

"Gary's head was down and he was just staring at the floor and squeezing the pew in front of him, and he said, 'Elzie, I'd give my life to have what you got.' And I told him that the Lord didn't want him to give up his life, the Lord wanted him to *live* his life for Jesus. I remember Gary hesitating, like he was thinking real hard, and then he said, 'I can't,' and he just turned and walked out. He just turned his back on God that night."[13]

Gary Tison was buried in an unmarked grave beside his oldest son. There were no plans for a tombstone. The family was advised that there might well be a problem with vandalism. After the family left, workmen lowered the casket and pushed the sandy soil in over it with shovels. As if wanting to be sure, a Casa Grande policeman watched from a patrol car parked nearby. When they finished, one of the workmen pushed a metal stake into the soft dirt to mark the head of the grave. A caretaker walked around picking up the flowers that had been strewn about when the helicopter left. When he was finished, he arranged them in a new makeshift bouquet and placed them neatly, with the others, on the mound of sandy soil that now marked the grave. A white ribbon fluttered loosely across a large basket of red and white carnations workmen had set beside the metal stake. The gold inscription read, "Our Loving Brother."

IV

Consequences

16

Seared with a Hot Iron

Not many days after the Tisons and Greenawalt were captured at the roadblock on Chuichu Road, John Judge flew to Yuma for their arraignment on the Quartzsite murder charges.

"I went over there," he said, "to try to negotiate with the Attorney General's Office some means to determine the location of my brother's and his wife's bodies. My parents and Margene's parents were in such distress about not knowing where they were, and I was also very upset at the time.

"Now, I'm an attorney, and I don't believe in capital punishment. Never have. I just don't think that's something the state should be doing. It's easier for me to understand personal retribution. Well, that's what was going through my mind when I flew over there. I thought about it. You know, sticking a gun in my briefcase and blowing them away right there in the courthouse for what they did to James and Margene. It was incredible. Two or three helicopters swarming around overhead, armed guards everywhere, deputies walking around with machine guns — I mean, it was a big show of security.

"Now, here's the funny part. Here I am, the guy with the best motive in the world to do harm to these three defendants, and I walk right into the courtroom with my briefcase and nobody says a damn word to me. No one asks me who I am. No one asks for identification. No one checks my briefcase. I just walk in and sit down. Then they bring in these three guys all shackled up in chains, and I find myself there sitting less than five feet away from my brother's killers. 'My God,' I said to myself, 'if I'd have brought a gun with me, I could've killed all three.' I guess you could say that I have a rather jaundiced view of the state of Arizona and the way it takes care of its prisoners."[1]

There were four trials altogether. In the first, in January 1979, Ricky and Ray Tison and Randy Greenawalt were tried together in Pinal County for the escape. When the guilty verdicts were announced on January 22, there were no surprises. Pinal County Superior Court Judge E. D. McBryde sentenced Ricky and Ray Tison and Randy Greenawalt to thirty years to life for assault with a deadly weapon, and four to five years on each of four lesser charges.* The only difference was that Randy's sentences were to run consecutively and the two Tison boys' were to run concurrently. It hardly mattered to Randy, who was already serving two consecutive life sentences.

The three defendants were tried separately in Yuma the following month for the murders of the Lyons family and Terri Jo Tyson. Randy went to trial first, followed by Ricky, then Ray, whose trial ended the first week of March. Convictions followed in each case. None of the trials was very interesting, except for the young girls — about Terri Jo Tyson's age — who would call and wave to Ricky and Ray when they were led in and out of the Yuma County Courthouse.

The evidence was overwhelming, and there just wasn't any doubt of guilt. The only questions that crossed some minds, especially a good number of friends and neighbors back in Casa Grande who had known the Tison boys all their lives, was the *degree* of guilt in their cases. To what extent were they actually involved in the homicides? And did they, as opposed to their father and Greenawalt, *intend* to kill the Lyons family and Terri Jo Tyson after the abduction? Not that anyone was for acquittal, but people who knew the Tison brothers just couldn't believe that they were aware of what their father and Greenawalt were going to do to that young family.

*On November 29, 1978, while awaiting trial, Ricky Tison and two other inmates overpowered a guard and escaped from the Pinal County Jail. Ricky was captured, without resistance, fourteen hours later in a cornfield less than a mile from the jail. The charges against him were dropped.

"I just don't believe those boys had any idea their father was going to kill those people," George McBride said, and his wife nodded in agreement. "We've known them, they've been in our house, grew up with our kids, and we know those boys are not killers. Their father was no good. Never was. But it just isn't right to make them pay for what he did. They should be punished for what they did at the prison, but not for those people their father killed. That's not right."[2]

As for Randy Greenawalt, there were no doubts about either his involvement or his criminal intent. Even in his own perverse mind. For a multiple killer like Randy, the chances of avoiding the gas chamber hinged only on legal technicalities — the hope that someone, the investigators or the prosecution, would make a mistake that could compromise an otherwise certain conviction.

The only big surprise, for some, came two months later in Yuma, when both Ricky and Ray were sentenced to death for the Quartzsite murders, along with Greenawalt. Up until then, the Tisons and their attorneys had been fairly confident in the knowledge that there was a significant difference between what Randy did and what the two boys did that night near Palm Canyon. But Yuma County Superior Court Judge Douglas C. Keddie didn't see it that way. When he handed down the sentences on March 29, 1979, it was the gas chamber for all three. The decisions were popular. A few people, however, in addition to the boys and their mother, wondered why no distinction had been made between Randy Greenawalt, a multiple murderer who had repeatedly fired a sawed-off shotgun at his victims, and two young men who, until that moment, were completely unaware of their father's deadly intentions. The only difference in Judge Keddie's three decisions were the names of the defendants. Otherwise the language was exactly the same.

But under Arizona law it didn't matter that Ricky and Raymond Tison hadn't killed anyone that night. Neither did it matter that they did not intend to harm anyone, nor that they did not anticipate their father's actions. Under Arizona's felony murder rule, the fact that they were participants in events that *led up* to the murders was enough to establish criminal intent. It was not even necessary under this rule to establish a defendant's *specific* intent to harm a *particular* victim. The prosecution had to prove only that a defendant participated in a crime in which someone — anyone — *might* have been killed. If that were proved, it was first-degree murder, regardless of whether the death was actually intended. As Yuma County prosecutor Michael Irwin explained it, "During the course of the [Lyons] robbery . . . four persons were murdered by *someone other than* these two defendants. However, as these two defendants were participants in the robbery [and abduction that preceded the murders], the felony murder rule would apply."[3]

It was a tough law and, some thought, constitutionally questionable. But it was the state law, and after Quartzsite the state was in a tough mood. Given that and the overwhelming case against the two boys, their court-appointed attorneys, Michael Beers and Harry Bagnall, decided a plea agreement was their best chance of saving Ricky and Ray's lives.

On January 25, 1979, before the trials began in Yuma, the court attorneys and the Tison brothers met with prosecutor Irwin and Judge McBryde to approve the terms of an agreement. The boys didn't like the idea, but they agreed to plead guilty to John Lyons's murder and thereby avoid trials. They also agreed "to appear and testify truthfully in any proceedings pertaining to criminal charges relating to an incident on or about August 1, 1978, in which the John Lyons family and Theresa Tyson were killed."[4] This meant they would be called to testify for the prosecution in Randy's murder trial two weeks later in Yuma. In exchange for their guilty pleas and testimony against Greenawalt, their sentences were to run concurrently with the sentences that were handed down in Pinal County for the escape. Most important, Irwin agreed not to ask for the death penalty. That would mean, the boys hoped — although it was difficult for two teenagers to contemplate — that they would be eligible for parole sometime when they were nearing sixty years of age.

But twelve days later, when the boys met with Judge Keddie in Yuma to go over the terms of the agreement, a misunderstanding developed. Ricky and Ray claimed that they understood the agreement to mean that they would be asked to testify *only* about what happened at Quartzsite. But Judge Keddie and the prosecutor interpreted the agreement much more broadly. It also means, they insisted, that Ricky and Ray would have to testify about events preceding and following the murders. They would have to answer questions about all the planning and activities that occurred prior to the escape, as well as what happened after Quartzsite, when they fled to Colorado. The brothers knew they couldn't do that without involving their mother, and that was something neither one was willing to do. It was also something that they could not, for the same reason, admit, even to their attorneys. Without ever mentioning their mother, Ray explained to Judge Keddie why they couldn't go through with the agreement.

"Okay, the plea agreement says *the* incident," Ray said indignantly, emphasizing the definite article. "I figured they were talking about the incident going on up at Quartzsite. I had no idea that you were going to be asking about *other* people involved, about the escape, all this, and maybe what happened afterwards. I thought it was just going to be that incident. But that's it, I'm not involving nobody else. I'm staying right there."[5]

Michael Beers and Harry Bagnall were dumbfounded. A plea agreement, or a second-degree murder conviction, they knew, was the best they could hope for for either boy. But they could not convince Ricky or Ray. The brothers were adamant in their refusal to go along with what they considered a change in the terms of the agreement. Attorney Kendra McNally, who was assisting Beers, argued that the boys' withdrawal from the agreement was not voluntary. Instead, she insisted, they were being forced to back out because Keddie's interpretation went beyond the scope of the original agreement. Not so, the judge insisted. He seemed to think that Ricky and Ray were unwilling to incriminate themselves on lesser charges of procuring weapons for the escape, even though they had already been tried and convicted on those charges. Keddie didn't realize that that had nothing to do with it. They weren't protecting themselves, they were protecting their mother.

Not that it mattered either way to anyone except Ricky and Ray, and, of course, their mother. Judge Keddie asked the two boys if they understood that if they rejected the agreement, they could be executed for first-degree murder. "I understand that we already got our lives in prison. What's it going to hurt?" Raymond asked in a rare flash of indignation, ignoring Keddie's warning, refusing to believe that he really meant it.[6] It was the wrong question, asked in the wrong way, at the wrong time, of the wrong judge. It was a question his attorneys regretted and Judge Keddie didn't forget.

It was cold and snowy on the morning of November 15, 1978, when searchers assembled at the Chimney Rock Café, along the highway west of Pagosa Springs, Colorado. Tom Brawley had notified Colorado authorities the day before that one of the defendants had said the bodies of James and Margene Judge had been buried in shallow graves in a canyon a few miles south of Chimney Rock. Charlie Kalbacher, an investigator out of the District Attorney's Office in Monte Vista, hunted deer in the area and knew it well. How far into the canyon? he asked. A little less than two miles, was the reply.

After coffee and doughnuts at the café, Kalbacher led a procession of four-wheel-drive vehicles to the snow-covered road that winds back into Cabison Canyon. It was about 9:00 A.M. when they stopped at the turnoff. Kalbacher explained that they were going to search an area on both sides of the road about 1.8 miles up the canyon. He had a hunch that the bodies wouldn't be too far from the road. The country was rough and the brush thick in that part of the canyon, he said, and Tison and Greenawalt were too fat and out of shape to walk far. He was right. Less than two hours later, he found a skull along the creek, a short distance from the road, then a pair of women's sunglasses amidst bones that had been chewed and scattered by animals, and then a wedding ring. Moments later, there was a shout from the other side of the road. They had found the remains of what appeared to be a man wearing Levi's and running shoes.[7]

Charlie Kalbacher was sure they had more than enough evidence to convict the three in Colorado for the murders of James and Margene Judge. But, much to the dismay of the young couple's parents, District Attorney Gene Farish had decided he would go to trial only if Arizona failed to hand down death sentences to all three defendants. It was just too expensive, he explained, and he didn't have the budget to go into a second expensive trial if they were convicted and given the death penalty in the first.[8] Farish's decision seemed insensitive to the grieving Davis and Judge families. They may have taken some consolation, though, in the fact that in March Kalbacher was called to testify in Yuma at the aggravation hearing required before sentencing. In the strictest sense, Ricky and Ray Tison were not being sentenced for what happened in Colorado. But surely Kalbacher's testimony was damaging to the defendants.

Kalbacher didn't testify about the abduction; he only described what he had found that cold morning a few months before along Cabison Creek.[9] Whether or not one believed that Ricky and Ray were completely surprised by the gunshots in Quartzsite, there could be little doubt that all three brothers were anticipating the shots that ended the lives of James and Margene Judge. And they had done nothing to stop the murders. Nor did they flee, as they could have when Gary left them alone in the pickup while he and Randy drove the young couple back into the canyon. Kalbacher didn't say — because at that time he didn't know — that one of the boys most likely had checked out the unsuspecting couple's van as they waited at the construction site and then reported back to his father. But even without that incriminating information, Kalbacher's testimony must have had a significant bearing on the sentences that Ricky and Raymond Tison received.

Jenelle and F. H. Davis thought that it did. They had driven over to Yuma from Borger to attend the trial. They were glad that Prosecutor Mike Irwin decided to call Kalbacher and other Colorado witnesses in for the aggravation hearing. Testimony was heard from the store clerks in South Fork and Bayfield who had seen the three defendants and also from F. H. Davis himself. Mrs. Davis lifted a handkerchief to her eyes as Linda Mae Carroll described how beautiful Margene looked when she came into the Foothills Market in South Fork.[10] When the court recessed, Jenelle rushed over to Linda Mae and introduced herself and F. H. She wanted to know more about how Margene looked that day. What was she wearing, again? Oh yes, I know that top. She liked to wear it with her windbreaker. You mentioned her smiling. That's Margene. She had a smile for everyone. She asked if Linda Mae would stand with them for a photograph on the courthouse steps. Linda Mae was embarrassed at first, but she understood.

When F. H. Davis was called to the stand, Mike Irwin asked him to describe the last telephone conversation he'd had with Margene the evening before the abduction. Then Irwin asked him to identify Margene's luggage and wedding ring. It was rough, but the toughest part came when Irwin asked about the last time he saw Margene. F. H. told how he had given her the hundred-dollar bill when he kissed her goodbye after the wedding reception. It was the same bill the Tisons used to buy cigarettes an hour after she was murdered.[11] He answered the question softly in that flat Texas drawl, but when the words started to thicken and catch in his throat, it was obvious to everyone in that courtroom that Gary Tison and Randy Greenawalt had left more than six victims behind in this tragedy. And that was the point Mike Irwin wanted to get across before the sentencing.

In both Ricky's and Ray's trials, the judge had instructed the jury that the charges would be limited to first-degree murder, excluding the possibility of a second-degree conviction. The jury had had to decide guilt or innocence on that very narrow basis.

It seemed an odd ruling, especially when even the prosecutor agreed that neither boy had fired a shot. Moreover, there was no evidence that Ricky and Ray (or Donny) had *intended* to kill anyone — or anticipated that that was their father's and Greenawalt's intent. The primary evidence was drawn from interviews both boys had had with Tom Brawley on January 26, 1979. Their description of what happened, which was accepted as truthful by everyone involved in the case, suggested that the Quartzsite murders were wholly unanticipated. Gary's decision to murder the family apparently was made impulsively only moments before the shooting began. Up until that time, it appeared that he intended to leave them behind, unharmed, with water, at the car.

Underlying the boys' behavior during events preceding the shooting were two assumptions about their father that proved to be tragically inaccurate. The first was that Gary would keep his promise, made before the escape, that no one would be hurt unnecessarily. The boys understood that to mean that no shots would be fired unless they found themselves in a life-threatening situation.

"We told Dad we will do this [break him out of prison] on one condition," Ray explained to Carl Cansler, a probation officer in Yuma County, "and that is no one gets hurt, and he told us, 'All right.' We had no intention to shoot anybody. Who ever said those guns were loaded?"

"You mean they weren't?" Cansler asked.

"Well, yes, they were, in case something happened."

"Do you think you could have shot someone if things had gone sour?"

"At the prison?"

"Yes."

Ray thought for a moment before replying. "It would have had to be a very close life-or-death situation," he said finally. "I could not have cold-bloodedly killed someone. No. But still I think I would have had some hesitation even then about killing anybody. I just really never thought about it. To kill all those people at the prison would have been a senseless killing. That is something I didn't want."

"Did you place all your trust in your dad for this whole deal?"

"Yeah, you see, I had never done anything like that before, and neither had my brothers. We didn't know the first thing about it. . . . We didn't have anything planned past the escape. You see, that's the only part we wanted."[12]

Gary's sons were also wrong in their second assumption: that their father was a man of normal emotions, empathy, and reasoned judgment. They could not imagine their father killing a baby; nor could some people who knew Gary much better than they did. They had only a blurred knowledge of the circumstances surrounding Gary's murder of a prison guard nine years before. That their father had a propensity for violence seemed implausible to three boys who knew him as a man who couldn't bring himself to spank them during the brief period he had spent with them as children. Moreover, like others who had watched Gary play with Martha LaBarre's grandson as well as other children in the prison visiting area, they had every reason to believe that he was fond of children — especially little boys like Christopher Lyons.

"After the escape, did your dad or Randy make any mention that there were going to be any killings?" Carl Cansler asked Raymond.

"Yeah, there was always the possibility, like we knew in Dad's 1967 escape, he killed the guard. We knew he was in there on a murder charge. There was a possibility, but we *didn't want to believe it.*"

"What about Randy? Did you ever consider him dangerous?"

"I didn't know what he was in there [prison] for. . . . He was my dad's man. Me, Ricky, and Donny had some control over it during the escape. After the escape, we lost all control."

"Was it taken away, or did you just give it up?"

"It was a little of both. My dad was a natural-born leader; now, you can check that out at the Pen and find that it's true. He was. He was a very intelligent man, lucky, and he had respect. He knew everything about it. It [control] was kind of relinquished because me, Don, or Ricky had no kind of knowledge at all about this. You know, all this running and hiding, you know, we knew only Dad had [the experience]."

"You mean that you were all just taking orders after the escape?"

"Yeah, that's about it."[13]

Any doubts the boys entertained about their misplaced confidence in Gary's good judgment and integrity didn't develop until after the shots were fired that night in the desert. Too late. What they didn't understand until after the escape was that their father was a full-blown sociopath. Guilt and fear were alien emotions to Gary. His sons mistook his shrewdness and manipulative skills for intelligence and sound judgment; his impulsiveness and independence they mistook for courage and integrity; his lack of empathy and toughness they mistook for strength of character. Gary Tison was not the person they thought he was. They could not have known that, except in a tightly restricted prison environment, their father was simply a killer without a conscience, whose love and concern for anyone other than himself — including his sons — were only fleeting and superficial.

Gary Tison's ability to manipulate people for his own purposes extended well beyond his children. It always had. Gary's ability to charm and influence was documented in his prison record. He had an uncanny way of impressing and winning the confidence of people, and getting them to do what he wanted, despite a record of offenses indicating that he was completely untrustworthy and dangerous.

Dan Deck, the journalism instructor who worked with Gary on the prison newspaper, testified that Tison's ability to manipulate people, to get what he wanted, was unsurpassed by anyone he had ever known. "He was able to cut through red tape that nobody else could do," Deck testified at Ray's trial. "He was able to come to terms with the administration. For instance, when we set up one of the inmate talent shows . . . the administration was absolutely adamant that it couldn't be done, that there would be too many complications in the security. And Gary just persisted and sat down and talked to them and, bit by bit, persuaded everybody in the administration that it would be a good thing and it needed to be done. The administration started cooperating, and pretty soon they became enthusiastic supporters."[14]

"Would you say then that he was the type of person that could by his extreme mental agility be able to influence people?" attorney Harry Bagnall asked.

"Very well," Deck answered. "Virtually anybody . . . Gary was the kind of person who was proud of his ability to get things across to people. He was good at it, and he wanted to make the point that people respected that about him. So, from time to time, he would do things to test me to see if he could con me into breaking a rule, or something like that. It was a game we played constantly, me trying to figure out what kind of game he was playing on me, and then afterward he would tell me what he had tried and we would talk it over and have a laugh about it."

Tison skillfully used his position as editor of the prison newspaper, Deck testified, to build respect and establish favor with the administration. He used the editorial page to convince prison administrators that he had been rehabilitated and now stood for traditional values. "He was one of the most persuasive people I have ever met," Deck said. "Normally when somebody tries to persuade you of something you are aware of the fact that he is putting on a sales pitch of some kind . . . Gary's technique was different. He always set an example. He never asked for more than he was willing to give, and he always made it so you were doing the *right* thing when you did what Gary *wanted* . . . Ultimately, everybody always ended up volunteering to do what he wanted."[15]

It was not only a misplaced confidence in their father's character that misled his sons that night. The logic and pattern of Gary's actions preceding the shooting reinforced their belief that the Lyons family would not be harmed. As frightening as it was, Gary's abrupt decision to shoot out the headlights and radiator of the car — while the engine was running — suggested that he did not intend to kill the family. If he intended to kill them, there was no need to disable the car to prevent the captives from signaling for help or leaving. When, after that, John Lyons asked them to leave water and Gary responded by first sending his sons to get it, the boys thought that it was for the people in the car. Leaving water behind, they reasonably assumed, also meant that no one would be harmed. Everything that Gary said and did up until then indicated that the family would be left behind, unharmed, with water.

It was only when Ricky returned and Gary called him over to give *him* the water that Ricky — and maybe Ray and Donny, if they happened to see — had the first hint that Gary might have changed his mind. Moments later, Gary had his brief whispered conversation with Randy, which only the four victims might have heard. Within seconds the shooting began, the shots ringing in the disbelieving ears of his three boys as they turned to witness the ghastly scene at the car.

The murders that night were brutally carried out and unnecessary. Unnecessary acts are difficult to understand; they are usually impossible to predict. Much of what we are able to anticipate in the behavior of others is based on insights we have about ourselves. Our capacity for empathy — what would *I* do in this situation? — becomes the basis of our expectations about what others will do. Gary Tison's three sons knew nothing of the dark pathological interior of their father's personality, and had no way of anticipating his actions.

"I hoped he knew what he was doing . . . I let him run the show," Ray said, expressing his growing uncertainty about his father's behavior. "I was just along for the ride. You know we never did have a life together [with Gary] on the street. About all we could do was see him on the weekends."[16]

The aberrant and extreme behavior of sociopaths like Gary Tison is very difficult even for mental health professionals to predict, because it has no reasonable basis. To ordinary people, sensitive to the guilt and fear that follow wrongdoing, sociopathic behavior doesn't make any sense. Means and ends, cause and effect — the bases of rational thought — lose their meaning, and when that happens, we are left perplexed, and sometimes horrified. The Tison boys were no different.

After his arrest, Ricky Tison told Tom Brawley that the killings that night near Quartzsite were "stupid" and "senseless." "They should have never happened," he said. "It made us very upset and very scared."[17] That was as close as he came to condemning what his father had done, or expressing remorse. It seemed odd, out of character. Or was it?

"I knew of Dad's past; I knew how he felt about things, but I didn't think he was dangerous," Ricky told psychologist James A. MacDonald. "Dad never showed any emotions . . . We were going to split up after the escape, but that didn't happen, and we got in real deep."

"Dad was in charge," his brother Ray explained to MacDonald. "He was running things like a military operation and there were no survivors, you know, that sort of thing — no witnesses. I couldn't see the point, I didn't agree, but I guess he had to do it."[18]

"What were your feelings when you realized people were getting hurt in this deal?" Carl Cansler asked.

"I didn't like it," Raymond replied. "It was all just going against my grain, and that's when I was really getting uptight about it. I was getting ready to leave . . ."[19]

Like his brother, that was as close as Ray came to expressing any remorse for the fates of the six people who had been killed during the thirteen days they spent with their father. It was also as far as either brother would go in expressing any reservations about their father and what he had done. Some regrets and symptoms of depression were observed in both young men after their arrest, but not many, and most of them had to do with their failure to make it across the border into Mexico. Ray and Ricky said that they didn't like what had happened to those six people, but no one actually heard them say they were sorry, either. There was little doubt that if Gary's sons — instead of Gary — had been making the decisions, no one would have been killed, but in their view it wasn't their decision, and so what happened was not their fault. Guilt, remorse, shame, a sense of responsibility — the ordinary emotions one might expect — were superseded by loyalty and love for their father. The two brothers didn't seem to comprehend why anyone would expect them to express feelings of conscience, or even that it might be in their self-interest to do so. When James MacDonald asked Ricky to define "remorse," Ricky replied that he had "no idea" what it meant. MacDonald then asked him what the word "calamity" meant. Ricky thought a moment and then said, "It's something that comes — went wrong — blew up in your face."[20] It was as if both boys had been in an automobile accident in which strangers had been killed. They felt bad about it, regretted that it had happened, but since neither had been driving, they didn't feel in any way responsible. They felt only compelled to defend their father and to rationalize, or ignore, what he had done.

"Remarkable is the observation," Pinal County Probation Officer John C. Woods wrote in his presentence report, "that neither of these defendants demonstrated discernible feelings of remorse during presentence interviews. Rather, Raymond Tison was preoccupied with explaining, in the present tense, that his father was a *great* man. Ricky Tison repeatedly emphasized, in commando-mercenary, military-type language, that the escape was well planned and was the product of precision execution."[21]

There was no shame, only pride in who they were and, paradoxically, what they had done. It was remarkable.

"Our old man had too much time to do," Ricky said to Woods, explaining why he had joined in the escape. "He had done enough time and it was time he got out and started leading a normal life; he had no one else to help, so we decided to do it . . . I was needed.

I volunteered for the mission." Then he added with pride, "My old man always taught me that you never run from anything, you attack."[22]

But his composure and bravado failed when he talked with the psychologist. There was nothing he could do to stop the killings, Ricky insisted to MacDonald, short of killing his own father. "This boy was nearly moved to tears," MacDonald wrote after the interview, "and verbal expression became very difficult for him when the events in Yuma County were mentioned . . . Ricky was placed in the position of having to shoot his own father in order to stop these events. He was simply overwhelmed by them, became immobilized and could take no action whatsoever."[23]

His brother also was emotional when he told Carl Cansler the same thing. "The only way to stop those murders was to kill our dad," Raymond said. "That would've been it. That would have meant putting a gun to my dad's head, and that's my father, and I respect and love him," he continued, emphasizing the present tense. "No way was I going to shoot my own father."[24]

But what about the murders ten days later in Colorado? Despite their lingering horror over Quartzsite and their realization, by then, that both their father and Greenawalt were killers, they had not only cooperated in the abduction of James and Margene Judge, they had waited behind in a pickup truck with weapons and plenty of gas while their father and Randy took the young couple back into the canyon and killed them. They'd made no effort to save the couple's lives, nor had they tried to flee when they were left alone. Why didn't they, if their father's actions were senseless and stupid as they both claimed?

"Raymond's judgment in this matter is poor," MacDonald concluded. "His social conscience is limited, his sense of comprehension of the enormity of the act was certainly inadequate . . . At this time, Raymond is experiencing some regret, although this appears to be quite limited . . . [He] appears to be obsessed with the *correctness* of the decision to help his father escape . . . [and] the necessity to have their family reunite. He is a very repressed and suppressed young man, whose emotions are deep beneath the surface. He is tough-minded, lacks insight, is affectually blocked, and in many ways is a very over-inhibited young man."[25]

MacDonald observed similar qualities in Ricky. "Social judgment, practical knowledge, and common sense appear to be definitely limited, and he appears to be unable to apply meaningful and emotionally relevant facts and relationships to his own life. Social mores, values, and the ability to make social judgments appear to be somewhat under-developed . . . When he does ponder and contemplate his life, it does appear that his judgment is somewhat impaired, socially, and his overall sense of moral values somewhat childish, immature, and underdeveloped . . . There were indications of a cold, flattened, often emotionless approach to life."[26]

It was impossible for either boy to criticize their father. Their love and respect for the man was too deep, too ingrained. They ignored or denied contradictory information, just as their mother had. Skirting the issue of the senseless murders he committed, they even strained to explain why Gary had abandoned them and their mortally wounded brother at the roadblock. For Gary, it was as it had been all along, "ev'ry man for hisself." When it came down to a choice between himself and others, his sons were as expendable as the people he killed. But neither boy was able to acknowledge that painful fact. It was one more facet of their father's unfolding personality that they didn't want to recognize.

Ricky, who had been splattered with his dying brother's blood and brain tissue, refused to confront such disturbing dissonant informa-tion. "It hit me real hard," he said, referring to the painful memory, "but now, like everything else, I just don't think about it."[27]

"[Ricky's] idealized notion of his father and his own need for a father figure who had been absent for years," James MacDonald wrote, "were important driving factors [in his behavior]."[28] Anything that was not consistent with that idealized view, Ricky simply blocked out.

Raymond was likewise defensive when he talked about the last time he saw his father. He tried to rationalize what Gary had done.

"With everything that happened after the escape," Carl Cansler asked, "do you think your dad knew what he was putting you into, or didn't he give a damn?"

"No. I don't think that he didn't give a damn about us," Raymond shot back. "Him being with us is what got him killed and our brother."

"You mean being with *you* caused your dad's death?"

"Five people together are pretty hard to hide."

"I still don't see how you can blame yourself for your dad's death."

"While we were on the run, law enforcement called my mom and told her they had orders to shoot on sight. They were calling us dangerous. They turned around and asked her to turn us in if we contacted her. I feel at that roadblock if they had caught him with us they would have killed us all right there."[29]

Raymond Tison's tortured logic omits mention of Donny's wounds and helplessness, while his father's callous abandonment of his sons is transformed into a selfless act of heroism in which Gary risks his own life to spare theirs.

"Gary Tison apparently lied outrageously to his sons," MacDonald concluded, "rationalizing and justifying his behavior to them by blaming all of his problems on the armed services. This is projection, of course, but he had convinced his sons he had been specially trained for 'secret' missions. These apparently included espionage, political murders, etc. He allegedly claimed to have been brainwashed by the military and trained to be a killer and discussed this freely and openly with his children, claiming it 'messed me all up — that's why I did it [killed the guard].' "

Ricky was convinced, MacDonald noted, that "no military record exists because . . . there is a 'top secret' plot to avoid having his father's military records come to light because of 'politics.' " Ricky told MacDonald that "only the FBI" could obtain the military records and prove that his father wasn't lying. But, he said, they would never do it. If his father was a killer, Ricky told MacDonald, it was because "the military" had made him one. It wasn't his dad's fault.[30]

In similar fashion, Raymond blamed the prison system for his father's violence. In a sentence-completion test, MacDonald asked him to begin with the phrase, "I despise." Raymond didn't hesitate. "I despise the prison for what it did to my dad," he said.[31]

In MacDonald's opinion, both Ricky and Ray were victims of a cunning sociopath whose true nature was concealed from them in a pathological family situation created by their mother's blind devotion and fantasies, which, in MacDonald's opinion, "permeated the entire household."[32] Such an environment, MacDonald suggested, greatly enhanced the inherent dominance of Gary Tison's personality and his practiced deviousness. He was a hero and a force in the lives of his children in a way few fathers ever are.

"Dad was running the show," Ray explained to Carl Cansler, "but he wasn't forcing us to do anything."

"Would your dad have let you leave anytime?" Cansler asked.

"Yes, as a matter of fact, just before we got arrested we were fixing to leave," Ray replied. "We were tired of running and we were wanting to get away from Dad because we figured something or other was going to happen, sooner or later. Just listening to those newscasts you knew how things were going, things were hot, but I thought *my* chances were better staying with Dad."[33]

Neither Ray nor his brothers could bring themselves to break with their father. Neither fear for their own safety nor revulsion over the brutal and senseless killings he had committed were strong enough to sever the bond they felt with him.

Ray's thoughts about what happened never extended beyond himself and his family. His father had already killed six people, and yet he explains that he was worried, at that time, that something was *going to happen*, as if nothing already had. He feels bad about the deaths of his father and brother, he worries about his mother being alone now that he and Ricky are in prison, but there is no mention of the six people his father and Greenawalt had murdered.

"Are you sorry you pulled that escape?" Cansler asked Raymond.

"Not at the time we pulled the escape," he replied, "because we just wanted to get Dad out. . . . In a way it's better now that Dad is dead instead of in that prison."[34]

Somewhere between the legacy of lawlessness they inherited from their grandfather and father and witnessed in their Uncle Joe, and the religious fundamentalism of their grandmothers and aunts, Ricky's and Raymond's personalities and values took form. It was an oddly contradictory moral environment to grow up in, but to them it seemed normal that their dad and grandfather and uncles filtered in and out of courtrooms and prisons, while their grandmothers and aunts faithfully went to church twice on Sunday and at least once during the week.

Religion for the women provided comfort and escape from the hardships of life. Theirs was a faith in absolutes that lifted away doubts and worries from lives lived at the margins of society. It was a theology based on a literal interpretation of the Bible and an apocalyptic view of the future, which promised redemption and a release from life's disappointments and burdens when Christ returned to claim his faithful. "O they tell me of a home far away . . . ," they would sing with smiles and misty eyes at hot Sunday evening services, "where no storm-clouds rise. O they tell me of an unclouded day."[35]

Such millenarian beliefs, religious scholar Elmer T. Clark suggests, have great appeal to the underprivileged, much more appeal than older, established faiths that represent the mainstream of society. The smaller sects provide, he writes, "a defense mechanism for the disinherited; despairing of obtaining substantial blessings through social processes, they turn on the world which has withheld its benefits and look to its destruction in a cosmic cataclysm which will exalt them and cast down the rich and powerful."[36]

Others have observed that such sects sometimes become flash points of social and political protest. And when that rebelliousness takes a different form, antiestablishment resentments may lead to aggressively antisocial patterns of behavior, as they did for Curt Tison and his sons. More often, however, religious sects serve to siphon off and contain the frustration and resentment of their followers with the promise of redemption and justice on Judgment Day. There is little doubt that it was that promise and hope that the Tison boys' grand-mothers found so comforting.

The members of these tiny, too brightly lit, starkly furnished churches practiced a demanding faith. Notions of right and wrong, heaven and hell, and redemption through unquestioning obedience to God were rigidly cast in the most unyielding scriptual terms. Preach-ers translated those beliefs into a world of the "saved" and the "lost," of superiors and inferiors, dominance and submission, authority and obedience. To appreciate the importance placed on unquestioning obedience, one need only recall the dramatic Old Testament story, faithfully repeated in the Sunday schools of these churches, of Abra-ham's willingness to sacrifice the life of his only son, Isaac, as God commanded him to.

There were few equals in this Biblically ordained chain of command, and many warnings about doubting or questioning minds. Irony and ambiguity were unwelcome and poorly understood. The key was obedi-ence. Wives obeyed their husbands, and children obeyed their parents. Love and respect, not to mention salvation, were defined within that rigid hierarchy of authority. Submission to God's will was the foremost condition of His love, and so it seemed down the hierarchy of authority.

In a classic study entitled *The Authoritarian Personality*, psychologist T. W. Adorno and his collaborators note that some persons are emo-tionally inclined toward excessively compliant behavior in certain rela-tionships. They labeled this tendency "authoritarian submissiveness."

Although variations are noted, authoritarian submissiveness is frequently caused by childrearing environments in which parental affection and approval are granted or withheld depending upon the respect and obedience the child accords its parents.[37] In these circumstances, children develop considerable anxiety about their self-worth. They attempt to satisfy their needs for love and approval through excessively conforming behavior. This behavioral adaptation to authority is carried into adulthood. Although not restricted to any particular social group, authoritarian submissiveness is most commonly observed in segments of the population characterized by lower educational levels, occupational marginality, economic insecurity, and cultural isolation — the same circumstances that seem to heighten the appeal of millenarian religions. Anxiety and uncertainty are common to people in both groups.[38] Some, like the followers of the Jonestown leader Jim Jones, are also frequently attracted by the appeals of authoritarian religious or political leaders who promise a release from life's burdens and responsibilities. The same social forces that define the appeal of such figures also sustain an unquestioning dependence on them.

The Tison boys grew up in an environment that, in important respects, created the very same abnormal feelings of dependency. Their dependency was so profound that their ability to make personal judgments was drained away by their father's extraordinary influence in matters that concerned him, whether exerted directly or indirectly through their mother. Gary Tison presided over a perverse patriarchy that evolved during his incarceration to assume both moral and psychological significance. It was, in fact, a cult, with all the accompanying authoritarian rituals, obsessions, and demands — and its focus was Gary himself.

Like the leader of another family cult, Charles Manson, Gary Tison was *the* unquestioned authority. Like Manson, he could inspire both awe and love, and always compliance, through the charismatic force of his personality. In his family's eyes, Gary's incarceration after his brief parole (like Manson's in the eyes of *his* "family" after his conviction in the Tate-LaBianca murders) assumed almost the level of significance that the Crucifixion has for Christians. Gary's needs dictated the weekly rituals of visitation; his hoped-for release was the persistent theme in household conversations. And their mother's worshipful devotion to Gary confirmed his importance to the family. She was the martyr, unyielding in her commitment to the man she adored. Like the followers of Manson and Jim Jones, Ricky and Ray accepted as normal the rituals, the social isolation, and the peculiar way they lived. Their loyalty to their parents and the recognition they received from Gary because of it became, over the years, the two most important elements in the way they thought about themselves, defining what psychoanalyst Erik H. Erikson has called the "identity" of each.[39]

Although the three brothers eventually stopped attending church after the move to Phoenix, the Pentecostal attitude toward authority and obedience stayed with them, reflected especially in Ricky's and Ray's diffidence and immaturity. Their excessive respect for their parents, their politeness, their deference to elders, their desire to *please* — these were the qualities that so impressed even tough old Frank Eyman when he met them.

Were they *ever* rebellious or difficult? Not that anyone can remember. On those rare occasions when they mildly took issue with their mother on some question (always minor, like ditching classes at school), she had only to mention that she would take up the matter with their father. That would end it. It wasn't Gary's anger they feared; it was the way he withheld affection and approval when he was displeased. That's the way he exerted his authority. He could be intimidating or encouraging, but his approval was the thing his sons valued more than anything else in their lives. Sadly enough, they always did what they were told, and what they could sense — without a word from Gary — he expected them to do. They were good boys, but hardly normal boys. They unquestioningly complied with their father's expectations, whether it meant cutting their hair, or holding up newspapers to shield his sexual activities, or participating in the abduction of a young couple they knew he was going to kill. In what amounted to a Faustian bargain, their independent judgment and consciences had been surrendered to Gary in return for his approval, and what they believed was his love.

Perhaps the most revealing insights into the psychological dynamics of such compliant and remorseless participation in morally objectionable acts are contained in a book by psychologist Stanley Milgram, *Obedience to Authority*. In experiments Milgram conducted at Yale University in 1963, 65 percent of his subjects administered what they thought were lethal electrical shocks to innocent victims, for no reason other than that Milgram told them to do so. This astonishing tendency — to do what one is told to do regardless of the consequences — appears to be a peculiarly human quality and is defined by particular situations rather than temperament or background.[40] One need only reflect on the methodically indifferent slaughter of women and children by American troops in the Vietnamese village of My Lai, or the mass suicide, on Jim Jones's command, of hundreds of people at Jonestown, to realize that Milgram's findings are not limited to laboratory experiments.

It is not that a person loses his sense of right and wrong, Milgram suggests; rather, in certain situations, that sense is simply subordinated to the will of the authority figure. Like a handful of the people who killed themselves at Jonestown, Milgram's subjects sometimes protested — some even wept — yet they continued to administer the shocks as they were told to do. "Though many subjects make the intellectual decision that they should not [obey such commands]," Milgram observes, "they are frequently unable to transform this conviction into action. . . . It is not so much the kind of person a man is," he concludes, "as the kind of *situation* in which he finds himself that determines how he will act."[41]

The essence of such compliant behavior is a psychological state in which a person's conscience is "externalized," or surrendered, to an authority figure — not just any authority figure, but a person whose authority is recognized as *legitimate,* either because of his position within a social hierarchy or through the charismatic force of his personality. When that occurs, the subject's normal concern with the rightness or wrongness of his actions shifts to an emergent, and paramount, concern with how well, or how poorly, he is functioning in the eyes of that other singularly important person.[42]

The most significant effect of this externalization of judgment and conscience, Milgram writes, "is that a man feels responsible *to* the authority directing him but feels no responsibility *for* the content of the actions that the authority prescribes." Thus, morality takes on a different meaning. A person feels shame and remorse only when he has failed in the eyes of the authority.[43] "For a man to feel responsible for his actions," Milgram explains, "he must sense that the behavior has flowed from 'the self.' " Ricky and Ray Tison correctly understood the murders at Quartzsite as their father's idea — and *not* theirs. Therefore, guilt was absent. Moreover, even though a person may disagree with an abhorrent action, as the boys did, Milgram suggests that he will probably not find it within himself to condemn what was done, regardless of how contrary to his own values the act may have been. Such condemnation, Milgram states, would betray the valued relationship with the authority figure.[44] Remaining loyal to their father seemed a less painful alternative to the Tison boys than the shame, embarrassment, and loss of self-respect they would have experienced if they had let him down.

But what about the *recurrence* of violence — such as the brutal murders that followed in Colorado? Wouldn't the horror of the Quartzsite slayings have been enough to inhibit further involvement in virtually identical crimes? Apparently not. In recurring situations, Milgram found that his subjects were usually unable to act on the basis of rational objections based on past experience. Instead, such inhibitions were suspended, and the subjects were driven by other anxieties to remain involved in the normally reprehensible activity.

"The recurrent nature of the action demanded of the subject," Milgram writes, "itself creates binding forces." Once integrated into a social structure and committed to a particular course of action, as the Tison boys were, it is extremely difficult to break free. Instead, Milgram observed, his subjects attempted to justify what had already occurred by continuing to administer shocks. To abandon the enterprise at that point, he explains, would be to admit that everything that had transpired up to that point was wrong, that a mistake had been made. Subjects opted for continuation and justification rather than termination and condemnation.[45]

As Ricky told Tom Brawley, he and his brothers suddenly found themselves "in real deep" after Quartzsite. After that, it seemed too late to turn back or to break loose. The stakes had risen dramatically with each shot that was fired. The only way to justify that slaughter was to keep going, to make sure their dad made it to Mexico. If Milgram is right, it was too late then to admit they were sorry.

Caught in a web of unanticipated circumstances, and intimidated by the personality of their powerful and charismatic father, the three Tison brothers, like Milgram's subjects, functioned within a separate subjective reality, defined by Gary and removed from conventional moral standards. They followed him masochistically, personal judgments suspended, as if under a hypnotic spell that deepened with the fatigue of the chase. Numbed in thought and feeling to the moral consequences of their actions, they continued to follow his instructions mechanically, long after they realized it was all futile and the flashing lights up ahead confirmed that it was.

But for how long would Gary's influence continue to hold sway over his surviving sons' thoughts and feelings, now that he was dead? Surely in the solitude of jail cells, after they had had time to reflect on all that their father had done, their perspectives would change. With that in mind, near the end of his interview with Raymond, James MacDonald asked him what he would change if he could do it all over again. Raymond's answer was revealing. There were no doubts in his mind about whether the breakout might have been a mistake; he expressed no recognition that his father had not been the kind of person he and his brothers had thought he was; nor did he acknowledge any regret for the sorrow they had brought to so many innocent people. In fact, there was no *moral* content to his answer at all.

"The way I figure — wishing to myself," Raymond told MacDonald, "if I could have known then what I know now, we'd find an airplane and fly to Mexico. It's something else to be on the run twelve days." Then he paused, heaving a big sigh and dropping his eyes. MacDonald waited, expecting to hear some other expression of regret. But it didn't come. "No matter what," Raymond finally said softly, still staring at the floor, "I will never quit loving my dad."[46]

"I don't know about all them psychological explanations for what people do," Reverend Elliott said as he stared at the cup of coffee he was stirring. "We all can be influenced by other people, we all make mistakes, wrong decisions from time to time in our lives, but what happened to those Tison boys goes beyond psychology. Those boys just had no idea *who* they were dealing with when they broke their dad out of prison. And I'm not sure *who* exactly they were dealing with either.

"Well, now, I know some high-toned people might laugh, but I'll tell you I think Gary Tison was demon-possessed. I've thought that for some time. What happened was the result of *sin*, pure and simple, not some kind of psychological illness. Years ago Gary turned his back on God — maybe it was that night he walked out of church when the Lord was speaking to his heart, I don't know. But the devil took over his life.

"You know in the fourth chapter of First Timothy, I believe it's the first couple of verses, it talks about 'seducing spirits and doctrines of devils, speaking lies and hypocrisy'; it talks about man having his conscience 'seared with a hot iron' so he doesn't feel anything anymore — no guilt, no sadness — when he sins. Well, that was Gary Tison, and, in my opinion, that's what happened to those boys. I think the things that they did happened when a demon spirit took control of their minds. What they did just wasn't natural. They changed. They weren't the same boys . . . Well, everybody's got an opinion, but I think it was the devil in Gary Tison."[47]

Sometime after she had buried her husband and oldest son, and listened to a judge sentence her two remaining sons to die in the Arizona gas chamber, Dorothy Tison sat down and struggled to compose letters to the families of John, Donna, and Christopher Lyons and Terri Jo Tyson. She wanted them to know how sorry she was, but worse than her sadness was the shame that now consumed her.

What had begun as a well-intentioned adventure had ended in horrible nightmare for Dorothy. Had the plan worked without bloodshed, and the escape been complete, there is little doubt that the story of the daring Tison prison break would have been accorded a niche in the folklore of the American West, right along with the stories of other western outlaw families, like the Jameses and the Youngers — a triumph of ordinary people over the system that would be told and retold by working men in saloons late at night.

But it didn't turn out that way for the Tison family. Instead, it was a tragedy, a nightmare you couldn't wake up from. Nothing had happened the way it was supposed to after the second flat tire. A man who was out of control was in control, and Dorothy Tison knew that as long as stories were told about the Tisons, they would be ugly stories of brutality, betrayal, and misplaced loyalties and values. She struggled for words, she wanted forgiveness.

"After the trials, I got a letter from their [the boys'] mother," Jo Ann Tyson said. "She said that she was sorry, and she asked me to please forgive her kids for what they did. It really hurt me because she's asking me to forgive them. Why? And what about her part in it all? I couldn't. Way down deep I know I should . . . I was raised that way, to forgive . . . but her asking that way made me very angry.

They didn't deserve forgiveness — not for killing my daughter and the baby and John and Donna . . . They were just so much a part of me, a part of me nobody knows, and now they're gone . . . Maybe it sounds wrong, because I have my church and my faith, but it still hurts so bad — too bad to say that I forgive them . . . I don't. I can't. I just can't raise that forgiveness."[48]

"Frank Reyes, the sheriff down in Arizona, sent it to me and I had it blown up and framed," Charlie Kalbacher said as he rocked back in his swivel chair to look up at the large color photograph hanging on the wall behind his desk. It was a close-up of Gary Tison's face, taken when they found his body in the desert. The face was blackened, the eyes watery pools above a nose trailing a column of maggots; the mouth was open and twisted down at the corners in what everyone thought was his final raging curse.

"Kind of looks like a devil, don't he?" Kalbacher observed without smiling.

"Doesn't it bother you to have to look at something like that every-day?" his visitor asked.

"A lot of people have asked me that," he replied, "but it doesn't. You know, being a cop can be pretty frustrating at times, the way the criminal justice system works a good part of the time. You know, plea bargains, all this concern about the rights of the accused, the time-consuming bullshit you have to contend with now to put people everyone knows is guilty behind bars. Who knows if they'll ever execute Greenawalt? But Gary Tison sure as hell is never going to hurt anyone again. Deterrence? You might say he's been permanently *deterred*. Every time I look at that picture, I think of that, and it makes me feel good."[49]

Epilogue

On August 23, 1979, a year and a day after Gary Tison's body was found in the desert, Dorothy Tison, Joe Tyson, Bob Adams, and Kathy Erhmentraut were arrested on conspiracy charges. Dorothy pleaded no contest to conspiracy; other charges against her were dropped in a plea agreement. On December 24, 1980, she was given a thirty-month prison sentence. A year later, she was released on parole, returning to her former job at a Phoenix insurance agency.

In 1980, Joe Tyson received a four-year sentence for his role in the escape. A plea agreement allowed the sentence to be served concurrently with one he was already serving for a 1979 drug conviction. Shortly after he was paroled in 1982, Joe Tyson was arrested by the Border Patrol, heading north from Nogales, Arizona, in a recreational vehicle with weapons and thirty-two illegal aliens on board. He was convicted of smuggling aliens and illegal possession of firearms and returned to prison.

Bob Adams pleaded guilty to conspiracy charges in 1980 and received a two-to-three-year sentence. That same year, Kathy Erhmentraut was fined and placed on probation.

In October 1978, Governor Bruce Babbitt named former prison warden Harold Cardwell to the post of state highway safety coordinator in the Department of Transportation. Less than two years later, Babbitt asked for his resignation. When Cardwell refused, the governor fired him. Cardwell returned to Ohio. In August 1980, he assumed the position of "trouble-shooter" in the Ohio correctional system.[1]

Director of Corrections Ellis MacDougall survived the scandal and remained in that position until 1982. At that time, he resigned to return to his former job as a criminology professor at the University of South Carolina.

In 1984, a federal jury awarded inmate Bobby Tuzon $58,000 in damages in his lawsuit against the state. Tuzon, acting as his own attorney, convinced the jury that prison officials had encouraged and permitted the danger he was exposed to before the Tison escape and the abuse he was forced to endure after it. Tuzon was placed on probation in 1985 and entered law school.[2]

In 1985, attorney Frank Lewis won a $975,000 out-of-court settlement from the state for the families of the six persons Tison and Greenawalt had killed. The Attorney General's Office was relieved. Asked to explain the state's decision, Richmond Turner, chief of the state's liability defense division, said the state had "a problem with the possibility of prior knowledge that [Tison] might escape, and then putting him in a position where he could escape."[3]

In Albert Camus's *The Stranger,* a novel about a killer and his execution, the condemned man observes, "nothing was more important than an execution . . . the only thing that can genuinely interest a man." Shortly before midnight on January 23, 1997, I watched Randy Greenawalt die. The witness room was packed.

Earlier, in the prison reception area, I visited over coffee with Pinal County sheriff Frank Reyes and deputies Dave Harrington and Perry Holmes. They reminisced about that dark desert night in 1978 and the shootout at the roadblock. Harrington still couldn't get over how his rifle had jammed. We smiled about how the time since then was showing on us all. No one had much to say about Randy except that all agreed that tonight was about nineteen years overdue.

In 1978, I had come within a few hundred yards of rutted road of becoming one of Greenawalt's and Gary Tison's victims. That was on my mind later that evening when the curtains were drawn and I saw Randy strapped to a gurney in the brightly lit, sparkling clean execution chamber. Everything looked so antiseptic, like an operating room. Randy was wearing a light blue surgical gown. He was covered to his chest with a white sheet. Two thick leather straps extended over his shoulders like oversized suspenders. A sheen of perspiration glistened on his broad forehead below neatly combed, now graying, hair. He turned his head toward the witnesses and, squinting through thick glasses, smiled—I thought, at me.

But then I realized it was directed toward his sister, who was standing directly in front of me. A tiny, gray-haired woman, she was the only member of Randy's family to attend. And you couldn't miss the connection; the facial resemblance to the doomed brother lying before her was eerie. When Randy smiled, she raised her right hand above her head and whispered something; it sounded like "Praise you, Jesus."

Moments later the prison warden, an attractive young woman with a grim expression on her face, entered the chamber and, standing at Randy's feet, read the death warrant in a loud, clear voice. Randy stared at the ceiling, a foot bobbing nervously beneath the sheet as the names of only four of his eight known victims were read: John, Donnelda, and Christopher Lyons, and Theresa Jo Tyson. Then the warden turned abruptly and left. As far as I know, Randy had never protested his innocence or admitted his guilt. His many appeals had been soley based on procedural technicalities, on which he had become as well versed as his attorneys. I once heard him make reference to "all the crimes I've been *accused* of."

It was very still for a moment. The shuffling and whispering ceased in the witness room. The only sound was the scratching of pens on pads as reporters scribbled notes. Then a disembodied voice from the darkness somewhere above our heads gave the order to begin the execution. As the lethal drugs took effect, Randy's lips parted slightly and he closed his eyes. His sister lowered her head and wept quietly as she raised her hand again. Over the next three or four minutes, his big chest heaved four times at irregular intervals. Then it was over. The peaceful expression on his face never changed.

Remorseless, repetitive, intelligent killers like Greenawalt in some sense forfeit their humanity. Such individuals have been described as wild beasts, but that is unfair. Wild animals kill out of joyless necessity in order to survive; Randy killed innocent men, women, and children senselessly for material gain. Moreover, he boasted about it. The "cruel and unusual punishment" prohibitions of the Eighth Amendment ring hollow in his case. Randy Greenawalt grew older, and died a lot easier, than any of his victims.

Meanwhile, Ray and Ricky Tison have been spared the same fate, thanks to years of skillful effort by their attorneys. Numerous appeals filed on their behalf traveled up and down the state and federal appeals processes, one making it all the way to the United States Supreme Court in 1986. The Supreme Court vacated their death penalties and remanded the cases back to the state for resentencing. In 1992, following new instructions imposed by the Arizona Supreme Court, a Maricopa County judge resentenced the brothers to four life terms each, two consecutive and two concurrent.

Since then, they no longer spend their time locked-down in the bleak, windowless confines of death row in Cell Block 6. Housed in separate cell blocks, the brothers have little direct contact with one another. Ray supervises work schedules and food preparation in a prison kitchen; Ricky, who completed his General Education Development degree is prison, now teaches basic literacy to fellow inmates in the same program.

They remain model prisoners. According to a prison officer who has observed them for years, "Those two really don't belong here. They're different—always courteous, responsible and, well, I don't know, but that alone sets them apart in here." But, unlike most of the other men living behind those walls, they will never leave.

Dorothy Tison, who never remarried, continued to visit her sons in prison faithfully every Sunday for more than forty years—since she first met Gary there in 1955—and that was the way it had been for as long as she had lived. "Rick and Ray are the most important things in my life," she had told an interviewer. "They're all I have left." Dorothy Tison died in 2006.

James W. Clarke
Tucson, Arizona

NOTES
ACKNOWLEDGMENTS
INDEX

NOTES

Prologue

1. *Arizona Cooperative Investigative Team Files,* Document 133; hereafter cited as *ACIT Files.*
2. Author's interview, Marquis Hodo, September 28, 1984.
3. Unless otherwise indicated, the dialogue is taken from the accounts of prison guards Wayne Wrisk, Marquis Hodo, Edward J. Barry, and George Goswick in *State of Arizona v. Randy Greenawalt, Raymond Curtis Tison and Ricky Wayne Tison,* Nos. 7979 and 8007 consolidated (1979), pp. 35–55, 97–105, 151–60, 178–200.
4. Based on the sworn statements of Ricky and Raymond Tison, January 26, 1979.
5. Ibid.
6. *Arizona Republic,* August 1, 1978, B1.
7. *ACIT Files,* Document 419.
8. Based on the sworn statements of Ricky and Raymond Tison, January 26, 1979.

Chapter 1

1. W. Eugene Holt, *The Southwest: Old and New* (New York: Alfred A. Knopf, 1967), p. 319.
2. Quoted in William Howarth, "Beyond the Dust Bowl," *National Geographic* (September 1984), p. 337.
3. P. P. Bliss, "Almost Persuaded," in *Songs We Sing Complete* (Fort Worth, Texas: Jacob A. Filbert, 1954), p. 48.

4. Author's interview, Elzia J. Elliott, January 13, 1984.
5. Author's telephone interview, Elzia Elliott, February 28, 1986.
6. Author's interview, Edward Vickrey, April 21, 1984; and Elzia Elliott, January 13, 1984.
7. Psychiatric evaluation, Gary Tison, January 16, 1968 (Richard E. H. Duisberg, M.D.); see also clinical interview, Gary Tison, October 5, 1961 (William B. McGrath, M.D.).
8. Clinical interview, Gary Tison, October 5, 1961 (William B. McGrath, M.D.).
9. Psychiatric evaluation, Gary Tison, January 16, 1968, p. 2.
10. *State of Arizona v. Gary Gene Tison and Earl Leroy David*, No. 3050 (1954).
11. *ACIT Files*, Letters, Gary Tison.
12. Author's interview, George McBride, August 23, 1983.
13. Clinical interview, Dorothy Tison, January 13, 1979 (James A. MacDonald, Ph.D.).
14. Clinical interview, Gary Tison, October 5, 1961 (William B. McGrath, M.D.).
15. Ibid.
16. Ibid.
17. Ibid.
18. Ibid., and author's telephone interview, William B. McGrath, M.D., October 25, 1984.

Chapter 2

1. Author's interview, Paul Chadwick, February 22, 1984.
2. The account of the abduction and murders is based on the Sworn Statements of Ricky and Raymond Tison, January 26, 1979.
3. Author's interview, Jo Ann Tyson, February 28, 1984.
4. *ACIT Files*, Escape Bulletin, July 30, 1978.

Chapter 3

1. *ACIT Files*, Document 84.
2. Sworn statement, Ricky Tison, January 26, 1979.
3. Author's interview, Tom Brawley, November 30, 1984.
4. Randy Greenawalt, "Just How Amazing Is His Amazing Grace?" cassette tape (ca. 1984).
5. Presentence report, Randy Greenawalt, February, 1974.
6. *ACIT Files*, FBI Report, Document 193, p. 34.
7. Author's interview, Tom Brawley, November 30–December 1–2, 1984.
8. The account of Kathy Ehrmentraut's interactions with the Tisons and Greenawalt is based on her testimony in *State of Arizona v. Randy Greenawalt*, No. 9299 (1979), pp. 601–24.
9. *ACIT Files*, Document 142.
10. Quoted by John Schroeder in "Punishment: Woman tries to wash stains of Tison gang out of her life," *Arizona Republic*, August 25, 1980, A1.

11. Ibid.
12. As quoted by Tom Brawley in author's interview, November 30–December 1–2, 1984.
13. Ibid.; *ACIT Files,* Document 96.
14. *ACIT Files,* FBI Report, Document 193, p. 79.
15. Author's interview, Tom Brawley, November 30–December 1–2, 1984; sworn statements of Ricky and Raymond Tison, January 26, 1979.
16. Testimony of Larry Young, *State of Arizona v. Randy Greenawalt,* No. 9299 (1979), pp. 479–502.
17. *ACIT Files,* Document 152.
18. *ACIT Files,* Document 132; author's interview, Paul Chadwick, February 22, 1984.
19. Quoted in *Arizona Republic,* August 8, 1978, A1.
20. *Arizona Republic,* August 8, 1978, A1.
21. Author's interview, Paul Chadwick, February 22, 1984; *ACIT Files,* Document 6.

Chapter 4

1. Author's interview, Shirley Gandy Elliott, March 28, 1984.
2. *ACIT Files,* Application for Commutation of Sentence, Gary Tison, August 3, 1965.
3. *ACIT Files,* Letter, Luther Leonard, August 7, 1965.
4. *ACIT Files,* Letter, Dorothy Tison, May 2, 1966.
5. These comments are drawn from two sources: "Fighters," by Pat Sabo, *Arizona Republic,* March 14, 1984, A1; and the clinical interviews of Ricky and Raymond Tison by psychologist James A. MacDonald, January 18–19, 1979.
6. *State of Arizona v. Gary Tison,* No. 4049 (1967).
7. *State of Arizona v. Gary Gene Tison,* No. 4998 (1968).
8. Statement of Gary Tison, September 19, 1967, for *State of Arizona v. Gary Tison,* No. 4049 (1967); see also his remarks, reported in psychiatric evaluation, Gary Tison, January 16, 1968 (Richard E. H. Duisberg, M.D.).
9. Author's interview, Frank Eyman, April 9, 1984.
10. *ACIT Files,* Document 302.
11. Clinical interview, Ricky Tison, January 18, 1979, p. 4 (James A. MacDonald, Ph.D.).
12. Ibid., p. 3.
13. Ibid.
14. Cited in psychological evaluation, Raymond Tison, January 19, 1979, p. 5 (James A. MacDonald, Ph.D.).
15. Author's interview, Mike McBride, February 10, 1984.
16. Ibid.
17. Quoted in *Phoenix Gazette,* Pat Sabo, "Fighters," March 14, 1984, A1.
18. Ibid.

19. Clinical interview, Ricky Tison, January 18, 1974 (James A. MacDonald, Ph.D.).
20. Clinical interview, Dorothy Tison, January 18, 1979 (James A. MacDonald, Ph.D.).
21. Author's interview, Marquis Hodo, September 27, 1984.

Chapter 5

1. Statement of Kay Wolfe, March 10, 1980; *State of Arizona v. Dorothy Tison, Robert Adams, and Joseph Tyson,* No. 108352 (1980).
2. *ACIT Files,* Statement of Carol Ericcson, Document 466.
3. Author's interview, Frank Eyman, April 9, 1984.
4. *ACIT Files,* p. 11.
5. Author's interview, Bud Gomes, August 24, 1983.
6. *State of Arizona v. Gary Tison, Duane Allen Warner, and George Richard Warnock,* No. 5789 (1972).
7. *ACIT Files,* Document 240.
8. *ACIT Files,* Statement of Harold Cardwell, August 31, 1978, Document 240.
9. Ibid.
10. *ACIT Files,* Letters, John J. Moran, June 4, 1974.
11. Author's interview, Bud Gomes, August 24, 1983.
12. *Arizona Republic,* March 6, 1977, A1.
13. *Arizona Republic,* August 19, 1978, A1.
14. *ACIT Files,* Letters, Randy Greenawalt, March 18, 1977.
15. *ACIT Files,* Letters, Gary Tison, July 8, 1977.
16. Author's interview, Bud Gomes, August 24, 1983.
17. *ACIT Files,* Statement of Bobby Tuzon, June 19, 1979, Document 412.
18. *ACIT Files,* Document 275.
19. Author's interview, Bobby Tuzon, September 6, 1985; and *ACIT Files,* Document 412, p. 11.
20. Author's interview, Bobby Tuzon, September 6, 1985.
21. *ACIT Files,* Statements of Martha and Marie LaBarre, Document 304.
22. Deposition of Lita Beigel, March 20, 1980, *State of Arizona v. Dorothy Tison et al.,* No. 108352 (1980), p. 2; *ACIT Files,* Document 472; and Statement of Karen Hacker, August 11, 1978 (K. Barton and R. Hopper, No. 73–45361), Maricopa County Attorney's Office.

Chapter 6

1. *Arizona Daily Star,* August 19, 1978, A1.
2. *Arizona Republic,* January 4, 1977, A1.
3. Ibid., August 13, 1976, A1; and January 4, 1977, A1.
4. Ibid., August 13, 1976.
5. Ibid., August 21, 1976, A1.
6. Confession of John Harvey Adamson, quoted in *Arizona Republic,* January 27, 1977, A1.

7. *Arizona Republic,* October 13, 1977; May 5, 1978.

8. Ibid., October 13, 1977, A1; June 25, 1978.

9. Ibid., July 25, 1978.

10. Ibid., January 4 and 6, 1977, A1.

11. Ibid., January 6, 1977.

12. Quoted in *Arizona Republic,* January 7, 1977.

13. *Arizona Republic,* January 7, 1977, A1.

14. *ACIT Files,* Statement of Joe Tyson, FBI Report, Document 193.

15. Deposition of Malcolm H. McMillan, investigator, Maricopa County Attorney's Office, *State of Arizona v. Dorothy Tison et al.,* No. 108352 (1979–1980); *ACIT Files,* Statement of Glenn Thornton, Document 459.

16. *ACIT Files,* Document 459; also Document 418.

17. Deposition of Malcolm H. McMillan, investigator, Maricopa County Attorney's Office, *State of Arizona v. Dorothy Tison et al.,* No. 108352 (1979–1980).

18. Quoted in *Arizona Republic,* January 12, 1978, A1; see also William C. Smitherman and Raymond P. Herand, "Prison Gangs — An Overview," *Report of the Arizona House of Representatives: Organized Crime Within The Arizona State Prison* (Phoenix: House Task Force on Organized Crime, December 29, 1977), pp. 45–48.

19. *ACIT Files,* Statement of Harold Cardwell, August 31, 1978, Document 240.

20. *ACIT Files,* Psychiatric Evaluation of Randy Greenawalt, Willard S. Gold, M.D., January 25, 1978, Document 282.

21. *ACIT Files,* Statement of William Lynn Dutton, Document 406.

22. Ibid.; Joe Tyson interview, Document 72.

23. *ACIT Files,* Statement of Joe Tyson, Document 72; Statement of Judy Tyson, Document 413.

24. *ACIT Files,* Document 150.

25. Ibid.

26. *State of Arizona v. Dorothy Tison et al.,* No. 108352 (1979–1980).

27. *ACIT Files,* Statement of Terry Tarr, Document 198.

28. *ACIT Files,* Statement of William Lynn Dutton, Document 406.

29. Interview, Joe Tyson, April 19, 1978 (to Al Stooks, Pinal County Deputy Attorney, and Casa Grande police officer Wes Stanford), case records.

30. *ACIT Files,* Document 12.

31. *ACIT Files,* Statement of Joe Tyson, Document 72.

32. Deposition of Irma Tuzon, *State of Arizona v. Dorothy Tison et al.,* Cr. No. 108352, November 2, 1979.

33. *ACIT Files,* Documents 275, 412.

34. *ACIT Files,* Document 412, p. 10.

35. *ACIT Files,* Statement of Terry Tarr, Document 198.

36. *ACIT Files,* Statement of Linda Smith, FBI Report, Document 193.

37. *ACIT Files,* Statement of Terry Tarr, Document 198.

38. *ACIT Files,* Statement of Edward L. Willingham, Document 464.

39. *ACIT Files,* Document 469.

40. *ACIT Files,* Statement of Joe Tyson, Document 72.
41. *ACIT Files,* Document 412, p. 11.

Chapter 7

1. *ACIT Files,* Statement of Harold Cardwell, Document 240.
2. Author's interview, Bobby Tuzon, September 6, 1985.
3. Interview, Robert Benjamin Smith, quoted by Michael Tulumello in *New Times,* May 1–7, 1985, p. 36.
4. Testimony of Dan Deck, *State of Arizona v. Randy Greenawalt,* No. 9299 (1979), pp. 125–43.
5. *ACIT Files,* Letters, Gary Tison, April 3, 1978.
6. *Arizona Republic,* January 12, 1978, A1.
7. Ibid., March 19, 1978, A1.
8. Testimony of Dan Deck, *State of Arizona v. Randy Greenawalt,* pp. 141–42.
9. Deposition of Irma Tuzon, November 2, 1979, *State of Arizona v. Dorothy Tison et al.,* No. 108352 (1979–1980).
10. Ibid.
11. *ACIT Files,* Statement of Bobby Tuzon, Document 412.
12. Deposition of Irma Tuzon, *State of Arizona v. Dorothy Tison et al.,* No. 108352 (1979–1980).
13. As described in the Statement of Florence Bauer Tuzon, June 25, 1979, *State of Arizona v. Dorothy Tison et al.,* No. 108352 (1979–1980).
14. *ACIT Files,* Documents 275, 424.
15. *ACIT Files,* Statement of Glenn Scott Thornton, Document 459.
16. Statement of Karen Hacker to K. Baron and R. Hopper, Arizona Department of Public Safety, No. 73–45861, August 11, 1978.
17. Author's interview, Bobby Tuzon, September 6, 1985.
18. *ACIT Files,* Statements of Bobby Tuzon, Documents 410, 412, and 419.
19. Ibid., Document 419.
20. Ibid., Document 410.
21. Ibid., Document 412.
22. Ibid., Document 412.
23. Statement of Florence Bauer Tuzon, June 25, 1979, *State of Arizona v. Dorothy Tison et al.,* No. 108352.
24. *ACIT Files,* Document 410.
25. *Arizona Republic,* May 12, 17, and 21, 1978.
26. Deborah Laake, "A Tragedy of Errors," *New Times,* April 30–May 6, 1986, p. 36.
27. Greg O'Brien, "Neal Roberts put off scheme to kill felon, former hit man says," *Arizona Republic,* June 25, 1978, A1.
28. Warnock quoted in *Arizona Republic,* June 25, 1978.
29. Greg O'Brien, "Neal Roberts put off scheme to kill felon, former hit man says," *Arizona Republic,* June 25, 1978, A1.
30. *ACIT Files,* Document 255.

31. *ACIT Files,* Document 255.
32. *ACIT Files,* Document 410.

Chapter 8

1. *ACIT Files,* Document 283.
2. Ibid.
3. Author's interview, Mike McBride, February 10, 1984.
4. *ACIT Files,* Document 356.
5. Statement of Karen Hacker to K. Barton and R. Hopper, Department of Public Safety, August 11, 1978, No. 73–45861.
6. *ACIT Files,* FBI Report, Document 193, p. 49; and Document 271.
7. *ACIT Files,* Statement of Linda Smith, FBI Report, Document 193.
8. Ibid., Document 301; and FBI Report, Document 193.
9. Ibid., Document 301.
10. *ACIT Files,* Statement of Rhonda Stanford, Document 288.
11. *ACIT Files,* Statement of Bobby Tuzon, Document 412.
12. *ACIT Files,* Document 412.
13. *ACIT Files,* Statement of Robert Flores, Document 312.
14. *ACIT Files,* Statement of Florence Bauer Tuzon, June 25, 1979, Document 421.
15. *ACIT Files,* Statement of Harold Cardwell, Document 240.
16. Ibid., p. 6.
17. *ACIT Files,* Document 312, p. 8.
18. *Arizona Republic,* June 7, 1984, A1.
19. Author's interview, Tom Brawley, December 3, 1986.

Chapter 9

1. *ACIT Files,* Document 254.
2. Ibid., Statement of Bob Adams, Document 75.
3. Ibid., Statement of Judy Tyson, June 29, 1979 (no document number).
4. Ibid., Statement of Terry Tarr, Document 198.
5. Ibid., FBI Report, Document 193, p. 33; author's interview, Dave Harrington, March 28, 1984.
6. *ACIT Files,* Document 238.
7. Ibid., Statement of Judy Tyson, June 29, 1979.
8. Author's interview, Dave Harrington, March 28, 1984.
9. Ibid.
10. Ibid.
11. Author's interview, Tom Brawley, September 8, 1986.
12. *ACIT Files,* FBI Report, Document 193, p. 3; and Document 254.

Chapter 10

1. Author's interview, Jenelle and F. H. Davis, January 28, 1984.
2. Author's interview, John Judge, January 28, 1984; *ACIT Files,* Document 141.

3. Author's interview, F. H. and Jenelle Davis, January 28, 1984.
4. *State of Arizona v. Randy Greenawalt,* No. 9299 (1979), State Exhibits 104–107; *ACIT Files,* Document 373.
5. Author's interview, F. H. and Jenelle Davis, January 28, 1984.
6. Testimony of Linda Mae Carroll, *State of Arizona v. Ricky Wayne Tison and Raymond Curtis Tison,* No. 9299 (1979), p. 41.
7. Ibid., pp. 42–43.
8. Ibid., p. 43–44.
9. Author's interview, Charles Kalbacher, August 2, 1983.
10. *ACIT Files,* FBI Report, Document 193, p. 89.
11. Since nobody has been tried for the Judges' murders, Colorado authorities are reluctant to say much about what happened, in case they do someday decide to go to trial.
12. Author's interview, Charles Kalbacher, August 2, 1983.
13. Author's interview, Bob Lewis, April 2, 1984.
14. Author's interview, Gloria Chisum, April 4, 1984.
15. Author's interviews, Tom Brawley, July 29, 1986, and September 28, 1987. Brawley is certain that it was one of the boys because it was consistent with a pattern of behavior that had been established since the escape. The brothers were less conspicuous looking than either Randy or Gary, and less likely to be recognized. For that reason, they were involved in most contacts with the public while the two convicts remained in the background.
16. Later, when he was standing trial in Yuma, Ray Tison told two fellow inmates at the Yuma County Jail that the Colorado couple were abducted at "a roadblock." *ACIT Files,* Documents 131 and 140.
17. Author's interview, Jenelle Davis, January 28, 1984.

Chapter 11

1. *ACIT Files,* Statement of Harold Cardwell, August 31, 1978, Document 240, p. 5 (transcribed copy).
2. Author's interview, Marquis Hodo, September 27, 1984, p. 15.
3. *Arizona Republic,* August 12, 1978, A1.
4. Ibid.
5. *ACIT Files,* Confidential Memorandum to Ellis C. McDougall from Arthur B. Huffman, August 16, 1978, p. 11; hereafter cited as Huffman memorandum.
6. Huffman memorandum, p. 9.
7. *Arizona Daily Star,* August 19, 1978, A1.
8. *ACIT Files,* Statement of Raymond Celenza, Document 404; see also, *Arizona Republic,* August 19, 1978, A1.
9. As quoted by Harold Cardwell in *ACIT Files,* Document 240, p. 5 (transcribed copy).
10. *Arizona Republic,* August 20, 1978, A1.

11. *ACIT Files,* Statement of Harold Cardwell, Document 240, p. 6 (transcribed copy).
12. *ACIT Files,* Statement of Raymond Celenza, Document 404.
13. *ACIT Files,* Document 400; and Statement of Raymond Celenza, Document 404.
14. *ACIT Files,* Statement of Harold Cardwell, Document 240, p. 7 (emphasis added).
15. *Arizona Republic,* July 10, 1979, A1.
16. *ACIT Files,* Statement of Harold Cardwell, Document 240, p. 7; see also Deborah Laake, "A Tragedy of Errors," *New Times,* April 30–May 6, 1986, p. 42.
17. *ACIT Files,* Statement of Harold Cardwell, Document 240.
18. Ibid.
19. Ibid; see also Deposition of Irma Tuzon, *State of Arizona v. Dorothy Tison et al.* No. 108352; and the remarks of Ellis MacDougall when he learned of Cardwell's denial: "I know for a fact that Tuzon talked with him [Cardwell] several times both from my conversations with Tuzon and through my interviews with Cardwell's staff." Quoted in *Arizona Republic,* July 10, 1979, A1.
20. *Arizona Republic,* July 10, 1979, A1.
21. *ACIT Files,* Statement of Harold Cardwell, Document 240, p. 7 (transcribed copy).
22. Ibid.
23. Ibid.
24. Ibid., p. 8.
25. *Arizona Republic,* July 8, 1979, A1.
26. Ibid., July 15, 1979, A1.
27. *ACIT Files,* Statement of Robert Flores, Document 312, pp. 7–8 (transcribed copy).
28. That was the original explanation given for the transfers to State Representative Peter Kay, as quoted in the *Arizona Republic,* August 12, 1978, A1; see also, *ACIT Files,* Document 400.
29. *Arizona Republic,* June 25, 1978, A1.
30. Quoted in Deborah Laake, "A Tragedy of Errors," *New Times,* April 30–May 6, 1986, p. 36.
31. Ibid.
32. Ibid.

Chapter 12

1. *Arizona Republic,* August 9, 1978, A6.
2. Paul Dean, "Justice: Something Is Awry," Ibid., B1.
3. As reported by Raymond and Ricky Tison, *ACIT Files,* Document 193, FBI Report, p. 62.
4. *State of Arizona v. Randy Greenawalt,* No. 9299 (1979), Exhibits 112–15.

5. Testimony of Charles Kalbacher, *State of Arizona v. Ricky Wayne Tison and Raymond Curtis Tison*, No. 9299 (1979), pp. 24–34.
6. *ACIT Files*, Document 369.
7. Testimony of Martha Jane Sauer, *State of Arizona v. Ricky Wayne Tison and Raymond Curtis Tison*, No. 9299 (1979), pp. 48–51.
8. *State of Arizona v. Randy Greenawalt*, No. 9299 (1979), Testimony of Dale Todeschi, pp. 779–84; *ACIT Files*, Document 132.
9. Author's interview, Tom Brawley, September 30, 1986. This is the explanation related to him by Ricky Tison.
10. Author's interview, Charles Kalbacher, August 2, 1983; *ACIT Files*, Document 184.
11. Author's interview, Jenelle Davis, January 28, 1984.

Chapter 13

1. *ACIT Files*, Document 275.
2. Ibid., Document 273.
3. Ibid., Documents 43 and 137.
4. Author's interview, Dave Harrington, March 28, 1984.
5. *ACIT Files*, Documents 95 and 148.
6. Ibid., Document 208.
7. Ibid., Document 347.
8. Author's interview, Dave Harrington, March 28, 1984.
9. Quoted in *Arizona Republic*, August 12, 1978, A1.
10. Author's interview, Wade Williams, September 28, 1983.
11. Testimony of Tom Scott, *State of Arizona v. Ricky Wayne Tison and Raymond Curtis Tison*, No. 7979 (1979), p. 389.
12. Dialogue based on the sworn statements of Raymond and Ricky Tison, January 26, 1979.
13. Author's interviews, Dave Warren, September 28, 1983; and Dave Harrington, March 28, 1984.
14. Author's interview, Dave Harrington, March 28, 1984; and *ACIT Files*, Document 347.
15. *ACIT Files*, Document 349.
16. Author's interview, Wade Williams, September 28, 1983.
17. Ibid.
18. Ibid.; and author's interview, Dave Harrington, March 28, 1984.
19. *ACIT Files*, Document 347.

Chapter 14

1. Author's interview, Jenelle Davis, January 28, 1984.
2. Author's interview, John Judge, January 28, 1984.
3. *ACIT Files*, Document 369.
4. Testimony of James D. Harville, *State of Arizona v. Ricky Wayne Tison and Raymond Curtis Tison*, No. 7979 (1979), pp. 34–40.
5. Testimony of Dwight G. Burd, ibid., pp. 103–20.

6. Testimony of Harold Cardwell, ibid., pp. 48–53.
7. Testimony of James D. Harville, ibid., p. 38.
8. Statement of Raymond Tison, August 11, 1978, 5:10 A.M., case records.
9. Statement of Ricky Wayne Tison, August 11, 1978, 5:30 A.M. (to Dan Martinez, Tom Solis, and Ed Harville), case records.
10. Quoted in *Arizona Republic*, August 23, 1978, A1.
11. Author's interview, Paul Chadwick, February 22, 1984.
12. Ibid.
13. Statement of Randy Greenawalt (by Tom Brawley), August 11, 1978, 1:46 P.M., case records; Author's interview, Tom Brawley, October 6, 1986. Proofread and approved by Tom Brawley, October 14, 1986.
14. In addition to Brawley, the members of the team were: Jim Erhart, Yuma County; Jim Harville, Pinal County; Matt McMillan, Maricopa County; Ken Barton and Dave Sanchez, Department of Public Safety; and Bill Richardson, Arizona Drug Control.
15. *ACIT Files*, Document 291.
16. Author's interview, Jo Ann Tyson, February 28, 1984.

Chapter 15

1. Author's interview, Dave Warren, September 28, 1983.
2. Author's interview, Frank Eyman, April 9, 1984.
3. Part of Eyman's statement; quoted in *Arizona Republic*, August 16, 1978, A1; also author's interview, April 9, 1984.
4. Author's interview, Dave Harrington, March 28, 1984.
5. Reyes quoted in *Arizona Republic*, August 25, 1978, A1.
6. Author's interview, Dave Harrington, March 28, 1984.
7. Deputy quoted in *Arizona Republic*, August 25, 1985, A1.
8. Lawrence quoted in *Arizona Republic*, August 24, 1978, A1.
9. Author's interview, Tom Brawley, October 17, 1986.
10. Author's interview, Dave Warren, September 28, 1983.
11. Joe Tyson quoted in *Arizona Daily Star*, August 25, 1978, A1.
12. Reverend Jerry Totty quoted in ibid.
13. Author's interview, Reverend E. J. Elliott, January 13, 1984.

Chapter 16

1. Author's interview, John Judge, January 28, 1984.
2. Author's interview, George and Mildred McBride, August 23, 1983.
3. *State of Arizona v. Ricky Tison and Raymond Tison*, No. 9299, January 25, 1979, p. 13 (hereafter cited as Trial record).
4. Ibid., p. 304.
5. Ibid., p. 308.
6. Ibid., p. 309.
7. Author's interview, Charles Kalbacher, August 2, 1983.
8. Author's interview, Gene Farish, August 2, 1983.
9. Aggravation Hearing, Testimony of Charles Kalbacher, March 14, 1979, pp. 16–36.

10. Ibid., Testimony of Linda Mae Carroll, pp. 37–44.
11. Ibid., Testimony of F. H. Davis, pp. 6–15.
12. Interview of Raymond Tison, by Carl B. Cansler, Jr., March 8, 1979, pp. 12–13 (hereafter cited as Cansler interview).
13. Cansler interview, Raymond Tison, pp. 15–16 (emphasis added).
14. Trial record, Dan Deck, pp. 128–30.
15. Ibid.
16. Cansler interview, Raymond Tison, p. 15; and James A. MacDonald, Ph.D., Psychological Evaluation of Raymond Tison, January 16, 1979, p. 3 (hereafter cited as MacDonald evaluation, Raymond Tison).
17. As quoted by Tom Brawley, author's interview, November 30, 1984.
18. James A. MacDonald, Ph.D., Psychological Evaluation of Ricky Tison, January 16, 1979, p. 4 (hereafter cited as MacDonald evaluation, Ricky Tison).
19. Cansler interview, Raymond Tison, pp. 15, 17.
20. MacDonald evaluation, Ricky Tison, p. 8.
21. Trial record, John C. Woods, Presentence Report, Ricky Tison, p. 24.
22. Ibid., p. 14.
23. MacDonald evaluation, Ricky Tison, p. 6.
24. Cansler interview, Raymond Tison, p. 15.
25. MacDonald evaluation, Raymond Tison, pp. 3–4 (emphasis added).
26. MacDonald evaluation, Ricky Tison, pp. 8, 5.
27. Ibid., p. 6.
28. Ibid., p. 5.
29. Cansler interview, Raymond Tison, pp. 12–13.
30. MacDonald evaluation, Ricky Tison, pp. 3–4.
31. MacDonald evaluation, Raymond Tison, p. 2.
32. James A. MacDonald, Ph.D., Psychological Evaluation of Dorothy Tison, January 18, 1979, p. 3.
33. Cansler interview, Raymond Tison, p. 17 (emphasis added).
34. Cansler interview, Raymond Tison, p. 17.
35. Reverend J. K. Alwood, "The Unclouded Day," in *Songs We Sing Complete* (Fort Worth, Texas: Jacob A. Filbert, 1954), p. 239.
36. Elmer T. Clark, *The Small Sects in America* (New York: Abingdon Press, 1949), pp. 218–19; see also Liston Pope, *Millhands and Preachers* (New Haven: Yale University Press, 1942), pp. 105–16.
37. T. W. Adorno, Else Frenkel-Brunswik, Daniel J. Levinson, and R. Nevitt Sanford, *The Authoritarian Personality* (New York: John Wiley & Sons, 1950).
38. See, for example, Seymour M. Lipset, *Political Man* (New York: Anchor Books, 1963; originally published by Doubleday, 1960), chapter 4.
39. Erik H. Erikson, *Childhood and Society* (New York: W. W. Norton, 1950).
40. Stanley Milgram, *Obedience to Authority* (New York: Harper & Row, 1974).
41. Ibid., pp. 148, 205.
42. Ibid., p. 146.
43. Ibid., pp. 145–46.

44. Ibid., pp. 146–47.

45. Ibid., p. 148–49.

46. MacDonald evaluation, Raymond Tison, p. 4.

47. Author's interview, Reverend E. J. Elliott, January 13, 1984.

48. Author's interview, Jo Ann Tyson, February 28, 1984.

49. Author's interview, Charles Kalbacher, August 2, 1983.

Epilogue

1. *Arizona Daily Star,* October 19, 1978; October 21, 1978, D8; July 13, 1980, B5; September 5, 1980, B11.

2. *Arizona Republic,* June 7, 1984, A1.

3. Richmond Turner quoted in *Arizona Daily Star,* October 2, 1985, B5.

4. As quoted by Ed Vickrey, author's interview, April 21, 1984.

5. *Ricky Wayne Tison and Raymond Curtis Tison, Petitioners v. Arizona,* No. 84–6075, April 21, 1987, p. 4497. Reprinted in *Law Week,* v. 55, no. 41, April 21, 1987, pp. 4496–509.

6. Ibid., p. 4502.

7. Ibid., p. 4508.

8. Dorothy Tison quoted in *Arizona Daily Star,* November 27, 1980, B2.

ACKNOWLEDGMENTS

I owe a special debt to three individuals: Tom Brawley, formerly a detective with the Coconino County (Arizona) Sheriff's Department; Dave Harrington of the Pinal County (Arizona) Sheriffs Department; and attorney Frank Lewis of Phoenix. Interesting lawmen in their own right, Brawley and Harrington both were willing to share information and perspectives that only men intimately acquainted with the people and events in this story could have. Brawley is as close to the whole story of the events that followed the prison escape as anyone I know. He served as Director of the Arizona Cooperative Investigative Team and coordinated the state's investigation of the prison breakout and the homicides that followed. Harrington, who grew up in Casa Grande, had known Gary Tison and other members of the Tison family long before they made the national news. He was also the officer in charge at the roadblock when the criminals were caught. Dave Harrington was kind enough to check the accuracy of significant portions of the manuscript; Tom Brawley insisted on proofreading it all.

Without Frank Lewis's help, it would have been very difficult to research the extraordinary circumstances and events within the Arizona State Prison that preceded the escape. In 1977, Lewis represented the American Civil Liberties Union in a lawsuit brought in behalf of inmates at the prison. Later he represented the families of the six victims Gary Tison and Randy Greenawalt killed after the escape. He won in both cases. Mr. Lewis very generously permitted me to review his extensive files and patiently answered the questions that followed. He was also kind enough to proofread those chapters pertaining to that part of the story.

I am especially grateful also to the families of those persons who were killed: Paul and Jean Chadwick of Fremont, Nebraska: Harry and Jo Ann

Tyson of Henderson, Nevada; F. H. Davis and his late wife, Jenelle, of Borger,
Texas; Pat Davis, of Hennessey, Oklahoma; John Judge of Amarillo, Texas;
and Francis Lyons of Omaha. Their willingness to talk with me about the
loved ones they lost and, in so doing, to endure the pain of reliving such a
tragic period in their own lives is something I will not forget.

There were a number of other persons — police officers, prison officials,
and attorneys — whose discussions with me were often enlightening: Pinal
County sheriff's deputies Dave Warren and Wade Williams; former Deputy
Warden Arthur "Bud" Gomes, and prison guards Marquis Hodo, Chuck
Ballard, and Steve Resler; Maricopa County District Attorney Larry Turoff;
Pinal County District Attorney Vic Cook; attorneys Michael Beers and Dwight
Callahan of Casa Grande; and attorney James Kemper of Phoenix. Charlie
Kalbacher, formerly an investigator with the Twelfth Judicial District in Monte
Vista, Colorado, was particularly helpful on the Colorado phase of my re-
search, as was Gene Farish, former district attorney in the same district.

Thanks to Pinal County Sheriff Frank Reyes, I was probably the last person
to interview former prison warden Frank Eyman, a legendary figure in Arizona
law enforcement, only a few weeks before he died. Reyes arranged the interview through Eyman's wife, Margaret. Mrs. Eyman graciously permitted me
to come into their home for the interview. Sheriff Reyes also made available
to me all the official photographs taken following the shootout and capture
at the roadblock, and the later discovery of Gary Tison's body in the desert.

I can't begin to name the scores of people I have talked with about this
case since 1978. Often they were just chance conversations with strangers
in cafés or saloons. So many people, in Casa Grande, Yuma, Flagstaff, Clovis,
South Fork, had a story to tell. Some are identified in the text, and a number
of those who aren't asked not to be. To all, I am grateful.

There were others I talked with who didn't think they were contributing
much; if they ever read this, I hope they will understand how wrong they
were: the Reverend E. J. Elliott and his wife, Shirley Gandy Elliott; George
and Mildred McBride, Mike McBride, Rick McBride, Mike and Georgia Petty,
Gloria Chisum, Bob Lewis, Mr. and Mrs. Ed Vickrey, and Pam Vickrey. I
would also like to thank the Gilmore family of Alamosa, Colorado, for permit-
ting me to spend a day tramping around their beautiful ranch on the banks
of the Rio Grande; and Ray Thomas, who took the time to show me around
the Papago Chemical Plant and to point out the spot where he discovered
Gary Tison's body. Thanks to the hospitality of my old friend Jack Soule, I
never had to worry about accommodations on my trips to Southern California.

The task of gaining access to the sometimes voluminous, sometimes obscure
trial records, transcripts, and documents that extend back over fifty years is
demanding. I was completely dependent on the cooperation of the court
clerks who manage these records. In Florence, Dolores Santillon and her
staff at the Pinal County Superior Court were most helpful, as were their
counterparts, Beverly Frame and her staff at the Yuma County Superior
Court in Yuma. State Representative Peter Goudinoff and, through him,
Arizona Supreme Court Justice Stanley Feldman were especially helpful on

my behalf at the Arizona Supreme Court in Phoenix. Without their assistance, it would have been a real struggle to get access to the materials I needed.

Newspapers provided an indispensable source of background information. Particularly helpful were stories in the *Arizona Republic* by Greg O'Brien, Marilyn Taylor, John Schroeder, Jack Swanson, Jack West, Charles Kelly, Albert J. Sitter, Earl Zarbin, Robert Barrett, Sam Negri, Vince Taylor, Randy Collier, and Frank Turco; as were articles by Pat Sabo in the *Phoenix Gazette*, Beverly Medlyn and John Rawlinson in the *Arizona Daily Star*, and Michael Tulumello and Deborah Laake in the *New Times*. I hope they will not object when, occasionally, I transposed a word or sentence, or deleted a word or two without inserting marks of ellipsis.

I would also like to thank William Shover, Veronica Mier, Laura Atwell, and Keela Kragenbring of the *Arizona Republic* and the *Phoenix Gazette* for their help in locating photographs. Donovan Kramer, Jr., of the *Casa Grande Gazette* permitted me to examine back issues of that newspaper.

The University of Arizona generously approved a one-semester sabbatical leave in 1985, during which a portion of the writing was done. In particular, I want to thank my department head, Jerrold Rusk, who was an unwavering source of encouragement throughout this somewhat unusual project; as was my cousin, Robert A. Weston, whose heroes, like mine, have always been cowboys. I am also grateful to five distinguished scholars: Vine Deloria, Jr., James C. Davies, Stanley Leiberson, Joel Feinberg, and Jules Coleman. Each was kind enough to put aside (let's assume) their reservations to endorse my futile attempts to fund a project that didn't fit neatly into any of the social science, or humanities, funding categories. I would also like to thank Sheila Tobias, Gloria Stern, and Peter Davison for the important roles they each played in getting this story into print in 1988. For the same reasons, I am grateful to Steve Cox, Chris Szuter, Kathryn Conrad, and the staff at the University of Arizona Press for the present edition. Finally, I am grateful to my agent, Patricia Burke, without whom this story would not have reached the silver screen.

For me, this story began during a strange night on the banks of the Delores River a couple of decades ago. A lot has happened on the interesting and memorable trip that has followed. I was very fortunate that night, but also, since then, to have Jeanne, Michael, and Julie—and now Courtney, Ed, and Pat—share it with me. For that reason, I would like to rededicate this edition to them, as well as to the memory of two wonderful parents.

INDEX

ABOUT THE AUTHOR

James W. Clarke is University Distinguished Professor Emeritus at the University of Arizona, former Fulbright Scholar, and occasional consultant to the U.S. Secret Service. He is the author of a number of articles that have appeared in leading academic journals, five nonfiction books on violent crime, and a novel. He and his wife live in Tucson, Arizona, and West Glacier, Montana. See his website, www.jameswclarke.net.